The Myth of Empowerment

The Myth of Empowerment

Women and the
Therapeutic Culture in America

Dana Becker

NEW YORK UNIVERSITY PRESS
New York and London

NEW YORK UNIVERSITY PRESS
New York and London
www.nyupress.org

Library of Congress Cataloging-in-Publication Data
Becker, Dana.
The myth of empowerment : women and the
therapeutic culture in America / Dana Becker.
p. cm.
Includes bibliographical references and index.
ISBN 0–8147–9925–6 (cloth : alk. paper) —
ISBN 0–8147–9936–1 (pbk. : alk. paper)
  1. Women—Mental health—United States—History.
  2. Women—Mental health—Social aspects—United States.
  3. Women—United States—Psychology.   4. Power (Social sciences)
  5. Women and psychoanalysis.   I. Title.
RC451.4.W6B426   2005
362.1'082'0973—dc22   2004019466

New York University Press books are printed on acid-free paper,
and their binding materials are chosen for strength and durability.

Manufactured in the United States of America

c 10 9 8 7 6 5 4 3 2 1
p 10 9 8 7 6 5 4 3 2 1

For Stan

Contents

Acknowledgments

If good fortune is measured in the number and quality of one's mentors, then I have been lucky indeed. My first and greatest mentors have been my parents, Betty and Marvin Becker, who created a secure, trustworthy, and encouraging world from which I could venture and to which I could return, trying out new ideas and new ways of being. My father, who died this year, was a teacher and scholar of formidable gifts and intellectual generosity. The pairing of these characteristics is uncommon, I think, and I and many others have benefited enormously both from his example and his encouragement.

It has also been my good fortune to have been mentored by some women scholars whose work has been critical in shaping my interest in the relationship between feminism and the therapeutic culture. I received particular support for this project from Sharon Lamb and Jeanne Marecek at a time when I was plagued with the certainty that a book like mine would be swallowed up by the tsunami of backlash against feminism. Jennifer Hammer at NYU Press was willing to buck that tide, and for that I am extremely grateful. Rachel Hare-Mustin, Paula Caplan, and Carolyn Enns have offered inestimable support for and interest in my work, and I thank Lyn Mikel Brown and the other readers who looked at several manuscript chapters early on, for their encouragement and helpful feedback. I would also like to thank Nicholas Taylor for copyediting the manuscript.

I was able to do research for the book uninterruptedly during the 2001–2002 academic year thanks to a year-long faculty leave granted by the Bryn Mawr College Graduate School of Social Work and Social Research. My colleague Sanford Schram brought Barbara Cruikshank's writing on empowerment to my attention early in the project, for which he has earned my thanks, as have co-Deans Raymond Albert and Marcia Martin and all the colleagues at the Graduate School who have made my late entry into the academic maelstrom smoother than it might have been. Peggy Calvarese has helped me enormously with administrative matters related to this book and other academic projects. Thanks should also go to Beth and the staff at my local Starbucks, whose good humor and caffeine helped fuel this project.

Finally, and most importantly, I could never have completed this book were it not for the unvarying support of my husband, Stan Tischler, without whose care and take-out Chinese nothing is possible.

Prologue

I confess it: I was tucked away at a good women's college, translating Homer and dating guys from the men's college next door while others were being jailed for protesting the Vietnam War. I was a hopeless bourgeois outfitted in tie-dyed, counterculture clothing. By 1969 I was holed up with my mother-in-law in New Jersey, fresh from the titillation of hearing my newly acquired married name pronounced by strangers and worrying about what effect the war might have on our future, while my new husband was in town insisting to his draft board that he was far from good Army material. By the following fall we were in New Haven and I was parsing Dante at Yale. I had no idea what the wives of our older friends were doing, sitting cross-legged in someone's living room, their peasant blouses barely covering unshaven armpits, talking about how the personal was political. None of this is to say that I wasn't a liberal. I was as liberal as you please, but I just didn't know much of anything. Although I did know that I couldn't see myself reflected in the glassy perfection of a Gothic Jell-O mold, I had no clear picture of the meaning of feminism as other than the struggle for occupational choice.

Let me reassure the reader who may worry that I am traveling down that confessional route so well-rutted of late that I will not open the door to further autobiographical accounts. I merely put before you, however shamefacedly, my non-activist past in order to say this: that my failure to have participated in key social movements through whose agency my life has been altered and my choices vastly expanded has, apart from engendering a sense of loss, regret, and remorse, catalyzed my interest, as a feminist, therapist, and academic, in looking critically at the difference between psychologizing and social action. Whereas in 1968 I knew that I was abjuring the political struggle by holding myself apart from it, today I know that I cannot protect myself from this unwelcome knowledge by the fictive notion that I am acting to change the world "one person at a time," and I have come to understand the deeply political nature of psychotherapy itself.

These days, many women are being encouraged to believe that by taking care of their psychological "selves" they are becoming ever more powerful. I believe that we owe it to ourselves, even if it makes us uneasy —and it certainly makes *me,* as a therapist, uneasy—to acknowledge that this is not so; to understand the limitations of the therapeutic culture and to see clearly our place in it. History tells us what happens when women are praised for tending to their—and society's—knitting, as well as what happens when they don't look up from it.

I am well aware that these ruminations would not be possible—or permissible—were it not for a particularly American self-consciousness that is a byproduct of the very heritage of individualism that I subject to scrutiny in this book. But, of course, as Ann Douglas has said, we are always more "alert to the lies of [our] predecessors" than we are to our own.[1]

1

Introduction

As the old adage goes, "knowledge is power." And, in our culture, self-knowledge—psychological knowledge—is often thought of as power, particularly for women. The term "empowerment" is now used to describe what women are supposed to gain from a variety of very personal activities, from exercise to psychotherapy. What empowerment promises women is control over their lives; however, when applied specifically to women, it is rarely a term that connotes more than self-knowledge or self-improvement. Power is not personal fulfillment, self-esteem, relational skill, or an improved ability to cope with or adapt to familial, social, or societal expectations, although these, singly or in combination, may be some of the spoken or unspoken aims of the therapeutic culture. Psychotherapy, as a product of an American individualist heritage that emphasizes personal change in the service of achieving personal goals, cannot furnish women, either collectively or individually, with power. In light of the promises of psychotherapy over the past three decades or more, this might sound like an unfair indictment, particularly to those women who have found therapy to be "empowering." Yet, the repackaging of the psychological as power reproduces what has long been the cultural norm for women: the colonization of both the interior world of the psyche and the small world of intimate relationships. There was a time when psychotherapy was primarily considered necessary for those whose behavior was considered abnormal. But now that the idea of psychotherapy for the "normal" has been institutionalized for more than fifty years,[1] now that women have been exposed to many decades-worth of psychologizing, it is time to question more closely how the therapeutic culture has served "normal" women with respect to the broader social and political problems they face.

Those of us who theorize about and practice psychotherapy rarely acknowledge the effects upon women of our society's individualistic understanding of humans and their problems as psychotherapy clients, as consumers of a vast self-help literature, and as frequent targets of media preoccupation with psychological matters. As I shall argue, the sense of women's strengths as primarily relational, their needs as primarily personal, and their expected roles in society as primarily unchangeable is the effect of our historical reliance on individualism. Decades ago, Philip Rieff argued that, within the culture of the therapeutic, socialization could be achieved without the symbolism of social goals.[2] What he meant by this was that Americans could reach adulthood without a sense of communal purpose enlarged much beyond the self and its pleasures. I argue that today, within the therapeutic culture, women are exposed to social goals *only* as symbols. The toothless notion of women's psychological "empowerment" constitutes one such symbol.

"Psychological woman"[3] is by and large not an activist, nor is her therapist—nor are the media experts that counsel her about how to handle relationships, how best to juggle work life and parenting responsibilities, and how to take care of herself as she tries to manage all of these. Even feminist therapists cannot assume that they are helping achieve the aims of social change in psychotherapy[4] when the cultural milieu makes upon therapists and clients alike the individualistic claims that have marked us as a nation. Of course, social activism is not the only means of producing social change. The therapeutic culture could help to create a different awareness of ourselves and the world, an awareness that, in theory, might promote social change. However, although the therapeutic culture does create its subjects, it is not generally creating subjects who are directed toward changing the status quo.

Mine is by no means the first discussion of psychotherapy as an individualistic enterprise; indeed, these discussions have become legion. But I am asking these questions: What kind of woman is the therapeutic culture as a whole producing? What sort of representation of women emerges from the understanding of self and the world that the therapeutic culture provides? The middle-class woman who is concerned about her health and her ability to care for others in an uncertain world is not as different from her late-nineteenth-century white middle-class predecessors as we might imagine. In the nineteenth century she was told that her moral virtue was her power; today her power is said to exist in her ability to relate to others or to take better care of herself and others. For tools she is expected to use primarily her *inner* resources.

It is as true now as it was in 1979, when Richard Cloward and Frances Fox Piven made the assertion, that "more and more women are being led to think of the tensions they experience as rooted in their health or mental health."[5] The "women's sphere" of the nineteenth century has been reborn in the therapeutic, emerging from the tradition of sentimental power that women have been expected to wield within families and in society at large. What the therapeutic culture offers women (particularly middle-class women, but, increasingly, women from all socioeconomic strata) is merely a type of compensatory power[6] that supports and reproduces the existing societal power/gender arrangements by obviating the need for social action to alter them, as women continue to perform the "emotion work"[7] of society, both domestically and professionally.

Power relations are implicit in the story of the professionalization of American "mind cure," and today's medical-therapeutic discourse represents women to themselves in a way that has significant social ramifications. If one's sense of oneself is influenced by what one takes in from the larger society—if, as Foucault believed, subjectivity and subjection are doubles—then the "truth" of women's experience of themselves in the therapeutic world is shaped by relations of power.

Individualism

In order to comprehend how a therapeutic culture geared in large part toward the perceived needs and the presumed identities of women has influenced and continues to influence women's understanding of themselves, I believe we must take into account the contexts both of feminism and therapy. Feminism is, indeed, the "daughter of individualism." Its language and goals are shaped within the historical and political context of its time, its "conditions, . . . limits, and . . . forms" established by society.[8] Although at times in our history women have engaged in communal efforts for the purpose of challenging societal traditions and structures, generally they have been responding to the tantalizing promise of individualism: the expansion of women's opportunities and individual rights.[9] It was, after all, through the consideration of individual rights that the powerful prerogatives many American women now take for granted—the right to own property, the right to vote—were gained.

One of the particularly American forms of individualism that has shaped feminism incorporates male discourses about the self, identity, autonomy, and agency that have long influenced our hypotheses and our conclusions about the origins of human problems as well as their "cures." As a result, the history of women alone cannot illuminate the association between individualism and power that has influenced women's relationship to the therapeutic. The reviled yet cosseted "hysteric"; the corseted, virtuous housewife; the mental healer; the suffragist; the feminist therapist—all occupy a central place in the story of psychological woman, but so do the mesmerist, the man of science, the general medical practitioner, the neurologist, and the psychiatrist. In the nineteenth century, it was men of science who formulated the "Woman Question"—the question of women's place in the modern world—hoping to answer it in a way that would allay their own anxieties. Today, science continues to pose—and to try to answer—many questions that speak both directly and indirectly to women's place. One such "answer," born of the unholy union of the medical and the psychological, can be found in our current preoccupation with stress. The discourse of stress attempts to address the question of women's place by locating her problems within a medical and psychological context rather than in the sociopolitical domain.

In this book, in order to demonstrate how psychological woman has been shaped by the discourses of individualism and of science, I turn to specific historical narratives, particularly to discussions of American "scientism," the place of men's interests in woman's sphere, and the origins and professionalization of psychotherapy in America. Men have pride of place in these stories; however, more recently, the feminization of psychotherapy has put women squarely at the center of their own psychological universe. Although some subjects addressed in this book will be well known to feminists and others interested in women's studies (e.g., "women's sphere"; the debates over equality versus difference; the artifact of hysteria as women's disease in the nineteenth century), in the chapters that follow these are frequently paired with subjects perhaps less familiar (e.g., the notion of "domestic individualism"; the professionalization of psychotherapy). The interplay of the themes I have outlined—science, subjectivity, and power—dictates the form of my discussion. My choice has been to illustrate specific social and therapeutic developments and practices in the nineteenth century in order to illuminate their relationship to the therapeutic context in which contemporary psychological woman finds herself.

Women and Psychotherapy

In the nineteenth century, when the practice of mental therapeutics began, there were many more men than women engaged in helping women to manage their emotions and their lives—clergymen, mesmerists, gynecologists, neurologists, psychologists—lecturing them about what was wrong with them and why, and offering treatment for what ailed them. As that century progressed, medical men emerged from the broad field of practitioners to become the dominant guardians of women's mental health, and women offered these new specialists a steady clientele and a good income.

Although middle- and upper-class white women have traditionally constituted the group most fluent in the vernacular of the therapeutic culture, in our time all women are increasingly exposed on a daily basis to the incessant psychologizing of a culture to which this psychologizing is mother's milk. And, indeed, psychologizing is almost *literally* mother's milk, for even though women have always been the primary consumers of psychotherapy and popular advice about ways to think and feel, now the practice of psychotherapy has been feminized, as women have become psychotherapy's chief professional purveyors. This development represents a new phenomenon in American life. The societal expectation that women will take up the work of the psyche and of fostering emotionally "healthy" relationships and that they will teach others, especially men, how to do this is not new; women have done society's emotion work for centuries. What *is* new is the sheer pervasiveness of therapeutic rhetoric in contemporary American society and the fact that more and more women are becoming professional psychotherapists. Women are now doing formally what they have always done informally, and men have taken and will continue to take comfort in women's psychological ministrations. History tells us that women's interiority and their claim to moral and emotional influence, their "domestic individualism," have always been championed by men, and for good reason.[10] If we continue fervently to privilege the inner world we will be less likely to foment trouble outside it.

The Culture and Discourse of the Therapeutic

In this book's title I refer to a "therapeutic culture" that I believe encompasses the professional or "expert" world of those who work in the psychological professions (e.g., psychologists, social workers, and psychiatrists); popular self-help books and self-help groups; media representations of the psychological; and the ideas that emanate from both the popular and the professional cultures, ideas that are often combined, transformed, recycled, and used for purposes other than the therapeutic (e.g., advertising, politics). Not only are all these domains—expertise, self-help, popular ideas—in continual and reciprocal interplay, but each in its own way owes its existence to one or both of two historical traditions. The first is that of American individualism (in one or another of its manifestations); the second, a belief in the application of scientific ideas to human problems.

Some therapeutic ideas have a short shelf life in our culture, whereas others become part of a more lasting discourse. Throughout this book, my use of the term *discourse* relates to the idea that when individuals inhabit the same culture, their discussions and their descriptions of what they see and experience are generated by the issues that worry them. Some of these discussions and their descriptions—discourses—become widely disseminated and broadly understood, both as embodiments and as reflections of a particular culture. In America, discourses on the nature of the self and its destiny have been ubiquitous. And, naturally, when the subject of the self arises, the subject of individualism is close at hand.[11]

Psychological woman is what society in general and the therapeutic culture in particular have made of her—her roles, her "place," her troubles, and her options for confronting them. And since the nineteenth century, individualistic psychological and medical discourses have been the vehicles through which she has been defined. These discourses, as I have previously suggested, have masked the need for structural changes—social, political, economic—in the gendered arrangements that have dictated women's roles and responsibilities with respect to domestic and emotional labor and have, in many cases, reduced women's struggles to purely personal problems.

In the nineteenth century, "hysteria" was the term given to the illness thought to result in the extreme changes in mood, excessive emotionality, nervousness, depression, sexual difficulties, and other symptoms that incapacitated some women. The medicalized "hysterical woman" discourse stood in contrast to the discourse of "true womanhood" that celebrated women's allegedly innate psychological characteristics of moral purity, patience, and tenderness. In my view, the contemporary replacements for the "hysterical woman" and "true womanhood" discourses are the "stress" discourse and the "relational woman" discourse. "Stress" is now blamed for women's shortness of temper, lack of sexual desire, sense of being overwhelmed, and, at times, their situational depression and anxiety. The relational discourse, in contrast, represents women as naturally affiliative beings and emotionally available, nurturing caretakers.[12]

A modern addition to these discourses has been the "empowerment" discourse. An emphasis on the ability of a person to experience a type of personal power through a sense of self-confidence or self-esteem, although not applicable to nineteenth-century women, nonetheless has its American roots in New Thought and other nineteenth-century mind cure movements. Currently, the empowerment and relational discourses are intertwined; psychological woman expects herself to "be her own person" as well as to be emotionally available to those she loves.

The medical and psychological discourses stand in reciprocal relation to each other. If the "stressed-out" woman cures herself or is cured of her symptoms, she can return to her position as the family's emotional center and to performing, in most cases, the lion's share of the household labor (and, today, she can also return to work);[13] if she has difficulty managing or balancing her myriad roles and duties, a primary social option is that of stress-related illness, a "curable" condition. To overcome *her* "disease," the nineteenth-century woman could try to "buck herself up" or call upon a male physician for help; in the twenty-first century, psychological woman can see a therapist, read a self-help book, or take the oft-recommended soak in a hot tub surrounded by scented candles.

If the "stressed-out" woman is a poor single mother who lives with her children in a dangerous neighborhood with bad schools (and this mother will more often be described as "overwhelmed" than "stressed"), her options will be different: she can look to similarly overwhelmed social service systems and/or to frequently over-stressed family members for support; look to the church for moral guidance and/or material assistance; and/or receive mandated therapeutic "help" if her children are not faring well. If the woman is childless and/or not heterosexual, she should not, according to contemporary judgments, be "stressed" in the first place.

It is probably clear by now that psychological woman is typically white, heterosexual, and middle class. She is, nonetheless, the "type" against which other normative evaluations and identifications will be made. And more and more women are taking after her, either looking to or *being told* to look to the therapeutic culture not only for answers to their problems, but for guidance on how to *be*.

Professionalization vs. Popularization

Although the feminization of psychotherapy may have begun in the aftermath of feminist consciousness-raising in the "second wave" of 1960s and 1970s feminism, the feminization of the *psychological* dates back to the popular culture of the nineteenth century, during which period journalists, women authors of sentimental novels, and advertising men made use of moral and psychological persuasion to influence middle-class women.[14] Since that time, the broad dissemination of many psychological ideas has helped create increasing numbers of psychological women who, if they do not actively seek out those ideas, absorb them unwittingly through the thin membrane that conveys the culture's prevailing ideologies. The advent of managed care, with its "deskilling, declassing, and degrading" of psychotherapists, although it has surely contributed to the feminization of psychotherapy practice,[15] has at least partly obscured the contribution of the older popular and professional discourses to that feminization.

Just as journalists, novelists, and advertisers once opened up the popular world of the psychological to women, an improbable pair of forces has enlarged the influence of the therapeutic culture more recently. One has been an ever-expanding consumer market that targets women; the other, the feminist consciousness-raising of the "second wave" that enabled many middle-class women to reflect on their situations in both personal and political terms (although, as I shall discuss later in the book, the weight was ever upon the personal). A generation of middle-class consumers, educated to advocate for themselves in every area of life from the medical to the relational, now expects to shop for answers and advice in the therapeutic marketplace. This is a form of "power" that middle-class women have only recently acquired. I question how far the professional can veer (even if, she, as a feminist practitioner, might wish to do so) from the accepted popular psychological canon without encountering deeply held beliefs derived by women from transactions with an intensely individualistic therapeutic culture.

Popular psychology and "expert" psychotherapy have never been as distinguishable as their advocates have alleged. Ever since William James, in *The Varieties of Religious Experience,* gave popular therapeutic ideas their due (and his was not an homage without reservations, as it later turned out), those who practice psychotherapy have sought to downplay the influence both upon themselves and their clients of popular psychological ideas and therapies. The rise of professionalism did not eliminate the influence of the popular psychological culture; it merely resulted in a lack of acknowledgment of the relationship between the popular and professional domains. What professionalism *did* accomplish was the active suppression of some forms of lay psychological practice and, initially, the almost total exclusion of women from the field of mental health practitioners.

The tension between the popular and the professional has its historical roots in the struggle of medical men for professional recognition in the mid- to late nineteenth century. At that time, exchanges between laymen and professionals often became vitriolic; popular purveyors of therapy had to be discredited and pushed aside if professionals were to dominate the marketplace. Although tensions between the popular and the professional worlds are more complicated—and more muted—today, professionals appear to feel the need continually to defend their territory against popular encroachments. Professional practitioners, when they are not co-opting their ideas for professional use, often identify self-help groups and "pop psych" books as the particular offshoots of the humanistic psychology movement of the 1960s and 1970s, as though the ideas that undergird the self-help culture were not associated with the American embrace of the very liberal humanist ideas that spawned psychotherapy itself. Associating popular psychology in its varied forms with one movement and one era in psychology (or with New Age and other "fringe" therapies, as is often the case) has seemed an effort to blunt its cultural force and imply its irrelevance to mainstream professional practice.

It is too late for professional psychotherapists to put the "pop" genie back in the bottle. The psychological universe is too vast, and women therapists (who, let us not forget, live in that universe) too numerous to exclude. Thus, what might be said to be occurring via the current feminization of psychotherapy is a nineteenth-century phenomenon with a twenty-first-century twist: a return of psychotherapy to its populist roots and a return of psychiatry and psychology to their origins in somatic medicine and neurology (the preoccupation of psychiatrists with psychobiology, and many in psychology with neuroscience, attests to this). Already, as Irene Philipson has pointed out, clinical practice is losing its allure (i.e., professional status and financial incentives) for men. Until quite recently, women had a "lay" or semiprofessional status in the therapeutic culture.[16] As psychotherapy is feminized and the allegedly scientific pursuits within psychiatry and psychology are favored by men, the retrograde forces can be felt.

Psychological Man, Meet Psychological Woman

In 1966 Philip Rieff's acid-etched portrait of "psychological man," who, in order to "limit the power of the culture in which he lives to sink deeper into his self" needed to "become something of a genius about himself," spoke to a fear that the therapeutic had become the religion of an age that was witnessing the cultural enlargement of psychological life.[17] Many male critics shared this concern about the undermining nature of the therapeutic culture. Christopher Lasch, following on Rieff's cultural analysis, inveighed against the intrusion of therapists and other experts into family life, arguing that they were undermining Americans' confidence in their parenting and turning the United States into a country of narcissists.[18] Lasch's 1970s narcissist was Rieff's 1960s "psychological man" revisited, his carapace of omnipotence concealing a soft core of psychological dependence on admiring others. But where would this male narcissist have been without that admiring other, without a woman's gaze to reflect his figure "at twice its natural size," as Virginia Woolf put it?[19] Lasch never adequately addressed the social conditions that set the stage for women's support of man's narcissism, the institutionalization of which he so decried.

American cultural critics, worriedly cautioning their compatriots about a falling away from the values and virtues of a communal past,[20] never suggested that men and women had not experienced that past identically; they never looked beyond the construction of psychological man to ask: "Who is psychological woman?" History tells us that it has been women, not men, who have truly been required to become the psychological "geniuses"—not only about themselves, but also about those closest to them—in a world in which they were required to make the relational universe go around. Psychological woman is not the antithesis of "public woman" in the sense that psychological man has been seen to be the antithesis of "public man";[21] rather, psychological woman is more continuous with the woman who earlier in our history inhabited a private, domestic world.

In 1962 the historian David Potter seemed indeed a lonely voice in the crowd when he took issue with David Riesman's formulation of the American character.[22] Riesman, a sociologist, had maintained, in his surprise 1950 bestseller *The Lonely Crowd,* that the American had been transformed over the course of a century into an "outer-directed" type of individual, exquisitely attuned to the expectations of other people as the result of the cultural requirement to "get along" in order to achieve worldly success. Potter felt that Riesman had gotten it all wrong, insofar as women were concerned. Since women had historically been dependent on men, he argued, they had *always* had to develop a keen sense of others' expectations, interests, and moods. *Their* "outer-directedness" had not been born yesterday. Potter was interested in what was happening to women as they became more and more socially and financially independent. With some prescience, it would appear, he outlined the dilemma of modern American women as he saw it:

> Other emancipated groups have sought to substitute a new condition in place of an old one and to obliterate the old, but except for a few of the most militant women in a generation of crusading suffragettes, now almost extinct, women have never renounced the roles of wife and mother. The result has been that their objective was to reconcile a new condition with an old one, to hold in balance the principle of equality, which denies a difference, and the practice of wifehood and motherhood which recognizes a difference in the roles of men and women.[23]

He continued:

> Society has given her the opportunity to fulfill her personal ambitions through the same career activities as a man, but it cannot make [a woman's] career aspirations and her family aspirations fit together as they do for a man. The result of all this is a certain tension between her old role and her new one. More of an individualist than women in traditional societies, she is by no means as whole-heartedly individualistic as the American male. . . . She is constantly holding in balance her general opportunities as a person and her distinctive needs as a woman, and

when we consider how badly these two go together in principle can we not say that she is maintaining the operative equilibrium between them with a remarkable degree of skill and success?[24]

If, instead of talking about women's "distinctive needs," Potter had spoken of the fact of male-female difference as socially constructed, he might have had it completely right. If his statement had read, "she is constantly holding in balance her general opportunities as a person and the *disproportionate responsibilities for childrearing and emotional and domestic labor that society demands,*" he might have described a generally agreed-upon dilemma experienced by many contemporary middle-class women.

Generalizations about the American character and the therapeutic culture have had limited applicability to women's experience in part because the dichotomization of individualism and communitarianism has left no room for considering the historical continuity of women's role as our society's chief instruments of informal social connection (Robert Putnam, who draws the distinction between formal and informal social connections in his book, *Bowling Alone,* does not make nearly enough, in my view, of this continuity).[25] When Robert Bellah and his colleagues fretted that an American redefinition of freedom as "freedom from the demands of others" would leave Americans morally at sea, they failed to consider how women, far from disconnecting from the relational world, might be looking for much-needed relief from the absolute requirement to nurture others.

Whither Psychoanalysis?

It has been widely assumed that the history of psychotherapy in America *is* the history of psychoanalysis, but this is far from the case. The profession of psychotherapy was influenced by particularly American religious and philosophical strains that long antedated the migration of European psychoanalytic thought to our shores, and women played key roles in a number of popular movements—the Second Great Awakening, Spiritualism, and New Thought, among these—that eventually contributed important precepts to the practice of "mental therapeutics."

Both critiques and revisions of psychoanalytic theory have long had pride of place in our cultural discourses of the therapeutic. Although it would be foolish to suggest that Freud's ideas have not had an enduring influence on our national psyche, I believe that for too long the examination of psychoanalytic ideas, the uses to which they have been put, and the debates they have engendered on the part of feminist academic theorists have dominated our discussions about women and the therapeutic.[26] In its focus on enduring aspects of the therapeutic enterprise rather than on specific psychological theories, as well as its emphasis on psychotherapy rather than psychoanalysis, mine differs substantially from other accounts.

When I discuss theory, as I do with respect to certain aspects of feminist object relations theory, it is because that theory's emphasis on women's relationality has exerted a persistent and enduring influence on the way many therapists view their women clients. Ideas about women's affiliative capacities are now far from the cutting edge, academically speaking; indeed, most feminist theorists have long since aimed their postmodern viewfinders elsewhere. However, both because academic wrangling over theory and method has recently been serving women less than it has been feeding academic machinery with "detached, metatheoretical discourse,"[27] and because many therapists are unfamiliar even with the less arcane feminist theoretical discussions, much of what is new in feminist theory has not been translated into psychotherapy theory or practice.

A number of us who practice psychotherapy, far from having overindulged in the excesses of postmodern theory, and despite recent forays into social constructionism (in the form of narrative therapy, for example), find that, all contentions to the contrary, our liberal humanist roots are still showing. Because therapists' exposure to undigested therapeutic ideas is far greater than their exposure to the cacophony of academic voices, it is imperative for us to understand the individualist legacy of those therapeutic ideas. It is this heritage that shapes therapists' understanding of the "self" and its meanings.

Organization of the Book

As part of my examination of the American ennoblement of the self in chapter 2, I critique several influential conceptualizations of therapeutic culture for their failure to take the representation of women and women's position within that culture into account. For all the caviling about the ruin that the therapeutic culture has visited on society in the form of the development of psychological man, the profound effects of that culture on the development of psychological woman is missing, in large part, from many contemporary accounts.

Extending the discussion of individualism, chapter 3 examines how nineteenth-century Americans became increasingly preoccupied with their inner lives. Shifts in Protestantism incorporated new elements of individualism into religious ideology in the form of subjectivity and autonomy. The growth and eventual professionalization of mental therapeutics was spurred by evangelical movements such as the Second Great Awakening and by the popular practice of mind cure, both of which promoted individualism in several ways: (1) through the increasing expectation that the individual take responsibility for his or her psychological life; (2) through relentless popular optimism with respect to the possibilities for individual change; and (3) through the interpenetration of popular and professional ("scientific") understandings of the individual psyche. I believe that the movement from mind cure to a particularly American psychotherapy demonstrates the origins of that persisting interpenetration.

The moral and ideological uses to which science was put with respect to the reification of male-female differences are discussed in chapter 4. In the "scientific" framing of the late nineteenth-century "Woman Question" one can find the origins of a persistent association between the establishment of societal gender arrangements and the medicalization of women's distress. This connection was vividly expressed in the relationship between the hysterical Victorian patient and her male physician as well as through the phenomenon of neurasthenia that ushered in the adoption in America of a stress paradigm of illness. The stress paradigm has come to be embodied in a twenty-first-century discourse that has increasing influence over the depiction of women's experience. It was not merely the "scientization" of woman that shaped that representation, however; nineteenth-century ideas about women's moral purity and their superior ability to influence others, explored in chapter 5, made equal contributions to it. Tensions between women's ideal of equality and the reality of a type of domestic individualism that positioned the woman as different, as literally and figuratively the keeper of the interior—both of man's hearth and his heart (i.e., the moral and emotional interior)—continue to resonate in the paradoxes that have come to define twentieth- and twenty-first-century feminism. The broad acceptance of the difference paradigm has had profound implications for the construction of psychological woman.

The nineteenth-century notion of women as "different" by virtue of their relationality has been revived in the twentieth and twenty-first centuries, and it forms the basis for much of the feminist therapy practiced today. In chapter 6 the paradigm of women's relational nature, a contemporary extension of domestic individualism, is viewed as the basis for the paradox of conservatism both in feminism and in some feminist psychotherapy practice. I examine the "self-in-relation" model widely employed by many feminist practitioners with respect both to its anti-individualist claims and its conceptualization of women's power, and I argue against the suggestion that women who become relationally "competent" —whether through therapy or otherwise—are able to remain uninfluenced by a cultural climate in which individualism has flourished. Self-in-relation theorists find the notion of power problematic for women; one reason for this, I believe, is that they define power narrowly, in the tradition of the most narrow of the utilitarian individualists—Jeremy Bentham—as being *out for oneself*. In decrying the idea of "power-over," these theorists set up a straw "man" that they then proceed to knock down in the name of countering an individualist heritage.

As I will discuss further in the interlude that follows chapter 5, from the time the term "feminism" began to be regularly employed, equality and difference have been debated, and for decades they have defined the poles between which feminism has slipped and slid. The idea of empowerment in therapy is paradoxical precisely because it attempts to embody both principles—difference and equality—within the culturally given framework of domestic individualism. Feminist psychotherapy forms a container for these twin aims of feminism, with the "rights/equality" question retained as a vestigial symbol that is subsumed under the aim of "empowerment," while the difference paradigm reigns supreme. In chapter 7 I examine the term "empowerment" as the slippery symbolic bridge between psychotherapy's inherent individualism and feminist therapy's tenuous attachment to feminist activism.

Chapter 8 revisits the stress paradigm of illness and its implications for the representation of women's experience through an examination of professional and popular discourses, as exemplified by the posttraumatic stress disorder discourse in the first case and by the stress discourse in the second. Maintaining the societal status quo in gender arrangements has demanded ever more sophisticated ways of viewing women's problems, involving representations that individualize causes and cures and point away from any requirement for profound sociopolitical change. The creation of psychological woman has taken more than a century, and we must examine the history of her development if we are to understand what forces in the twenty-first-century culture of the therapeutic are helping to keep her in her place.

2

In the Self's Country
Individualism in America

> Seldom do we . . . ask the question whether social attitudes do indeed become "ideas." When the historian talks of "popular" ideas, he rarely sees them as part of the world in which "ideas" . . . are born.
> The problem of self . . . becomes a fundamental one for almost all modern cultural development. The effort to achieve both a moral and a social order and a freely developing self shapes the cultural products of the times.
> —Warren I. Susman[1]

In a national survey reported in the *New York Times Magazine* exploring "what's really on Americans' minds," 85 percent of those polled answered in the affirmative to the question: "Is it possible in America to be pretty much who you want to be?"[2] I can't vouch for the methodological accuracy of the survey other than to note that the Americans came from a wide range of demographic groups; nonetheless, the results have a disturbing relevance for anyone interested in the phenomenon of individualism, and American individualism in particular. It was surprising how many of those questioned felt that race, education, and parental income did not have a major influence on their identities (it does not appear that the respondents were asked about gender). Richard Powers, dispirited by the results of the survey, questioned how such opinions could be so widespread. Perhaps, he hypothesized, people don't really believe that they have limitless opportunity; perhaps they just don't "want to be what [they] pretty much couldn't be," and the American love affair with infinite opportunity cloaks "an equally happy acceptance of normative social control." Powers grumbled:

We're not afraid of losing all we have. But we're terrified of losing a chance to have it all. Perhaps for this reason more than a third of us sometimes lament that our lives did not turn out as we wished. A third have visited therapists. Half know someone who has tried to commit suicide. Half of us think we don't get enough credit for what we do. We seem to be free to be everything we want—except content.

For possibility and contentment may be sworn enemies. Pure potential and its despair combine to create the ideal late-capitalist perpetual-motion engine, with self-realization powering the drive train. So long as we believe there is no ceiling, there will be no end to the effort we'll expend on the way to self-making. Be all you can be. Go for the gusto. Such cheerleading cloaks the sharpest spurs ever invented. For in this country, if you don't become all that you pretty much want, you've only your own indolence to blame.

Powers's suggestion that "possibility and contentment may be sworn enemies" hints at the dangers of individualism that Alexis de Tocqueville had warned of in the early nineteenth century, when the term "individualism" first made its appearance. The culture of the therapeutic is a culture of *individualisms* that is increasingly becoming a woman's culture, as I have suggested. Before we can fully understand the effects of the therapeutic culture on psychological woman, we must examine the notions about personhood—the self—that culture espouses and examine the particularly American forms of individualism in which ideas of the self are grounded. Cultural analyses of how the American "character" has been reshaped from the eighteenth century through modern times, analyses that have largely excluded the experiences of women, are in themselves prisms through which ideas about the psychological have been both distilled and transformed. All of these are subjects that will be tackled in this chapter, but let us begin with a discussion of individualism.

A Brief History of Individualism and Its Meanings

Modern individualism was forged in response to the rule of monarchy and an oppressive class system. Throughout the history of the Western world, there have been fears that the individual would be crushed by society or, alternately, that the rational order of society would be overturned by the uncivilized expression of untrammeled individuality.[3] The term "individualism" has come to have many meanings, some of them contradictory and paradoxical.[4] It was Alexis de Tocqueville's trenchant observations, made during his travels in America, that significantly influenced the meaning of the term "individualism" in France. Although in his writings on America Tocqueville took care to distinguish American individualism from American selfishness, he warned that in practice the two might come to look very much alike. For all the virtues of democracy, the individualism spawned by it, if left unchecked, "at first, only saps the virtues of public life; but in the long run . . . attacks and destroys all others and is at length absorbed in downright selfishness." Individualism, he proposed, encourages the severance of an individual from his community and his retreat into the bosom of family and friends, "so that after he has thus formed a little circle of his own, he willingly leaves society at large to itself." The past is soon forgotten, the future is unknown, and the interest of the individual attaches primarily to those closest to him. Along with the equality that accompanies democracy, the aristocratic visitor maintained, a condition can arise wherein, owing nothing to anyone, people "are apt to imagine that their whole destiny is in their own hands." Democracy "threatens in the end to confine [man] entirely within the solitude of his own heart."[5] In this environment, the political power of the state might grow without restraint. Only the particularly American antidotes to this destructive power of liberty—"free institutions and active citizenship"—prevented such an encroachment.[6]

Although, to the French, individualism came to signify social atomization, quite another use of the term was associated with the German Romantic ideal. This representation, perhaps more accurately referred to as "individuality," emphasized the tension between the individual and society, often symbolized by the struggles of the artist. As Steven Lukes has pointed out, a premium was placed on "the . . . value of subjectivity, solitude and introspection."[7] It was not until the 1860 publication of Jacob Burckhardt's *Civilization of the Renaissance in Italy,* however, that the term "individualism" began to take on multiple meanings—the meaning of individual personality taken from the German Romantics; Tocqueville's idea of withdrawal from society; and the concept of competitive self-assertiveness characteristic of a new middle class freed from the yoke of imposed authority.[8]

In America by the mid-nineteenth century some were beginning to employ the term individualism more frequently, although the terms "self-reliance," "self-culture," and "self-help," among others, had more favor.[9]

It was not until the end of the Civil War that "individualism" became a fixture in the vernacular. The primary significance of individualism in a burgeoning capitalist society and a liberal democracy was, in Lukes's words, as an expression of the "realization of the final stage of human progress in a spontaneously cohesive society of equal individual rights, limited government, laissez-faire, natural justice and equal opportunity, and individual freedom, moral development, and dignity."[10] But alongside this meaning another was also developing. This was the modern notion of self-actualization, with its emphasis on fulfillment through retreat into a private world apart from society, an idea that descended from Romantic ideas of expressive individualism and formed a cornerstone of the emerging Transcendentalist movement of the mid-nineteenth century (of which more will be said in the next chapter). The notion of self-gratification could not have taken root at a time when the common belief was that heavenly salvation was the preordained goal of human potential; it could only flourish when men became able to see themselves apart from the roles they played in society.[11] This development made it possible, historians tell us, for individuals to experience conflicts between self and society, struggles which, even as they eventually led to greater flexibility in social arrangements, left individuals with less "guidance . . . as to how to live."[12] For men, the relaxing of social constraints brought with it uncertainty and a quest for yet greater certainty. Women, however, had a great deal of "guidance," given the social necessity in a patriarchal society of their adhering to the roles and rules rigidly prescribed for them.

One hypothesis Richard Powers failed to explore in his quest to understand the naiveté of Americans' ideas about their identities was whether his fellow citizens' responses merely represent what Gillian Brown has referred to as "the banality of utopianism in American visions of the self."[13] A banal utopianism is one shorn of uncertainty and, therefore, of anxiety. As we continue, we shall glimpse how the search for secure meanings as well as the goal of self-fulfillment, of "being all that you can be" in an uncertain world, became translated into the language, aims, and practices of therapeutic. Now, however, we will briefly examine the interrelationship between culture and conceptions of the self.

Construction of the Self

If culture is "the system of significances attached to behavior by which a society explains itself to itself," understanding the vision of the self that is endorsed by a particular culture opens the door, as perhaps no other knowledge does, to that system of meanings, because "as cultures change, so do the modal types of personality that are their bearers."[14] To Émile Durkheim, personality is cut to the cloth of current societal norms; personality *is* the individual, socialized. In this view, as Nikolas Rose explains, the self does not

> pre-exist the forms of its social recognition; it [results from] the social expectations targeted upon it, the social duties accorded it, the norms according to which it is judged, the pleasures and pains that entice and coerce it, the forms of self-inspection inculcated in it, the languages according to which it is spoken about and about which it learns to account for itself in thought and speech.[15]

Over time, the self has come to be viewed as a describable entity with "specific psychological boundaries, a deep interior core of initiative and mastery, and a private life of subjective emotion," an entity that must be nourished and helped to grow, whose autonomy must be protected from the constant dangers that the world can pose to it.[16] But it was not ever thus.

There is ample historical evidence that wrestling with the problems of the self is quite a modern preoccupation.[17] In fact, the emergence of consciousness of the self has much to do with what *made* the world modern.[18] There was no distinction made centuries ago between an internal and an external self, nor was the self understood, as it is now, as something abstract and also hidden. The self of the individual was viewed as the sum of his[19] behaviors and public commitments, not, as today, the cause of these same phenomena and separate from them. The domain of the hidden self enlarged as the idea of personality supplanted the primacy of social rank and social roles in importance.

Today the idea that humans can look at themselves—that is, that they can take a reflexive position and say "I"—seems obvious to us. But it is not every culture that makes of *self* a noun, and the fact that our culture began to do so represented a historical sea change in the understanding of the self.[20] This change originated in the late sixteenth and early seventeenth centuries, particularly with Descartes, who believed that the individual had a unique, protected entrée into his own inner world.[21] Rationality requires subjective thought, not, as the ancients had believed, the taking in of a preordered cosmic reality. The individual was now viewed as sufficiently disengaged from himself that he could order his thoughts according to rational principles.

For all the resistance to Descartes' ideas from empiricist quarters, his perspective has continued to prevail in modern times. In the contemporary rendering of those ideas, the individual can "remake himself by methodical and disciplined action," as Charles Taylor contends, assuming an "instrumental stance" vis-à-vis [his] own "given properties, desires, inclinations, tendencies, habits of thought and feeling, so that they can be *worked on,* doing away with some and strengthening others, until the desired specifications are met."[22] Inwardness is requisite to this disengaged, reflexive position, and inwardness has played an important role in Western thought ever since Augustine held that humans discover God within themselves, that *in interiore homine habitat veritas* ("in the inner man (human) dwells the truth").

Of course today this inwardness is not necessarily related to the search for God, but is directed more often toward the particularly modern end of making meaning in our lives.[23] In the ancient view, even as humans were buffeted by the vicissitudes of the world around them, they had a constant, true nature. Only in modern times has the idea taken root that what we are in need of is to be found within ourselves as unique beings. A central cultural assumption is that we do not yet know who we are. For the task of self-exploration that our culture demands, what is called for is a reflexivity that allows us to explore our "selves" in order to establish our identities. And because this examination of ourselves is not a disengaged, objective analysis of a stable psychological landscape, it has the potential to transform the self that it examines.[24] If, in fact, the self is a social construction, then the crucial question is not how it happened that identity came to be internalized, but for what purpose both "interiority" and the distinction between inner and outer have permeated the culture.[25]

As we have just discussed, ideas about subjectivity and inwardness are intertwined with a culture's system of meanings. When there is no one traditional cultural framework such as religion that is universally shared, Philip Cushman asks, how are we to know what to "strive toward, . . . what is worthwhile, who is worthwhile, and which institutions determine worthwhileness?" Cushman frames this question in terms of an "ongoing moral negotiation over what it means to be human."[26] From this vantage point, there are no boundaries between the moral and the psychological. Selfhood cannot exist separately from the sphere of the moral, the good.[27]

The particular ideas that constitute American individualism—the dignity of "man," autonomy, privacy, self-development, among others—have moral sources that are deeply embedded in the past.[28] In our culture the presumed freedom of each person to develop in his or her own way—to develop his or her personality, to have self-control—is paramount to a sense of well-being. But there are other ideas about the meaning of life. Charles Taylor believes that although we are no longer living in a society in which human endeavors are guided by traditional, unassailable frameworks that define "the good" or "the higher," neither are we living in a society in which anything goes. Rather, although our notions of the higher are no longer to be found through the contrast between the ordinary and the extraordinary—heroism in war, say, or asceticism—they are present in the qualitative distinctions we make among *ways* of living ordinary life, *ways* of working and of organizing family life. In the absence of traditional frameworks the quest is not for valor or martyrdom, but for meaning or sense *itself*. And we find meaning or sense through articulation. As Taylor puts it, "Moderns have become acutely aware of how much sense . . . depends on our own powers of expression. . . . Finding a sense to life depends on framing meaningful expressions that are adequate."[29]

Some critics believe that such meaningful expressions are not readily found. Robert Bellah and his colleagues have argued that we should not underestimate the influence in America of Locke's idea that society is formed only through the voluntary actions of individuals attempting to "maximize their own self-interest."[30] They insist that a language of radical individualism is not useful in the search for meaning because "we never get to the bottom of ourselves on our own."[31] The language of "values" espoused by many Americans these days, they maintain, does not speak to real moral choice, but issues from a common view of the self as acontextual, as unattached to society. It falsely assumes that values can be independently chosen by autonomous individuals when, in fact, everything we do takes place within a society governed by institutions and is understood through patterns of meaning provided by our culture.

Bellah and his associates draw a rigid boundary between individualism and the communal life that Tocqueville believed was the antidote to the perils of individualism in America. From the Frenchman's vantage point, the exercise of the individual's abilities and strengths could be accomplished only through participation in family life, in connection to religious tradition, and through relationship to the larger political community. From Plato and Aristotle through Tocqueville, the therapeutic and the moral were viewed as intertwined.[32] The healthy man and the good citizen were identical. From the mid-twentieth century to the present, however, the transformation in the relationship between public and private life brought about by modern individualism has been consistently under scrutiny.

A common theme in the analysis of American cultural transformation is that, as the biblical religion and classical republicanism of the seventeenth and eighteenth centuries lost ground to an extreme, modern form of individualism, a "loosely bounded" cultural pattern took hold.[33] There is a commonly shared fear that what Tocqueville warned against may have come to pass, namely, that individualism has undermined vital connections between public and private life, since the private life of Americans provides little preparation for engagement in a public, political life that is essential for supporting democracy.[34]

The idealization of tradition and of communal life should not blind us to their excesses, however. Although none of the critics of American individualism suggest that Americans should turn the clock back to an earlier time of oppressive community intrusion into the affairs of individuals, they have been accused of failing to offer up any new, viable models of collective action.[35] In fact, one criticism of their handwringing has been that it has enabled these social analysts to circumvent any challenges to fundamental institutions, challenges that might involve "painful and divisive efforts to rearrange political structures and economic rewards."[36]

As I noted in the previous chapter, women had no "public" world in which to live, and their experience of community was considerably different from that of men. Cultural critics' preoccupation with the dichotomization of individualism and communitarianism, character and personality, not only fails to capture the reality of men's and women's different experiences, past and present, it also renders women's experience nearly invisible.

Women's Absence from Men's Cultural Analyses

In theory, although the notion of the self is neither male nor female, both women and men construct specific representations of themselves from the discourses that are available to them, discourses that are shaped by time, place, and, of course, gender. Gender is a way of structuring human experience socially, politically, economically, intellectually, and psychologically. As Elizabeth Fox-Genovese maintains, the self, whether male or female, is not separable from history: "Women's consciousness, like that of men, results in large measure from women's historical experience: the roles to which society has assigned them, their relations with men, and prevailing discourses with which they have been invited to identify."[37]

Theories describing a unitary American character (e.g., "public man," "psychological man," the narcissistic personality of our time) can be read as cultural texts that both interpret and mirror the culture from which they emanate.[38] The ease with which we Americans have accepted being summed up may stem from a cultural need to reduce complexity in our view of ourselves and, thereby, to reduce anxiety. In its reductionism, this characterological typecasting also obscures differences—of class, race, and gender, to name just a few.

To survey the literature on the self and American character types, one might conclude that, generally, in the 1950s the social or "character" problem was that of conformism (e.g., David Riesman's notion of the "lonely crowd"),[39] and that by the 1970s and 1980s the problem was one of isolation and alienation.[40] Over the years, some cultural critics have fretted over what they viewed as the tightening grip of therapeutic and bureaucratic institutions on American families.[41] Some have talked of weakened identities and loose boundaries,[42] others of "empty selves."[43] Despite the apparent diversity in these perceptions, a common fear underlying them, as Rupert Wilkinson has pointed out, is "the fear of being owned and controlled."[44]

The fear of being owned and controlled—the fear of dependency—permeated Christopher Lasch's description of the narcissist, who, he insisted, was the ugly American character type of our age. In this selection from his popular 1979 book *The Culture of Narcissism,* Lasch discussed how, as the importance of self-reliance waned, an increased dependence "on the state, the corporation, and other bureaucracies" was represented in the psychological phenomenon of narcissism. What follows is his description of the narcissistic American:

Notwithstanding his occasional illusions of omnipotence, the narcissist depends on others to validate his self-esteem. He cannot live without an admiring audience. His apparent freedom from family ties and institutional constraints does not free him to stand alone or to glory in his individuality. On the contrary, it contributes to his insecurity, which he can overcome only by seeing his "grandiose self" reflected in the attentions of others, or by attaching himself to those who radiate celebrity, power, and charisma. For the narcissist, the work is a mirror, whereas the rugged individualist saw it as an empty wilderness to be shaped in his own design.[45]

It is interesting to note how many of the characteristics of the narcissist as Lasch described him one might ascribe not just to modern "man," but to "man" over the ages. Lasch seemed to be just discovering the substrate of dependence underlying male narcissism, and he was certainly deluded in believing that modern man was alone in his dependence on others "to validate his self-esteem." As I shall discuss further in chapter 5, women have been delegated this job over the ages in Western societies, frequently in the absence of men's acknowledgment of their own dependence upon them.[46] Woman has provided the mirroring and the day-to-day attention to childrearing and other domestic matters that have permitted man to indulge his "grandiose self."

Many sociologists and historians have contrasted the present with an American agrarian past in which communities were more organic and less homogenous and goal-oriented than they are today. These theorists share with each other a preoccupation with the opposition of individualism and communal life (communitarianism), a focus that has restricted the scope of their work.[47] In the introduction to *Habits of the Heart,* Bellah and his associates asserted that

> there is something missing in the individualist set of values, that individualism alone does not allow persons to understand certain basic realities of their lives, especially their interdependence with others. These realities become more salient as individual effort alone proves inadequate to meet the demands of living. At such times in the past Americans have turned to other cultural traditions, particularly those we termed the biblical and civic republican understandings of life.
>
> The key point of connection between these traditions, one which sets them off from radical individualism, is their appreciation for the social

dimensions of the human person. [They] remind us that being an individual—being one's own person—does not entail escaping our ties to others.[48]

This talk of a modern lack of appreciation for the "social dimensions of the human person" fails to consider what feminist historians and psychologists have known for decades: that women have long held the "appreciation for the social dimensions of the human person" on men's behalf. When Bellah and his associates assert that "American individualism resists more adult virtues, such as care and generativity, . . . because the struggle for independence is all-consuming,"[49] they not only overlook their own insistence that individualism is not monolithic, but they also bypass the criticism that Jean Baker Miller, Carol Gilligan, and others have justifiably leveled at theories such as Erik Erikson's that do not emphasize caring and interdependence as goals for human development throughout the life span.[50] To say that "American individualism" resists the virtues of care and generativity is more than a bit disingenuous. Women have never "resisted" these virtues; far from it. And how can one cleanly separate individualism from care and caretaking? Caring and caretaking take place within the context of an individualistic culture and bear its impress (we shall return to this discussion in chapter 6).

The failure to address gender contributes to a notion of individualism as experienced identically by men and women. Here, Margaret, a middle-class woman, interviewed by Bellah and his colleagues during the course of their research, discusses her views on values and freedom:

> What I think the universe wants from me is to take my values, whatever they might happen to be, and live up to them as much as I can. If I'm the best person I know how to be according to my lights, then something good will happen. . . . I do think it's important for you to take responsibility for yourself, I mean, nobody else is going to really do it. I mean people do take care of each other, people help each other, you know, when somebody's sick, and that's wonderful. In the end, you're really alone and you really have to answer for yourself, and in the end, if you don't get the job you want or, you know, meet the person you want, it's at least in part our responsibility. I mean your knight in shining armor is not going to meet you on the street and leave messages all over the world trying to find you. It's not going to happen.[51]

What follows is Bellah's interpretation of the statements of Margaret "and . . . others influenced by psychological ideals":

> To be free is not simply to be left alone by others; it is also somehow to be your own person in the sense that you have defined who you are, decided for yourself what you want out of life, freedom as much as possible from the demands of conformity to family friends, or community. From this point of view, to be free psychologically is to succeed in separating oneself from the values imposed by one's past or by conformity to one's social milieu, so that one can discover what one really wants.[52]

Although it would be difficult not to see Margaret's vision of an almost contextless "self" as naive, Bellah and his colleagues' interpretation of her remarks does not take into account the possibility that Margaret's definition of freedom from the demands of conformity may refer primarily to shedding some of the constraints imposed upon women both by the mythology of Prince Charming and the "happily ever after" that determines their roles in relationships and in families. The idea of freedom as "freedom from the demands of others"[53] to which Bellah and his associates refer is a relative affair. In the 1980s Margaret's vision of such freedom, as now, might be a vision of release from female imperatives.

Another idea that is commonly subscribed to in cultural analyses is the notion that in the mid- to late nineteenth century "character," as defined through hard work and ethical behavior, was supplanted by the idea of "personality," as defined by personal qualities such as dominance, creativity, forcefulness, and the like that were considered necessary prerequisites for getting ahead.[54] The central thesis of this argument is that the great machinery of the industrial age ground away at a psychological level in popular exhortations to succeed through competition, to win. The Protestant ethic that had rendered discipline, frugality, industry, and temperance virtues in their own right yielded to the idea of success as an end in itself, as a confidence game, with personal magnetism as its trump card.[55] As denizens of a mass society Americans were encouraged to stand out from the crowd and develop their individuality. But where were women in the land of the glad hand and the ready grin? The alleged evolution from character to personality does not describe the psychological transformation of women at the turn of the century. In Theodore Dreiser's novel *Sister Carrie,* Carrie Meeber begins *her* quest for material goods and distinction in the arms of men. She takes *her* first step toward the American dream by sleeping with a successful salesman—a "drummer"—and glad-hander. If Carrie had begun as a middle-class instead of a working-class girl, she would have married and joined the ranks of the "cult of true womanhood," as a beacon to the men around her of older days and traditional values, a reminder of the triumph of character over personality.

What have women had to fear from individualism? Certainly not what men have feared. Although Wilkinson maintains that, historically, the desire to be in connection with others represented a "check against the pull of loneliness, selfishness, and aggression that lies within individualism,"[56] the fear of these forces was men's fear. For women, their own socialization, which dictated immersion in the "invisible web"[57] of domestic connections, was pull enough, and women themselves have often acted as buffers against loneliness, selfishness, and aggression for men. I would argue that what women *have* had to fear from individualism is an overfocus on the personal at the expense of the political; a search for the sources of their problems in the psyche that obscures their view of the social forces that frequently define those problems and prescribe their solutions.

Many Individualisms: Let Us Count the Ways

Despite the critical stance taken in relation to individualism throughout this book, I am by no means suggesting either that the effects of individualism are altogether adverse or that, as a society, we can or should shake off its toils; indeed, to abandon it, in the words of Robert Bellah and his associates, "would mean for us to abandon our deepest identity. But individualism has come to mean so many things . . . that even to defend it requires that we analyze it critically."[58] Individualism is not monolithic; indeed, "its power lies precisely in its ambiguity and plasticity," in the ways its meanings can be put to quite different and even contradictory uses.[59] Those who emphasize self-reliance and those who stress nonconformity are frequently—and unnecessarily—at loggerheads with one another.[60] But as Rupert Wilkinson suggests, "a particular kind of individualism is not something you have or don't have—people practice or believe in it to different extents (as well as showing it in different forms and situations)."[61]

Individualism and collectivism, often assumed to oppose each other absolutely, actually have a dialectical relationship. Americans do not appear to want either to subordinate the individual to the group or to yield the interests of the group to one individual or an elite group; thus, as David Potter contends, "while philosophers are engaged in pursuing one or the other of these two to their logical extremes and even their logical absurdities, people in everyday life will go on, trying . . . to accommodate these two and imperfectly to reconcile the indispensable values which are inherent in them both."[62] In the domain of mental health, adopting the liberal individualist notion that one can choose his or her own values and goals in a world in which others have the same freedom makes it possible for therapists to speak of the effectiveness of diverse therapies in assisting clients in becoming "healthier" or achieving a state of "well-being" without necessarily understanding that anything other than a purely "natural developmental process" is unfolding.[63] As a culture, we seem to fear collectivist goals as paving the road to totalitarianism. However, as Edward Sampson reminds us, this does not mean that we need to convert this worry into theories "about some fundamental, objective psychological truth regarding human growth and development."[64]

Individualism and Psychotherapy

There are a number of forms that contemporary liberal individualism can assume, and these, taken alone or together, establish, in good measure, the basis of many psychotherapies practiced today. The impact of the therapeutic enterprise as a whole depends upon them, and its deficiencies are in part attributable to them.[65] Two central forms of individualism are what Bellah and his associates term "utilitarian" and "expressive" individualism.[66] Utilitarian individualism refers, in its most strict construction, to the notion originally put forward by Jeremy Bentham that human action is based on a calculus of material interests. Benjamin Franklin put it in a somewhat gentler American form: work hard to improve yourself and you will be "healthy, wealthy, and wise." Utilitarian individualism is embodied in the institution of a competitive, capitalist economy. In therapeutic terms, this vision of individualism has influenced the discourse of effectiveness and "mastery."

On the other hand, expressive individualism, which we have mentioned in connection with Romanticism, defines success in terms of the triumph of individual self-expression over societal repression, and it is represented in such psychotherapy concepts as self-fulfillment and self-realization. The therapeutic nostrum that one must love oneself before one can love others is related to its tenets. Expressive individualism, in the tradition of Emerson, Thoreau, and Whitman, while strongly emphasizing emotions and self-expression, also endorses autonomy. Bellah and his colleagues view the therapeutic relationship as an amalgam of the expressive and the utilitarian strains of individualism. Therapy, they believe, furnishes a strange type of intimacy, and yet its exchange of money for service and its rule-bound structure tie "it into the bureaucratic and economic structure of the larger society."[67] From their perspective, the therapeutic relationship is emblematic of a more general contemporary form of contractual relationship in which the consideration of self-interest is preeminent.[68]

Although the expressive and utilitarian strains of individualism are quite easy to trace to their parent, the legacy that the postmodern concept of social constructionism owes to individualism is less distinct. Social constructionism, which stresses the socially constructed nature of the self, claims, in fact, to offer an alternative to "self-contained individualism." As applied to psychotherapy practice, constructionism encourages a "not-knowing" stance on the part of therapists. Theoretically the client and therapist together will look beyond the narrative of the client to find a new story more useful to the client than her/his old one.[69] Constructionism has been critiqued for its moral relativism, but this kind of relativism only makes sense from a highly relativistic standpoint. For all constructionism's anti-individualist bias, the notion that one can continually "remake the self," as Jane Flax argues, is, in fact, strongly reminiscent of a romantic/expressive perspective.[70]

The Empire of Self-Esteem: Self-Governance and the Culture of the Therapeutic

In a democratic society, Tocqueville believed, freedom can isolate individuals from each other. Even the right to associate would not suffice to guarantee stability in a democracy if citizens could not be brought to exercise their political liberties. Tocqueville found within democracy two contradictory and dangerous possibilities: either citizens might, in their independence, produce anarchy, or they might travel "a more roundabout . . . but also a [more] certain road to servitude" by giving over their will to an authority capable of sufficient strength to rule them. Barbara Cruikshank believes that had Tocqueville realized how much authority would be vested in the social sciences—in their position of helping individuals to govern themselves—he might have worried less about the possibility of despotism encroaching upon a democratic society. His statement that "each individual lets them put the collar on, for he sees that it is not a person, or a class of persons, but society itself which holds the end of the chain" was meant to apply to the possibility that one despot or a class of people might come to exercise tyranny, but it could pertain equally well to the idea that a society might exercise a control that emanated from inside the selves of individual citizens.[71]

In America, individual fulfillment has come almost to represent a social responsibility. The discourse of self-esteem has been transformed into a way of governing or managing ourselves through expert knowledge.[72] Michel Foucault in *Discipline and Punish* employed Bentham's design of the Panopticon, a model prison, as a metaphor for the way in which power is exerted over individuals in modern society. In this prison, inmates, each in his own cell, would be rendered continually visible, via backlighting, from a central tower. The effect of constant scrutiny on the inmates would be to induce in them "a state of conscious and permanent visibility that assures the automatic functioning of power."[73] This power, designated in Foucault's writings as both "bio-power" and "disciplinary power," is evidenced in the inmate's ongoing self-observation. To Foucault the Panopticon is a metaphor for societal institutions, and self-scrutiny represents the manner in which institutions exert power over individuals through a sense of continual self-consciousness—what Foucault terms a "technology" of the self.[74]

Consider the establishment in the 1980s of the California Task Force to Promote Self-Esteem and Personal and Social Responsibility, formed to study the relationship between self-esteem and a variety of social problems. The bill that established the task force states that "government and experts cannot fix these problems for us. It is only when each of us recognizes our individual personal and social responsibility to be part of the solution that we also realize higher 'self-esteem.'"[75] The idea was that Californians could become better citizens by developing this sense of personal and social responsibility. The task force reported that self-esteem is the likeliest candidate for a *social vaccine,* something that empowers us to live responsibly and that inoculates us against the lures of crime, violence, substance abuse, teen pregnancy, child abuse, chronic welfare dependency, and educational failure. The lack of self-esteem is central to most personal and social ills plaguing our state and nation as we approach the end of the twentieth century.[76]

In this conceptualization one can observe the pairing of self-esteem and empowerment in the idea that power derives from feeling good about oneself—that self-esteem can empower individuals to overcome a whole host of social ills. One of the goals of the California program was to get clients to narrate their personal stories so that they would see how their personal lives were bound up with the greater social good.

The project of confession, as Foucault describes it, is the technical key to many modern models of psychotherapy. By putting into words who we are and what we do, we become subjects in "a certain game of authority —bound to the languages and norms of psychological expertise" in ways that influence how we come to explain ourselves to ourselves.[77] What is viewed by experts as normal plays a significant part in the construction of our identities. In contemporary America, what does "low self-esteem" signify if not a deviation from the desired norm of "high self-esteem"? (One never hears anyone speak of "normal" self-esteem; so much for a psychological middle ground in the definition of what is normal.)

When people adopt self-esteem as a social aim they enable themselves to be governed: they take it upon themselves to establish, of their own accord, relationships with tutelary experts (e.g., therapists or social workers) in which power is the medium of exchange. Power need not be exercised from without because it is already being exercised by the individual on her- or himself. A "state of esteem" is not arrived at through public acts and public talk; its foundation is an interior dialogue "between self and self."[78] The notion of self-esteem forms the bridge between subjectivity and power; as Nikolas Rose maintains, self-esteem "binds subjects to a subjection that is the more profound because it appears to emanate from our autonomous quest for ourselves." From this perspective, freedom entails "slow, painstaking, and detailed work on our own subjective and personal realities, guided by an expert knowledge of the psyche."[79] Those who perform the self-esteem vaccinations—therapists, politicians, mothers—are not the people responsible for making "citizen-subjects," however,[80] and self-esteem is only one among an array of technologies of selfhood. Governing the self continues to be requisite to democracy; and yet, as Celia Kitzinger and Rachel Perkins suggest, it becomes "harder and harder to ask . . . serious . . . questions about what is meant by the 'self,' why it is considered necessary to discover, fulfill, and validate it, and how we theorize the relationship between 'self' and 'society.'"[81]

When Gloria Steinem, long a feminist activist, became a champion of self-esteem (see her book *Revolution from Within*)[82] she did not account for the ways in which what appears personal—the ways in which we "act upon ourselves"—are influenced by relations of power. Women cannot tap into a pure wellspring of "authentic" self-knowledge. As Cruikshank has pointed out, their subjectivity is not a "natural subjectivity that is hindered or repressed by power; [it is] shaped and constituted by power"—subjection rather than subjectivity.[83] Although Foucault identifies the institutions that regulate women and men, Sandra Bartky contends that it is not just institutions such as schools, family, and the media that regulate femininity; many strictures not bound to any institution profoundly affect women. The ubiquitous nature of feminine imperatives "creates the impression that the production of femininity is either entirely voluntary or natural." A woman is not marched off to the nail salon at the point of a bayonet; nonetheless, her sense that her body is deficient and requires transformation must be viewed as part of an enterprise of much broader scope—sexual subordination—whose goal is to make women the "docile and compliant companions of men just as surely as the army aims to turn its raw recruits into soldiers."[84] The male gaze is internalized and comes to shape a woman's awareness of herself as a corporeal being:

> Whatever its ultimate effect, discipline can provide the individual upon whom it is imposed with a sense of mastery as well as a secure sense of identity. There is a certain contradiction here: while its imposition may promote a larger disempowerment, discipline may bring with it a certain development of a person's powers. Women, then, like other skilled individuals, have a stake in the perpetuation of their skills, whatever it may have cost to acquire them and quite apart from the question whether, as a gender, they would have been better off had they never had to acquire them in the first place. Hence, feminism, especially a genuinely radical feminism . . . threatens women with a certain de-skilling, something people normally resist: beyond this, it calls into question that aspect of personal identity that is tied to the development of a sense of competence.[85]

Although Bartky refers here to the female body, I believe that her statements apply to the idea of relationality as well. While those feminists who emphasize the ubiquity and "naturalness" of women's relational powers clearly would never want to see women chained again to their "separate sphere," they accept a female identity based on conventions established within that sphere, as we shall discuss in chapter 6.

In the metaphor of the Panopticon, knowing that he may be observed from the tower at any time, the inmate takes over the job of policing himself. Women, who are on display to a greater extent than men, subject themselves not to outward regulation, but to an inner "self-surveillance" that observes patriarchal norms. Bartky believes that resistance is possible if women are able to understand how during the period when they have made enormous gains in the economic and political realms they have, paradoxically, become increasingly subject to "the dominating gaze of patriarchy."[86] What seems critical is the ability to change the terms of the contest, to see where we are located within the terrain, and to make our response from another position.[87]

Power exists in society's representation of individuals to themselves. Women have been both the subjects of and subjected to the observations, ministrations, and regulation of medico-psychological experts who limit and control "what it means to be a woman" in terms of the "truths" that suit the needs of the psychotherapy profession.[88] What are these truths and how have we come to subscribe to them? The story of how psychotherapy emerged as a profession, related in the next chapter, offers a number of answers to this question. It is a story about how men developed those "technologies of the self" that we have been talking about— the means by which we come to evaluate ourselves, to correct ourselves —and about how those technologies came to be broadly employed and adopted.

3

Romancing the Self
From Mind Cure to Psychotherapy

Psychotherapy is one of the significant "creations of modernity." It has attained cultural significance as both a creator of present-day mores and beliefs and as a mirror of them.[1] To discuss the creation that we call psychotherapy we must consider both the development of the way of understanding life that we now call "psychological" as well as the growth of the psychological professions. From the mid-nineteenth century to the present that thinking and that professional scrutiny have played an ever-expanding role in defining how we understand ourselves as specific kinds of actors in our own lives.[2] In the nineteenth and early twentieth centuries women were not at the center of theory-building, nor were they the majority of psychological and psychotherapeutic "experts." In this chapter, then, we enter a predominantly male world of ideas, commerce, and professional activity, one in which women were profoundly affected by men's theories, methods, and practices.

During the period from the early 1800s through the 1920s Americans' preoccupation with their inner lives proceeded apace. As I mentioned in chapter 1, both religious revivalism and popular mind cure movements promoted individualism through the message that people take responsibility for their own psychological well-being and by means of an unmerciful popular optimism about the possibilities for remaking the self as well as through the dissemination of popular and professional/scientific ideas about the nature of the mind. The product of these forces was, in the end, an unmistakably American psychotherapy.

As is the case today, the reciprocal influence that popular culture and professional expertise exert on each other often remained unacknowledged—at least by the experts—and this lack of recognition has furthered the notion of psychological expertise as removed from the everyday. In fact, as I will demonstrate, it was the very exploration of the mundane that first gave men interested in the psychological realm the power to reach into the ordinary lives of "normal Americans." To the extent that domestic life came under scrutiny, women's mothering and their "selves" necessarily became targets of acute and ongoing interest by experts. The increasing focus on the inner life of individuals that had its origins in the nineteenth century had important ramifications for women, given the expectations that were to grow up around their role as guardians of the moral life of the family and, later, of the family's emotional/relational life.

Religion, Medicine, and Mind Cure

> The advance of liberalism, so-called, in Christianity, during the past fifty years, may fairly be called a victory of healthy-mindedness within the church over the morbidness with which the old hell-fire theology was more harmoniously related. We now have whole congregations whose preachers, far from magnifying our consciousness of sin, seem devoted rather to making little of it. They ignore, or even deny, eternal punishment, and insist on the dignity rather than the depravity of man. They look at the continual preoccupation of the old-fashioned Christian with the salvation of his soul as something sickly and reprehensible rather than admirable. . . . I am not asking whether or not they are right, I am only pointing out the change. . . .
>
> We see the ground laid for a new sort of religion of Nature, which has entirely displaced Christianity from the thought of a large part of our generation. The idea of a universal evolution lends itself to a doctrine of general meliorism and progress which fits the religious needs of the healthy-minded so well that it seems almost as if it might have been created for their use. Accordingly we find "evolutionism" interpreted thus optimistically and embraced as a substitute for the religion they were born in, by a multitude of our contemporaries who have either been trained scientifically, or been fond of reading popular science, and who had already begun to be inwardly dissatisfied with what seemed to them the harshness and irrationality of the orthodox Christian scheme.
>
> —William James[3]

Psychological vocabularies articulated more than a century ago have made it possible for many Americans to believe that they can achieve desired objectives (e.g., contentment, productivity, sanity, intellectual ability) through the systematic oversight of their own inner lives.[4] In the early portion of the nineteenth century it could hardly have been imagined that, by the early decades of the twentieth, a therapeutic way of life would begin to be established that would reach beyond any single discipline to shape our ideas of the normal and the pathological, and, eventually, by setting the standards for "normal" self-actualization, influence how we should conduct our private lives—how we should understand ourselves and act upon ourselves.[5] Although some critics have posited that the culture of the therapeutic has become the twentieth century substitute for religion (or, indeed, that it has become an antireligion),[6] ample evidence exists to show that people have continued to consult with clergy, friends, and family about their problems, even as professional psychotherapy has flourished.[7]

The historical record shows that early nineteenth century transformations in religious thought paved the way for new considerations of the self in the United States. Although the reasons for it are in dispute, the fact is that traditional Calvinist Protestantism, the most pervasive religious influence following the Revolutionary War—the Protestant ideology that championed predestination for the pious and damnation for the unconverted—became less dominant as the nineteenth century progressed, and by mid-century many Americans were plunged into a crisis of faith.[8] Nostalgic renderings of nineteenth-century small-town American life do not come close to portraying the diversity and confusion that existed during that century among attitudes, ideas, and practices in each sphere of life from the social, religious, and political to the medical. Theology underwent a progressive liberalization, and the country was embroiled in religious ferment such as has not been experienced before or since, making way for new forms of religious expression, from revivalism to other "religious" movements, some purely American and some imported from abroad.[9]

The Second Great Awakening

The revivals of the Second Great Awakening, a large Christian evangelical movement that swept the country from about 1800 to 1840, introduced new elements of individualism into religion in the form of subjectivity and autonomy.[10] The movement brought a dramatic intensity and an expressive emotionality as well as an element of individual decision making to the religious experience.[11] Now the validation of the authenticity or meaning of religious experience, rather than, as formerly, residing in doctrine or in the religious community, began to be located in the self as the supreme evaluator, able to make choices and to *feel*. Extreme states of emotion "proved" the action of God in the self, and subjectivity displaced rationality as the principal means of apprehending the divine. Whereas in the older Calvinist theology salvation was viewed as deriving from God, preachers like Henry Ward Beecher (1813–1887) began insisting that individuals had the ability to find God for themselves. The self became the agent and God, a passive entity, awaited human agency to activate Him.[12]

Roy Anker maintains that the Awakening, as a movement that infused Protestantism with a new individualism, was but one of two cultural strains that had enormous influence on the American cultural climate. The other was Transcendentalism, an offshoot of American Romanticism.[13] Transcendentalism brought the human and the divine into a more intimate relation with each other than the Puritans would ever have allowed. If God were omnipresent in nature, as Emerson and the Transcendentalists believed, there could be no rigid boundary between humankind and God. The Transcendentalist theme that emanated from the revival movement, that health resided in harmony between self and the universe, not in an ultimate reconciliation with God, persisted in many forms of mind cure.[14] Harmony derived from "insight and intuition," suffusing individuals with an inflow of power and joy.[15] In a moral and spiritual universe in which contrition and repentance were no longer seen as necessary for entrance to divine realms, the path to God appeared to be eased—a significant alteration in the American religious landscape, or heavenscape, if you will.

Transcendentalism aside, all was not harmonious in America. As I shall discuss further in chapter 4, Americans seemed to be paying a steep price for social change as the nineteenth century progressed. Many physicians believed that contemporary existence was not conducive to health, rest, or security. Psychosomatic illnesses were on the rise, and Americans, increasingly subject to the need to devote attention to their inner lives, worried about their mental health as they "threw responsibility" for their problems "pitilessly inward."[16] Physicians observed more and more patients who were not coping well with the pressures of life, and from their observations these physicians developed hypotheses not only about what ailed their patients but also about what ailed society.

cf.
also
Rothman
+
Paul Starr

In the Gilded Age health was viewed as "an absence of illness rather than as a quality in its own right."[17] As one woman physician put it, "Health is like the silent existence of those happy nations that have no history. But disease represents the commotion, the storm and stress, the drama and the convulsions into which the disturbed history of our race has usually been thrown."[18] Nineteenth-century doctors had no explanations for the mind-body relationship that underlies psychosomatic illnesses, nor did they apply themselves to the treatment of symptoms for which there was no apparent physiological basis. In fact, they showed little general interest in methods and models of mental therapy until the turn of the next century and beyond.[19] Neurologists, of whom more will be said later, had been establishing themselves as experts in the treatment of nervous disorders during the period between 1850 and 1870. In their bid for professional recognition they attempted to make a firm demarcation between their medical specialty and that of general practitioners and asylum superintendents. Although their experience in treating nervous diseases, it is true, opened up the possibility that some diseases believed to be organic might be treated through the use of mental methods, the fact that psychosocial factors might play a part in the healing process was not obvious to them.[20] The exploration of *that* thesis was left for the mind curists to cultivate; it was only later that physicians accepted it, and, then, not without a struggle.

A Brief History of Mind Cure

> The plain fact remains that the spread of the movement has been due to practical fruits, and the extremely practical turn of character of the American people has never been better shown than by the fact that this, their only decidedly original contribution to the systematic philosophy of life, should by so intimately knit up with concrete therapeutics. To the importance of mind-cure the medical and clerical professions in the United States are beginning, though with much recalcitrancy and protesting, to open their eyes. It is evidently bound to develop still farther, both speculatively and practically.
>
> —William James, 1902, *The Varieties of Religious Experience*

In an age entranced with the possibilities of science and technology, psychological theories had particular allure. Rather than depending upon transcendent theological principles alone, Americans could now depend upon "natural law" to help them feel that they had a measure of power over parts of their lives that seemed to be careening out of control. Psychology, in the form of mind cure, began taking on "the religious cure of souls."[21] Although there was often bitter factionalism among mind cure practitioners, to the public—as to William James, who lumped all mental healing philosophies together under the aegis of "mind cure"—mental healing was a single phenomenon. In a sense the public saw more clearly than the mind curists themselves the common aim of the movements—to provide Americans with alternatives to traditional medical materialism and the increasing dominance of physicians.[22] A blending of medicine and morals, a faith in individuals' right to, responsibility for, and control over their own mental well-being—these spoke to the particularly American nature of mind cure. And new methods of mental healing, as well as a new type of relationship between patient and practitioner, spoke to the ingenuity and practicality for which, as James had duly remarked, Americans were noted. The combining of "science" and subjectivity was not only characteristic of mind cure but came to typify all "mind cures" to come, including psychoanalysis and beyond.

Mesmerism

The mind cure movement had its genesis when mesmerism first came to America from Europe in the 1830s.[23] Although at that time its attraction may well have been its apparent ability to provide the answer to human illness, Robert Fuller makes the point that mesmerism, by unintentionally melding Enlightenment rationality with Romanticism, gained in popularity because it could serve as a ready vehicle for "whatever ideological currents were underfoot."[24] The mesmerist who gained the widest following in America was one Phineas Parkhurst Quimby (1802–1866),[25] a relatively uneducated clock maker and a highly practical and curious man who is frequently credited with transforming mesmerism into an early form of psychotherapy.[26] Quimby came to believe that the truly curative elements in mesmerism were the subliminal suggestion of healing and the patient's faith in the prescribed cure.[27] Although other mesmerists subscribed to the idea that patients' expectations played a part in their cures, Quimby went beyond this, concluding that the mind controlled the body and that beliefs themselves could be responsible for causing illness and effecting cure. Quimby felt that with his "spiritual science" he could correct faulty beliefs (usually about the body, God, or the self) by setting the mind in the "true direction."[28] He did not agree with his contemporaries that the ultimate rewards for hard work, persistence, and self-denial lay in religious salvation and the building of a strong character.[29] Instead, Quimby avowed that the goal of these virtues was to defeat unhappiness: "Happiness being man's aim, it is what we are all striving for. . . . My method is based on a science . . . which destroys opinions on all subjects which tend to disturb man's happiness."[30]

Quimby employed clairvoyance in his practice, as did all mesmerists of the day. However, when some of his cures did not hold up over time, Quimby, unlike his fellow practitioners, came to the realization that deep-seated and enduring emotional conditions were at the root of many of his patients' complaints. This insight led him to rely more completely on empathy, understanding, and influence[31]—talk—to help patients understand the relationship between their illnesses and their mistaken beliefs about God, themselves, and disease, among other matters. He wanted his patients to understand what his clairvoyance had taught him about *them*. "This," he maintained, "is the science or cure."[32]

Although one cannot stretch the comparison too far, Quimby, like Freud (who also eventually abandoned hypnosis in favor of psychoanalysis), saw a need for his patients to achieve a conscious understanding of their problems. One patient of Quimby's described his method thus: "Instead of telling me that I was not sick, he sat beside me, and explained to me what my sickness was, how I got into the condition. . . . The general effect of these quiet sittings with him was to lighten the mind, so that one came in time to understand the troublesome experiences and problems of the past in the light of his clear and convincing explanations."[33]

Psychological self-exploration was a new and fascinating activity. Quimby, who understood that many Americans longed for an ethical or moral guidance that mesmerism alone could not provide, was able to supply this tutelage through his methods of mental healing, outside any formal religious context. For American practitioners of psychoanalysis and psychotherapy, "talk" methods have never lost their preeminence.

As Quimby's ideas took hold throughout the country, schools of mental healing proliferated. So popular was the new talking form of self-discovery that eventually the practice of mesmerism was entirely abandoned in favor of its new incarnation, named "mind cure philosophy" or "New Thought,"[34] a movement that was to achieve wide recognition as one of the dominant mind cure philosophies to spring up during the latter 1800s and to endure, albeit in a changed form, into the early 1900s. A number of Quimby's most prominent disciples, many of whom had themselves been cured by him, expanded upon Quimby's ideas, among them Mary Baker Eddy, the founder of the Christian Science movement, whose *Science and Health* (1875) stands out as the first important work to emerge from the mental healing movement.[35]

New Thought and the "Powerhouse of the Universe"

In *The Varieties of Religious Experience* (1902) William James described mind cure as a "gospel of healthy-mindedness" and delineated its central precepts: "That the controlling energies of nature are personal, that your own personal thoughts are forces, that the powers of the universe will directly respond to your individual appeals and needs." A rather primitive notion of the unconscious sprang from the idea that spirituality was experienced through the subconscious. As James put it: "We are already one with the Divine without any miracle of grace."[36] A few years later a by-now popular American view of the subconscious was reiterated in *Colliers* magazine: that dreams and desires originated from "One Great Will, lying at the foundation of all consciousness and subconsciousness."[37] In this formulation the universal was viewed as not only *within* the individual, but *within* the individual's subconscious.

For the New Thoughters, as for Quimby, health, the Divine, and psychological well-being were located within the individual. In 1902 one of William James's female correspondents described her condition and her New Thought cure in this fashion:

> Life seemed difficult to me at one time. I was always breaking down, and had several attacks of what is called nervous prostration, with terrible insomnia, being on the verge of insanity; besides having many other troubles, especially of the digestive organs. I had been sent away from home in charge of doctors, had taken all the narcotics, stopped all work, been fed up, and in fact knew all doctors within reach. But I never recovered permanently till this New Thought took possession of me.
>
> I think that the one thing which impressed me most was learning the fact that we must be in absolutely constant relation or mental touch . . . with that essence of life which permeates all and which we call God.[38]

Psychological exploration was deemed necessary if individuals were to counter the power of thoughts to subvert happiness. As one advocate of New Thought opined, "You will never be perfectly well until you have brought forward into light those dispositions as lie quiescent in the past and even buried in oblivion."[39] Good health and happiness demanded *self*-consciousness, and the individual, with proper training and "practical guidance," of course, carried the major responsibility for achieving these goals.[40]

New Thought ideas were widely disseminated, not chiefly through practitioner-patient contact, but through an onslaught of publications. Magazines offered guidance to readers on the specific problems that plagued them.[41] Elizabeth Towne, editor of the preeminent New Thought journal *The Nautilus*,[42] published a regular column called "Family Counsel," which offered the following advice to one reader, R. E. G., in 1905: "I believe that a cheerful right-thinking attitude of mind along with fasting properly and persistently applied will cure any kind of disease except broken bones. You are on the right track. Keep cheerfully along"; and to a shy and lonely H. L. B.: "Accustom yourself to meeting people and you will outgrow self-consciousness. And when you are alone at work, think of yourself as working before lots of people and not caring a darn whether they admire your actions or not. . . . Be proud of yourself; consider yourself as good as the best."[43] Not only was the primary audience for this advice female; the preponderance of New Thought writers, teachers, and healers were white middle-class women. From about 1875 to 1905 leaders of the woman movement, early progressives, neurologists, and physicians found in New Thought a popular intellectual forum. The movement in its early incarnation developed a reputation for highly effective mental healing, offering new ways of thinking about the relationship of mind to matter, heredity, desire, and selfhood.[44,45]

Mind cure was helping Americans believe that the world outside themselves was not responsible for their miseries; it was *how* they viewed that world that had significance (today we might say that what mattered was how they "internalized" perceptions of the world). When, in the 1890s, a psychologist from Clark University interviewed patients and practitioners, he found that, whereas prior to the healing sessions the patients had believed that their emotional difficulties might have been caused by such external factors as governmental bureaucracy, crowded streets, or unkind spouses, after their healing they were convinced that all their problems were in their minds.[46] Patients expressed relief at finding that they had more control over their happiness or unhappiness than they had believed.

Ever optimistic about natural man's "capacity to transcend human limitations,"[47] those who espoused New Thought ideas railed against the notion of a vengeful God and embraced a God whose might could be used for their purposes, as this example from Ralph Waldo Trine's best-selling 1897 book *In Tune with the Infinite: Fullness of Peace, Power, and Plenty* illustrates:

> In just the degree in which you realize your oneness with the Infinite Spirit, you will exchange dis-ease for ease, inharmony for harmony, suffering and pain for abounding health and strength. To recognize our own divinity, and our intimate relation to the Universal, is to attach the belts of our machinery to the powerhouse of the Universe.[48]

Here, building upon—some might say bastardizing—Romantic and Transcendentalist ideas about the intimate relationship between humans and their God, Trine articulated an idea of God as the turbocharger of individual will. Movements such as Alcoholics Anonymous, "human potential" movements such as Lifespring, as well as New Age philosophies are the not-so-distant cousins of New Thought; the popular philosophy espoused on *The Oprah Winfrey Show* and the rhetoric of codependency, too, would be recognizable to nineteenth-century New Thought practitioners.[49]

New Thought philosophy had relied on thought or belief to heal and to establish both physical and emotional/spiritual well-being; Trine extended "the power of thought to the world of the material, specifically, to the promise of 'plenty,'"[50] and the New Thought movement began to give currency, literally and figuratively, to the idea that financial success could be attained through the power of thought. No longer was it, as in the Puritan tradition, one's treatment of and behavior toward others that ensured material success; as Fuller maintains, "now what mattered was the strength of one's thoughts about oneself."[51] Eschewing altogether the traditional virtues of interdependence—community, cooperation, compassion for others, compromise, delay of gratification—the later-minted variant of New Thought placed the self and its actualization at the center of the individual's universe.

The Emmanuel Movement and the Medicalization of Mind Cure

Whereas Trine appears to have sown the seeds for the further seculariztion of New Thought philosophy,[52] it was the Emmanuel Movement that inadvertently propelled the medical establishment toward the adoption of psychotherapeutic methods.[53] When, in 1906, the Reverend Elwood Worcester began a class for the "moral and psychological treatment of nervous and psychic disorders" to inaugurate "a cheerful crusade combining liberal Christianity, the powers of the Subliminal Self, and the latest in medical psychotherapy,"[54] little did he anticipate that these classes would spawn a movement that would have a profound influence upon the development of psychotherapy in the United States.

The Emmanuel Movement, a unique and literal combining of science and religion, began as a partnership of Episcopalian ministers and physicians working together in a Boston public health venture to aid poor people suffering from nervous diseases. The program that developed out of this collaboration was comprised of the establishment of a medical clinic; a weekly health class to which well-known doctors, psychologists, and clergymen gave lectures on subjects pertaining to mental, spiritual, and physical healing; and individual psychotherapy sessions with a minister. This individual meeting with a minister, lasting anywhere from fifteen minutes to an hour, was the most controversial aspect of the program. A typical session was described by a participant as follows:

> After the discussion and prescription of good books the patient is seated in the comfortable morris chair before the fire . . . [The patient] is taught by rhythmic breathing and by visual imagery to relax the muscles, and is led into the silence of the mind by tranquilizing suggestion. Then in terms of the spirit, the power of the mind over the body is impressed upon the patient's consciousness, and soothing suggestions are given for the relief of specific ills.[55]

Loneliness and fear of failure seemed to afflict many who came for help, and, of these, women were in the majority. Richard Cabot, a physician of the time, attributed this to the fact that "most psychoneurotics are women . . . [and] [m]ost women care deeply for religion."[56] There seemed no need to venture beyond this reasoning to consider why women were flocking to the Emmanuel Movement in such numbers to

obtain relief from their distress; no thought was given to the social
sources of their unease.

The rhetoric of the Emmanuel Movement, not unlike that of New
Thought, emphasized the individual's ability to control his or her own
destiny. In 1908, the journalist Ray Stannard Baker wrote that

> The basis of the whole system is a vital belief based partly on religion,
> partly on the applications of the new psychological knowledge that a
> man is, indeed, largely the master of his fate; that there is new hope for
> the weakest and the lowest; that if a man will place himself where he is
> in the current of good and high thoughts, if he says, "I do," "I will," in-
> stead of saying weakly and hopelessly "I cannot, I do not," his life will
> become a new thing.[57]

For all its commonalities with other movements, however, the Emmanuel Movement distinguished itself from the less respectable Christian
Science and New Thought movements, "despised by select and superior
people,"[58] and attracted important advocates such as Richard C. Cabot
and James Jackson Putnam from the ranks of professionally prominent
physicians.

The Reverend Worcester's belief that neurotic individuals had "moral
symptoms"—weak will, poor powers of concentration, impulsivity, and
apathy, among others—greatly expanded both the domain and the role
of the therapist.[59]

Over a two-year period *Good Housekeeping* magazine became a
home for articles by and about the founders of the Emmanuel Movement
and a source of advice to its largely female readership on topics ranging
from "housekeeper's anxiety" to childrearing.[60] The 1908 book *Religion
and Medicine,* written by Worcester and his colleagues, was wildly popular. However, in an irony lost on its founders at the time, the very popularity of the book galvanized opposition from the medical establishment
that was to prove the undoing of the movement, for in the book the authors had had the temerity to assert that in order to adopt their practices
professional training was not required.[61] In the late 1880s American
physicians had begun to lobby for restrictive licensing laws, one effect of
which would be to squash mental healing. As the Emmanuel Movement
increased in popularity, it drew increasing fire. Cabot withdrew his support, and Putnam penned an article in which he decried the practice of

allowing clergy to treat neuroses when, in fact, expert medical knowledge and ability were essential to this practice.[62]

Although the Emmanuel Movement had claimed a basis in the newest science, religion still played a pivotal role in its philosophy and practices, and the physician played but an ancillary role in the movement; he was "not yet the 'scientific man' of a new cultural order" that he was to become.[63] But this condition was not to last for long. Medical men were soon knocking on the door to get into the business of psychotherapy. Eric Caplan maintains that physicians were motivated less by their professed desire to rid the public of unscientific therapies than by a venality that cleared the field for what they now recognized was a booming market for their own professional services.[64] Over several decades neurologists, viewed as egotistical and "little better than commercial adventurers" by those in the next generation, had seemed permanently wedded to somatic therapies that failed to produce either effective treatments for nervous diseases or sound explanations for their causes, and their professional rivals, the asylum superintendents, were doing no better.[65] Even though it could be said that the neurologists owed their renewed openness to mental therapeutics at least in part to the success of the mind curists, physicians feared association in the public imagination with practitioners whom they viewed, for all their disturbing success, as unscientific charlatans. Putnam, one of the elite Boston neurologists who formed a small nucleus of psychotherapy advocates, wrote in 1895, "In a sense, I grudge the irregulars every case that they win from us, be they few or many, because I believe that with a deeper knowledge of human nature, a better understanding of psychology, a wider range of methods and greater skill in applying them, we could cure more of these patients ourselves."[66] There was—and continues to be—a strong need on the part of professionals to differentiate popular from professional mental "treatments."

Up to this time psychiatrists had been largely isolated in their work of managing asylum inmates, and psychiatry itself was an employment distinctly lacking in stature. But by the time psychoanalysis had begun to exert its commanding influence in America psychiatrists had already constructed a new basis for their profession. Had it not been for the interest shown by early-twentieth-century institutional psychiatrists in helping patients disclose aspects of their private lives—"the filigree psychic interior of many a personal situation," as Boston psychiatrist Elmer Ernest Southard put it—the analytic perspective would never have met with its subsequent great success in the United States.[67] At the same time, one must credit the enormous influence of earlier mind cure philosophies and techniques with preparing the ground for the neurologists and psychiatrists who took up the new project of psychoanalytic understanding. Long before psychiatrists began to question their patients about their daily lives, for example, Phineas Quimby had encouraged his patients to talk to him so that he and they could come to a more thorough understanding of their distress.

At the turn of the century science and its enchantments beckoned the individual increasingly looking for secular answers to life's most puzzling questions,[68] and in less than two decades mental therapeutics, once thought faddish and laughable, had been embraced by medical professionals as their natural sphere of activity. Professional interest and energy were increasingly focused on the improvable self, the conceptualization of which had been more easily sold by the New Thoughters and their kin than the idea of the curable soul. Soon the idea of the self as a unitary phenomenon would be vanquished, and the hunt for the "real" self would be on, an exploration for which psychoanalytic ideas, or at least a sanitized, Americanized version of them, seemed ideally suited.[69]

An American Psychotherapy

The beginnings of psychotherapy in the United States are often closely associated with Freud's first visit to America in 1909. However, there were almost no references made to Freud's ideas in medical periodicals and none at all in the popular magazines and other sources before 1910. Far from a European invention, psychotherapy derived from a number of interpenetrating sociocultural discourses abroad in America during the waning days of the Victorian era, and the ideas that eventually became accepted by the newly professional group of physicians who practiced psychotherapy bore the strong impress of those discourses. At the time of Freud's visit, mental therapeutics were part of both American culture and of American medicine. But even so, as late as 1907 very few American doctors understood the central role that psychotherapy would come to play in their own professional lives and in the culture at large.[70]

In 1876 the captain of the war on American nervousness, George M. Beard, had been mocked for suggesting that mental healing might be employed to treat disease.[71] Given the stranglehold the somatic paradigm had exerted on the treatment of nervous and mental disorders, the handful of American physicians who had reposed their confidence in mental therapeutics just fifteen to twenty years before Freud's appearance in America had needed to wage an uphill battle to gain professional recognition for their theories,[72] and they were ultimately successful. By the first decade of the twentieth century, the interaction of mind and body could be seriously discussed and debated.

The word "psychotherapy" itself entered the lexicon specifically to differentiate the physicians' approach to mental therapeutics—their medical movement—from popular lay movements. The charge to fellow physicians was clear: if they were to save patients from error and beat back the competition, as Charles L. Dana insisted in 1908,

> there ought to be some definite form of psychotherapeutics approved by the profession so that people would not go after "soul massage" or other faked forms of psychotherapeutics. What are we going to do with the large number who won't come to us and will go to anyone who will raise his psychic standard? We must find out the good behind these false methods and organize it into some wise scientific measure which we can prescribe. Until we do this there will be a continual succession of new cults . . . to the discredit of medicine and more especially of psychiatry and neurology.[73]

Rather than invoking the ideas of the New Thoughters or other American mind curists, the medical proponents of mental therapeutics preferred to cite writings of their European counterparts in the medical and scientific communities—Charcot, Janet, Bernheim, Breuer, Freud, and others.[74]

The status of Putnam and his fellow neurologist Morton Prince, Harvard men with university affiliations, enabled them, as campaigners on behalf of mental therapeutics, to put forward a methodical analysis of the part played by mental phenomena in specific nervous diseases and to be heard within their professional ranks without fear of denigration.[75] Professionals and the public alike were becoming familiar with concepts such as the subconscious, complexes, suppressed memories, and trauma. A handful of Americans had become the world's most sophisticated practitioners of psychotherapy. Although methods were diverse and training in a particular method was neither required nor promoted by any specific professional organization, American theorists and practitioners gave prominence to some European ideas over others, thereby shaping the first American rendering of psychoanalytic ideas.[76]

Despite the lingering use of hypnosis in psychotherapy and psycho-analysis, physicians increasingly helped their patients develop new per-spectives and new habits through reeducation and suggestion. In addi-tion to addressing patient symptoms, Prince, a chief proponent of the new "scientific" psychotherapy, took pains to consider the moral realm —the ideals of the true, the beautiful, and the good.[77] The domain of the psychotherapy practitioner was turning out to be a very extensive one indeed.

New Conceptualizations of the Self

The ideas of Prince's colleague, James Jackson Putnam, seem to bridge the distance between the Prince's therapeutics and the psychoanalytic move-ment yet to reach ascendancy in the United States.[78] They also speak to an evolving conceptualization of the self that would increasingly gain credibility among therapists and laypersons alike over the next century. Putnam had a strong belief that consciousness and the unconscious rep-resented the "ultimate reality."[79] Whereas the revivalists and the Tran-scendentalists had maintained that health was achieved through harmony between self and universe, in this newer vision harmony was seen to re-side *within* the self. Putnam, like William James, Henri Bergson, and Pierre Janet, believed that the operations of mind and body were com-prised of many independent processes, some operating outside con-sciousness.[80] If the self achieved consistency through the integration or harmonious interplay among its various processes, then the disharmony that nervous disease implied might be reversed through the *remaking* of the self. The individual with a nervous disorder had to be ready to relin-quish the "acting out" of morbid fears and thoughts in the interest of cre-ating an "image of himself freed from harassing . . . feelings."[81] If "per-sonality" could be improved by attending to cues in the outside world, the self could be remade through attention to the inner one.

Often disproportionate to its outcomes, popular interest in medical psychotherapy was helped along by journalistic enthusiasm. Defects of character could be transformed into virtues; illnesses could be cured purely through psychological methods. There was no end to man's ability to overcome any human barriers. New discoveries in abnormal psychology buttressed popular beliefs in the power of "mind." According to journalists of the period, popular and professional theories proved that America was turning away from its materialistic ways in an idealistic and spiritual direction; it was "as if the age of Transcendentalism were being reborn and its claims endorsed by modern science."[82]

William James and his former student, psychologist and psychotherapist Boris Sidis, put forward an idea that gained tremendous popularity: the notion that by pushing past depleting inhibitions and routines humans could, by effort of will, gain access to "deeper and deeper levels of energy," and that this energy could spur individuals on to ever higher levels of achievement.[83] Psychotherapists were frequently put to work assisting those who had failed or shoring up the confidence of the ambitious.[84] There was no one—not even the poverty-stricken—who could not lift him- or herself up. Even when a disease appeared to have social causes, there remained a focus on individual accountability.[85] Will or character, agencies fundamental to the individualism of the early to mid-nineteenth century,[86] could be shored up by outside experts. In the parlance of the twenty-first century, individuals could be "empowered" through psychotherapy.

Cleaning Up the Psyche:
Science, Mental Hygiene, and the Psychoanalytic Revolution

Virginia Woolf once remarked that "in or about December, 1910, human character changed,"[87] and it well may be that the period from 1905 to 1910 was critical to the movement of American society toward "psychologization." During this period Freud traveled to America, delivering his lectures and receiving an honorary doctorate from Clark University, and the mental hygiene movement was founded. Psychoanalysis and mental hygiene made a potent ideological combination that formed the foundation of the modern mental health industry. As Joel Kovel has maintained,

[pairing] the cleansing of the mind with that of toilets and streets . . . establishes a material-symbolic link between evil, rejected wishes and thoughts on the one hand, and dirt on the other. . . . In the new order, people are no longer undesirable, bad, mad, or possessed, they are sick,

and need the ministrations of a mental hygienist, the technically skilled, impersonal practitioner of remunerable skill.[88]

The distinction between sanity and insanity was discarded in favor of looking at how far a given patient had strayed from what was deemed "normal." When individuals exhibited distressing symptoms, their day-to-day existence—marriage, family life—was examined for indications of trouble. Interest in the everyday activities of patients led to a science of the mundane, as psychiatry began to prescribe as well as to define what was normal.[89] As Foucault has noted, following the institution of the case study and the assessment, the written history of a man's (or a woman's) life became a way of judging, measuring, and comparing individuals. A "case," by virtue of its ability to be described, offered to the professional a means of exercising control and authority. In examining the patient, the doctor and the social worker combined both "hierarchical surveillance and normalizing judgment."[90] According to Foucault:

> The examination as the fixing, at once ritual and "scientific," of individual differences, as the pinning down of each individual in his own particularity . . . clearly indicates the appearance of a new modality of power in which each individual receives as his status his own individuality, and in which he is linked by his status to the features, the measurements, the gaps, the "marks" that characterize him and make him a "case."[91]

From the perspective of mental hygiene in the 1920s and 1930s, personality was shaped by the environment, but "environment" was narrowly defined as the home, with a particular emphasis on the emotional climate in which childrearing took place, since childrearing was seen as profoundly affecting adult personality development.[92] If children were quarrelsome or lied or wet the bed, their behavior was seen as potentially leading to social problems (e.g., crime) up ahead. Discourse on the life of the family and the behavior of children linked an intimate psychological vernacular of wishes, fears, and guilts to relationships and early experiences. And "naturally," as I shall discuss in chapter 5, the focus on childrearing brought women and mothering under intense scrutiny.

"Adjustment" and "maladjustment" were the operative words in the brave new world of mental hygiene. Institutions such as factories and courtrooms could be viewed as sites that might promote "health, contentment, and efficiency. The new language was disseminated to family members through broadcasts and popular writings of . . . experts. . . . Mental hygiene was both a 'public' and a 'private' value: it linked social tranquillity and institutional efficiency with personal contentment."[93] Even during the Progressive Era, when the impetus for social reform was at its height, many Progressives believed that the safekeeping of democracy and the fate of cities lay in the hands of experts.[94] The psychologization of the normal had begun.

The status and influence of psychiatrists increased with their distance from the mental hospital. By 1940 when William Menninger stated with brio that "even though we regard ourselves as normal, all of us need some help every now and then," he accurately indicated the enlarged domain of therapeutic activity that had, within a century, moved from asylum to private office and outpatient clinic.[95] What historians have termed "therapy for the normal" began gradually to spread beyond the well-educated and well-off classes during the 1950s as more and more Americans became acquainted with various psychotherapies, not only through popular media (e.g., movies, newspapers), but, more directly, through experience. Clinicians encouraged the public to consider therapy as a natural way to manage the vicissitudes of day-to-day life. Anyone could become neurotic;[96] as Karen Horney had suggested in 1937, even an entire era could be characterized by its predominant neurosis.[97]

For those who believe that the age of mental hygiene has passed I offer an example from the days after the terrorist attacks on the World Trade Center. At that time Albert Fernandez, director of the crisis center at Bellevue Hospital, was asked whether individuals exposed to the trauma of 9/11 would need professional help; his answer: "Everybody needs professional help." He then went on to describe the professionals who were offering assistance in terms likely to be unfamiliar to most Americans watching the program: he called them "mental hygiene workers."

By 1970 there were as many as twenty thousand psychiatrists and ten thousand psychologists treating one million individuals in outpatient settings. Middle-class Americans were entering therapy for reasons very different than those that had motivated previous generations—not necessarily to fix themselves, but to enlarge and understand their personalities.[98] Today the "psy" professions are expanding at a much faster rate than the general population, and it has been projected that, if current rates hold, there will be a doubling of the number of psychiatrists every twenty years, of social workers every fourteen years, and of clinical psychologists every ten years.[99] Individuals who a few decades ago would never have considered their problems psychological in nature now openly describe them in psychological terms.[100]

Psychoanalysis and Its American Uses

Although psychoanalytic theory was to become the prominent medical psychology in America, not all of Freud's ideas survived their trip across the Atlantic intact. Within about ten years of Freud's visit to Clark University, not only had the mental hygiene movement pretty well cleaned up the "dirt"—the perceived excesses of sexuality and aggression—in Freudian theory,[101] but interpretations of his teachings took on a more optimistic and more moralistic tone.[102] Freud's interest in civilization's discontents and his lack of consoling answers to pressing human questions was not compatible with the cultural climate of the United States. As Philip Rieff put it, in Freud's work there

> is no large new cosset of an idea. . . . Freud's was a severe and chill anti-doctrine. . . . Freud maintained a sober vision of man in the middle, a go-between, aware of the fact that he had little strength of his own, forever mediating between culture and instinct in an effort to gain some room for maneuver between these hostile powers. Maturity, according to Freud, lay in the trained capacity to keep the negotiations from breaking down.[103]

Freud harbored no illusions about human perfectibility. When James Jackson Putnam asked him in a letter why psychoanalysts who had undergone psychoanalysis were not "perfect persons," Freud replied, "The unworthiness of human beings, including the analysts, always has impressed me deeply, but why should analyzed men and women be better? Analysis makes for integration but does not of itself make for goodness."[104]

The American version of psychoanalysis was cut to the cloth of the culture. It seems that the eager reception of psychoanalysis in the United States was based both on "real collective needs and . . . certain wishful misunderstandings." Sanford Gifford contends that

> the real needs were for a practical treatment of neuroses and a theory of unconscious motivation, both of which had been partially met by the

psychotherapies of suggestion. The wishful elements included the need to see Freud as a more active social reformer than he actually was, both in overthrowing sexual taboos and in creating the possibility for a better political system.[105]

Modernists did not appear to find any contradiction in the notion that people could simultaneously turn inward toward self-understanding and outward toward the pursuit of social change. However, modern American bureaucracy soon weighed in on the side of the individual; the focus on personal problems and their solutions usefully obviated the need to acknowledge societal problems.[106]

The particularly American psychoanalytic attitude gave a conservative message to the individual: that he or she face up to "reality" in the interest of understanding his or her inner desires, the better to keep those desires under control. It would seem that the new mandates made a strong bridge between the older cult of character and the newer cult of personality. In Nathan G. Hale Jr.'s words,

> what had once been "good" was now "adapted," "conscious," "civilized," and "mature." What had been "bad" was "unconscious," "primitive," "childish," "emotional," "unadapted." Mere pleasure, sexual indulgence, passivity, laziness, and selfishness were "immature." Rationality, unselfishness, control of instinct, independence, were "evolved," "scientific," and "progressive."[107]

Early popularizations of psychoanalysis frequently described how neuroses interfered with the fulfillment of the individual's social role, and early case histories show patients who seemed to have internalized the harsh moral strictures of the day in the form of shame, guilt, and fear of punishment for failures to measure up to prevailing moral standards.

The American rendering of Freud's ideas as both more medical and more social than he had intended seems to have been a symptom rather than a cause of historical change.[108] Girls like Edna St. Vincent Millay, arriving in Greenwich Village seeking freedom from convention, could just as easily have found their Mecca in the philosophy of social liberation as in psychoanalytically based encouragements to shed their inhibitions.[109] Although I will not count—or even recount—the myriad social uses to which Freud's teachings were put, suffice it to say that Americans, in their selective reading and interpretation of Freud, were able to use his work to take—or to protect—whatever position they wished. There is no doubt that Freud's ideas contributed mightily to the Western tradition of individualism. Americans could find the causes of indecipherable actions in "instinctual drives and defense mechanisms rather than [in] the devil or economic man."[110] And, after the 1920s, popular accounts of psychoanalysis had more and more to say about uncovering one's "wants, needs, and desires . . . and gratifying them."[111] Practitioners of psychoanalysis claimed for their approach an effective, systematic, and rigorous method whose scientific aura appealed to the physicians then treating nervous problems. Although it was never Freud's desire that psychoanalysis become a medical profession, he could never win this battle in America.[112]

Psychotherapy and the Culture of Professionalism: From Horse Sense to Higher Education[113]

Psychology was a growing empirical, academic discipline that in the ensuing decades was to be responsible for exposing many Americans to the psychoanalytic vernacular.[114] And it was the late-nineteenth-century thrust toward professionalization, in medicine as in other fields, that made the growth of the "psy" disciplines and the dissemination of their ideas possible. For mid-Victorians professionalism had come to mean more than the training in a body of knowledge that culminated in the earning of an institutionally sanctioned license or degree; it was a natural outgrowth of Americans' historical rejection of authority, and the science that undergirded professionalization provided the expert with a unique understanding of the world that protected him from insinuations of political, partisan, or personal motives or bias and left him accountable to very few.[115] Those untutored in his specialization were ill equipped to determine his competence; they were required to have confidence in his judgment. The authority with which a profession was invested seemed proportionate to the recondite nature of its knowledge base and the fussiness of its rituals. That the professional could see beyond the confusions and ambivalence of everyday life offered reassurance to those who sought his help or advice.

Unfortunately the advantage of what on the face of it appears a quite radical notion of the "autonomous professional" as a member of a democratic society had unusually conservative consequences. The professionalization of social problems such as poverty rendered them more readily isolable and controllable, placing all domains of living under the professional's authority and helping to maintain the societal status quo.[116] The culture of professionalism also reinforced individualism by deracinating social causes from social problems in the interest of science; the social system could not be held responsible for life's vicissitudes, nor could it be blamed for people's "nerves."[117] A "space of objectivity" had been discovered between the body and behavior, an interior site for scientific knowledge and practice. How that space has been inhabited by psychological professionals and what psychological understanding has been produced by them can be analyzed as a historical series of what Nikolas Rose calls "problematizations": the types of problems that psychological expertise seems to be able to solve, and "reciprocally, the kinds of issues that psychological ways of seeing and calculating have rendered problematic."[118] In the nineteenth century the woman's trouble called hysteria was one of those problematizations; the constellation of nervous symptoms labeled neurasthenia was another. In the chapters to follow, the bearing that gender and gender distinctions had on the types of problems that came into the professional's purview will come more sharply into focus.

As I have noted, in the mid- to late nineteenth century nervous diseases proved to be the making of many neurologists, garnering them patients in the fierce competition waged among specialist groups,[119] and it was this competition that fueled their struggle for a greater degree of professional organization, eventually enabling not only neurologists, but also psychiatrists and psychologists to corner the market on mental therapeutics. At stake was a large fee-paying clientele with a middle- to upper-middle-class pedigree. Beyond the establishment of a professional monopoly, however, the insistence on grounding theories and practices in a presumably rational and objective science bound "subjects to experts in new and potent ways."[120]

The medicalization of stress began with the panic of medical men over how to treat the nervous diseases that seemed to be sweeping the country in the wake of social upheaval at the turn of the century. The newly forming American psychological professions accepted the notion that strain or anxiety caused by social and psychological factors could lead to a wide spectrum of disorders, from stomachaches to schizophrenia.[121] This association between particular types of disorder and particular kinds of stress forms the backbone of the Western classical or "scientific" stress paradigm that has persisted into the present, and although the model may have had its roots in psychoanalytic theory, its applications have been solidly attached to the ideological foundations of American psychotherapy that we have just explored—the belief in the controllability of human actions and emotions; the faith in human perfectibility; the insistence on personal responsibility; the search for inner harmony. The following chapter will examine the stress paradigm and its particular implications. How we conceive of the "social" in relation to the personal and psychological—what permits us to conjure up the idea of a purely psychological "empowerment"—is one of the problems and paradoxes of the therapeutic culture, and one that has particular meaning for women.

4

American Nervousness
and the Social Uses of Science

> For doctors have to operate in the public domain, jostling with rivals
> in expertise and authority, and their services ultimately have to
> please paying patients. So medicine cannot afford to bury itself in
> sprains and pains but must engage with wider issues—religious, eth-
> ical, social, and cultural. The public wants from doctors explana-
> tions no less than medications; society looks to the profession for ex-
> hortation and excuses. Medicine is called upon to supply stories
> about the nature of man and the order of things. Moreover, because
> medicine has never enjoyed monopoly—nor has it been monolithic
> . . .—it has developed multiple strategies for securing its place in the
> sun.   —Roy Porter[1]

Medicine and the Stress Paradigm of Illness

The story of women and the medicalization of disorder, closely associated
with the stress paradigm of illness and mental illness, has its roots in the
late nineteenth century. Then, as now, a great deal of attention was given
to the effects of social change upon individuals in the form of stress-related conditions. And science in general and medicine in particular have
played central roles in explaining the effects of stress upon individuals.
The historical canon, particularly "the triumph of individualism," has
had quite a bit to say about the relationship between mind and matter, the
victory of reason (male) over disorder (female).[2] The question before us
here is how these discourses have influenced practitioners through whose
agency women have come to understand themselves. In the nineteenth
century, most of those figures were men; in the shifting therapeutic culture of today, women are in the majority. In the Western world, practi-

tioners tend to adopt an intrapsychic perspective that persistently emphasizes individual experience. The stress model is a mainstay of Western popular culture that has been, as Arthur Kleinman puts it, "'scientified' into a professional paradigm."[3]

Sorting out the relationship between stress and social change has been a complex business for historians and psychological theorists.[4] Indeed medicine has often been caught short when it has had to address common problems such as stress, a task that requires close examination of the relationship between mind and body.[5] This relationship was a great deal easier to forge in the nineteenth century when American physicians viewed the conclusions arrived at through their explorations as essentially compatible with moral truths. The body possessed materiality and divinity, and disease was the punishment for both material and moral transgressions, not because God intervened directly into the affairs of humans, but because He was the Creator of the human body. Thus "moralism . . . drew upon the prestige of science, while medicine was pleased that its findings supported the dictates of morality."[6] Today, no less than in the nineteenth century, moralism exists in science even though its presence is not readily acknowledged.

Whereas the authority of medicine[7] may be attributed to its territorial claims of expertise over the human body, its popular seductiveness has rested equally on its ability to adjust itself to public sensibilities.[8] That attunement has required taking into account changes in ideas about the self, morality, and culture. Science has had an expository role, lending to American thought a language that has been used to suggest, explain, justify, and at times to help determine societal values.[9] The relationship of science to social thought is also shaped by the needs and beliefs of society, and these needs and beliefs can influence scientific ideas and their expression. Although it is often believed that science, which provides assessment and critical objectivity, is far removed from ideology, which offers apology and justification, science and ideology are hardly dichotomous.[10]

Despite the lack of internal consistency in some "scientific" ideas, those ideas may be accepted by Americans for the social functions they perform. Indeed, the more insecure a domain of scientific understanding, the more readily it lends itself to social uses.[11] In fields most closely associated with social problems, society may make more insistent claims on and exert more influence over "scientific" work. The biological and behavioral sciences, touching most closely on social problems not always easily reducible to mathematical equations or amenable to controlled experimentation, are ever vulnerable to such pressures.[12]

Science and Scientism

Although in the nineteenth century science ascended to a position of new authority—of greater "emotional relevance"—its values were in no way incompatible with those of religion. The language of faith and the language of science are very different, it is true;[13] but American faith in the effectiveness of rational solutions and the romantic inclination toward natural phenomena assured their complementarity. Far from conflicting with religious ideologies, scientific progress seemed to complement morality, sharing the ideals of altruism, integrity, and the potential for spirituality.[14] Science, embraced by such radical Victorian thinkers as Karl Marx and Charlotte Perkins Gilman in the name of liberation, no less than by the middle class in the name of the status quo, was invoked to explain virtually every social problem.

As science took on an increasing significance as a moral force, particularly among the middle classes, the scientist became something of a cultural hero. He was an intellectual, although not an aesthete or an airy philosopher (he was more of a man than that); he was a pragmatist, a materialist, as tough as any businessman going. And yet he was selfless, working for the betterment of society without concern for financial gain —indeed he was a kind of secular god. This transformation of science into "scientism" (science worship) and scientist into idol was only able to be accomplished because belief in the transcendent objectivity of science made it the captive of no one class or group.[15]

For all the luster that clung to the man of science, however, the "regular" medical practitioner of Victorian times was not a member of the "scientific elite"; in fact he was likely to have attended no more than two years of medical school and to have had little or no clinical experience.[16] He was a product of the new bourgeoisie, prey to all its desires and fears; an individual who retained the mind of a small-town businessman, more worried about earning his daily bread and the competition that might interfere with his gaining that livelihood than about his profession's future. Indeed, he was no more a public authority than the local pharmacist. If he *did* happen to have a scientific bent this had less to do with his being a physician than it had to do with his membership in a group that had put all its eggs in the basket of expertise and professionalism. Although the world of scientific medicine was a male world, a universe from which female healers had been systematically banished, a place in it could not be ensured for the white, male physician unless he could prove he had something to sell.[17] It was only after medicine had been commodified that it could be fortified against its competitors through a marriage with science. Physicians looked to science to remove the stench of commercialism from medicine and, as we have seen, to fortify it against those who threatened to rob them of their territorial prerogatives.[18]

At the same time, whereas the vista of Jacksonian America had seemed to open up a world of near-limitless opportunity for the industrious man, late-nineteenth-century science's disappointing acknowledgment of human limitations threatened to cast as deep a shadow over that view as did the damask portieres over the Victorian drawing room. On the one hand, as I will soon discuss, even American nervousness could be fashioned into a flattering commentary on an endlessly aspiring American bourgeoisie.[19] At the same time, Darwin's biological determinism, with its suggestion that just beneath the polished surface of civilization roiled unthinkable savagery, was not easily dismissed. It was frightening to consider that human beings could be capable of harboring uncontrollable instincts or of experiencing feelings that seemed at variance with their reasonable selves. William James plaintively asked in 1909: is it absolutely necessary to "believe human experience to be fundamentally irrational?"[20] As science situated the mind more firmly in the body, it became clear that mind was prey to the same ills to which flesh succumbed, and that thought and emotion exacted their toll on the body's vital force.[21] The Victorian globe wobbled uneasily on its axis.

The neurologist George M. Beard, of whom more will be said later, frequently compared nervous energy to Edison's electric light:

> The force in this nervous system . . . is limited; and when new functions are interposed in the circuit, as modern civilization is constantly requiring us to do, there comes a period, sooner or later, varying in different individuals, and at different times of life, when the amount of force is insufficient to keep all lamps actively burning.[22]

There were dire warnings about draining one's limited reserve of nervous energy and exhortations to achieve moderation in all things, from actions (conventional actions were safe because, unlike daring ones, they did not endanger one's control) to emotions (excessive happiness could be just as dangerous as "depression of spirits"). Ambition and overwork were the bane of middle-class men, as were worry, novelty, and risk.[23] On the other hand, extravagance and idleness were thought to be even more taxing to the nervous system.[24]

The Stress Paradigm of Mental Illness

Mind and body are not discrete categories; rather, they can be viewed as representations that are negotiated between medicine and society.[25] The language of suffering varies from culture to culture. As cultural anthropologists have long understood, in some societies the somatic articulation of suffering is legitimized, in others the psychological. Discussions about the relationship between stress and disorder must necessarily take into account the social structure within which stressful conditions exist. Stressful conditions and the options available to individuals in coping with those conditions are shaped by the social and historical contexts of people's lives. The classical view of the causal connection between stress and disorder is both persistent and pervasive. Social changes increase stress and lead to alterations in the forms that disordered behavior will take.[26]

Allegedly scientific arguments become particularly entrenched when social change indicates that there is stress in the existing social order, and when that stress is related to gender[27] there can be a rise in scientism and a "radical medicalization" of illness.[28] As the nineteenth century wore on, stresses upon existing gender arrangements could not have been more acute, and concern over the definition of gender roles created tensions sufficiently palpable as to bring forth a distinct set of ideological correctives.[29] Medical specialists exerted increasing power over women by virtue of their interpretations of and intervention into individual and social domains such as sexuality, hygiene, and morality. They alchemized "scientific" understanding into socio-moral edicts, pronouncing not only upon what they thought to be true, but what they believed to be appropriate.[30]

Science and the "Woman Question"

> Throughout history people have knocked their heads against the riddle of the nature of femininity. . . . Nor will *you* have escaped worrying over this problem—those of you who are men; to those of you who are women this will not apply—you are yourselves the problem.
>
> —Sigmund Freud

> For most men, when she seizes the apple, she drops the rose.
>
> —Silas Weir Mitchell

As industrialization and commercialization seemed to bring with them potential power and roles for women, the new social and economic arrangements ushered in demands from some women for new rights. It was unclear where all this was heading. Among the middle classes both marriage rates and birthrates were falling. Mounting male fears of what these changes might portend for existing domestic arrangements created a yet more constraining atmosphere for women.[31] The Woman Question —the question of women's position in the modern world—became compelling by virtue of the potential threat that the increasing autonomy of women posed to the social order. There were two available answers to the question of Woman as Social Issue. Ehrenreich and English call these the *sexual rationalist* and the *sexual romantic* positions.[32] The rationalist answer, a demand for equality, espoused by "public" feminist reformers such as Charlotte Perkins Gilman (and in our time Betty Friedan) was assimilationist: women must join men in the market economy, unquestioning of its male-defined precepts. In contradistinction the romantic position, which depended upon a rigid delineation of the differences between men and women,[33] put woman partially outside man's universe, as mystery, as emotional, intuitive—as the consolatory prize for Adam Smith's rational "economic man." She is described in an 1830 edition of *Ladies Magazine*:

> See, she sits, she walks, she speaks, she looks—unutterable things! Inspiration springs up in her very paths—it follows her foot-steps. A halo of glory encircles her, and illumines her whole orbit. With her, man not only feels safe but is actually renovated. For he approaches her with an awe, a reverence, and an affection which before he knew not he possessed.[34]

This is woman valued only insofar as she can "work a kind of religious transformation in man," woman as "the register of man's capacity for personal experience."[35] Later more will be said of feminism's travels between the poles of equality and difference; for the present suffice it to say that at this time in history it was the sexual romantic solution to the Woman Question that triumphed, and science, that trusted friend of the bourgeois and reformer alike, was there to lend its authority to the proof.

The Governed Body and the Reification of Male-Female Difference

> For me the grave significance of sexual difference controls the whole question. . . . The woman's desire to be on a level of competition with man and to assume his duties is . . . making mischief. . . . She is physiologically other than man. I am concerned with her now as she is, only desiring to help her in my small way to be in wiser and more healthful fashion what I believe her Maker meant her to be, and to teach her how not to be that with which her physiological construction and the strong ideals of her sexual nature threaten her as no contingencies of man's career threaten in like measure or like number the feeblest of the masculine sex.
>   —Silas Weir Mitchell, *Doctor and Patient,* 1888

The "Woman Question" was not openly debated; instead, it was couched in the language and metaphors of science and medicine that, beyond reflecting the status quo, helped it to persist.[36] As Carroll Smith-Rosenberg maintains:

> On the very simplest level these ideas served as an absolute biological justification for woman's restricted role. They served as well to express and explain traditional empirical observations and folk wisdom concerning the real biological, emotional, and social significance—and stress—of puberty, menstruation, and menopause. They created, moreover, an ideal metaphor in which the Victorian physician could express a characteristic and revealingly inconsistent ambiguity toward woman's sexual and social nature.[37]

The justification for woman's subordinate place in man's universe was to be found in the careful delineation of her differences, from the physiological and anatomical to differences in her identity, defined by such ideal qualities as domesticity, caring, intuition, moral purity, and passivity. The ways in which her suffering differed from his were naturally subjects for medical scrutiny. Medical men used the raw material of Darwinian theory to fashion a view of women as more primitive than men, as less differentiated in the evolutionary hierarchy.[38] A lack of empirical data posed no barrier to theorizing. Women were more frail than men, physicians insisted: "The nerves themselves are smaller and of a more delicate structure. They [women] are endowed with greater sensibility, and, of course, are liable to more frequent and stronger impressions from external agents or mental influences."[39] Naturally the nervous system and emotions overwhelmed the female capacity for the kind of rational thought of which the Anglo-Saxon male was so capable.

Women were captives of their reproductive systems, dominated by their ovaries, physically and emotionally buffeted by variations in their reproductive cycles from puberty to menopause. At puberty the fragile balance between mind and body could be easily subverted—with disastrous results for their health and the ability to conceive. Throughout pregnancy women must remain preternaturally inactive; if all had gone well during their previous reproductive years, they might prosper. If not, menopause—the gateway to old age—would bring with it depression, the high probability of disease, and even the possibility of an early death. Since it was believed that the uterus and the central nervous system were connected, any shock to the nerves might affect the cycle of reproduction; conversely, changes in the reproductive cycle would necessarily influence the emotions. Nervous excitements of various kinds, then, could affect women's ability to produce healthy offspring, thereby interfering with women's larger social responsibility. Because of its ability to cause nervous distress and sap her vital energies, education, particularly during puberty and adolescence, might pose dangers to the development of a girl's reproductive organs.

In books and health manuals published between 1840 and 1900, references to the large number of middle-class women stricken with hysterical symptoms were plentiful, and some authors even went so far as to comment on how fashionable illness had become.[40] A sense of powerlessness had found expression in nervous diseases such as hysteria, which afflicted women in unprecedented numbers. Nervous illness became a socially sanctioned means of expressing unhappiness with the status quo—and a far a safer alternative than agitation for legal, political, and economic rights.[41] Hysteria, as it turns out, was neither new nor did it remain fashionable, but the meanings it took on during this period *were* new, and the illness became the gateway for a new profession with a predominantly female clientele.

The American Crisis of Nerves

Although the symptoms of hysteria and neurasthenia were frequently confounded, what is clear is that the pairing of "nerves" and symptomatic distress in the formulation of hysteria, the "female" disease, preceded the appearance of neurasthenia, the "American" nervous disease. To those who might ask what this distinction will yield, beyond a historical splitting of hairs (or, perhaps more to the point, a fraying of nerves), I would respond that the artifact of female hysteria made possible the development of the American preoccupation with stress and the reliance on the individualistic stress paradigm of illness that has persisted beyond the nineteenth century into the twentieth and twenty-first centuries. The widening scope of our cultural discourse about stress and the effects of stress upon individuals that began with the nineteenth-century epidemic of hysteria and proceeded with the "discovery" of the all-American disease of neurasthenia has been resurrected in our time, on the backs of women, and to their detriment. Even today, to speak of "female hysteria" is to commit redundancy.[42] Historically there has always been a category of male nervous disease that, depending upon the age, went by a different name—and a more "honorable" name at that. As I shall soon discuss, late in the nineteenth century the opposed categories were hysteria and neurasthenia.[43]

Hysteria and the Medicalization of Women's Distress

The historian Carroll Smith-Rosenberg has viewed hysteria as a social role option for some middle-class women crushed by the pressure to occupy two conflicting roles, that of the "True Woman" (delicate, dependent, emotional) and that of the "Ideal Mother" (strong; competent in the many tasks of her caretaking role; offering support to those around her; and able to bear up in the face of the pain, illness, and death that were frequent concomitants of nineteenth-century life). For some women who could neither meet societal expectations on the one hand nor release themselves from the pressure of those internalized standards on the other, the sick role provided respite from stress in the protective and cosseting environment of the family.[44] Their early years—the indulged girlhoods and languid courtships—had ill-prepared many of these flowers of Victorian womanhood for the agonies of childbirth, the isolation of domestic life, and the care of household and children. The women who felt most overwhelmed, physicians noted, were prone to succumb to nervous illness. Hysteria's symptoms, through what Porter has termed the "sickness pantomime," seemed both to undermine and to mimic the stereotype of femininity.[45] Whereas "fits" or other unseemly emotional displays to which hysterical individuals were prone ran counter to all that was ladylike, other debilitating symptoms created a helpless victim, a caricature of feminine delicacy.[46]

Just as the sick role prescribed the behavior of the hysterical woman, it likewise served to legitimate the relationship between doctor and patient.[47] Long ago religious men had performed exorcisms on witches afflicted with hysterical symptoms; now male doctors were expected to rid women of those same hysterical symptoms.[48] Physicians viewed both the disease and their patients as challenges to be overcome. Hysteria was a puzzle to them. Silas Weir Mitchell, perhaps the most famous of the specialists in nervous disease, once stated that hysteria "were as well called mysteria."[49] Physicians saw wildly varying constellations of symptoms in their patients, symptoms that, even as they were observed, seemed to twist and tangle into new configurations. As men of science they were required to find an organic cause for hysteria, but their efforts to do so proved immeasurably frustrating.[50] The result of the constant widening of hysteria's diagnostic boundaries was that increasing numbers of women were diagnosed with the disease. (In chapter 8 I will take up this phenomenon of the enlargement of diagnostic boundaries in relation to the evolution of the posttraumatic stress disorder [PTSD] diagnosis.)

Neurasthenia

Civilization is the one constant factor without which there can be little or no nervousness.   —George M. Beard

In 1881 George M. Beard, a New York neurologist who treated disorders of the nervous system, stated boldly that "American nervousness is the product of American civilization"[51] and predicted that nervous exhaustion might increase for at least another twenty-five years, or until human neurological development had advanced to the point that it could withstand the overload to which modern civilization exposed it. Many educated women felt the pull of traditional social role expectations as they strained toward an independent existence; for men, the characteristics required in order to become successfully self-made contravened earlier social dictates. As was also the case with hysteria, while an increase in choices led to an increase in the sense of tension or stress, nervous illness gave individuals a means both for expressing these societal contradictions and for dealing with them.[52]

Neurasthenia was an important development in the increasing medicalization of emotional distress, creating new roles for patients and physicians. As Tom Lutz has pointed out, the discourse of nervousness was an encompassing one. It was popular as well as medical; it was determined by notions of class, gender, civilized life, and psychology.[53] "Nervousness" became the term used to describe almost every "nonspecific emotional disorder short of outright insanity . . . from simple stress to severe neuroses" from the late nineteenth century until Freud's terminology gained popularity in the 1910s and 1920s. For a period of time neurasthenia was *the* respectable diagnosis. Several other diagnoses of the day were tainted in ways that the diagnosis of neurasthenia was not: hysteria through its association with women, hypochondria because of the implication of malingering, and melancholia by virtue of its symptom of delusions. Prior to Beard's formulation the symptoms now described as neurasthenic—fatigue, anxiety, ill-defined physical ailments— had been dismissed by physicians as trifling.

George Beard's description of neurasthenia,[54] if such a hydra-head of symptoms can be said ever to have constituted a unitary "disease," showed it to be a nervous ailment protean in its scope. Beard once listed forty-eight illnesses with which it could be confounded. His list of symptoms, only partially reconstructed here, will give the reader an idea of the diverse conditions subsumed under the diagnostic label of neurasthenia:

> Insomnia, flushing, drowsiness, bad dreams, cerebral irritation, . . . atonic voice, mental irritability, tenderness of the teeth and gums, nervous dyspepsia, desire for stimulants and narcotics . . . sweating hands and feet with redness, . . . fear of lightning, or fear of responsibility, of open places or of closed places, fear of society, fear of being alone, fear of fears, fear of contamination, . . . fear of everything, . . . lack of deci-

sion in trifling matters, . . . pains in the back, . . . cold hands and feet, . . .
a feeling of profound exhaustion unaccompanied by positive pain, . . .
involuntary emissions, partial or complete impotence, . . . certain functional diseases of women, . . . decay and irregularities of the teeth, . . .
dryness of the hair.[55]

Beard, who believed that he had been neurasthenic as a young adult,
viewed neurasthenia as an authentic and curable functional disorder
brought on by depletion of the nerve cells. Earlier in the century, without
the legitimation of this diagnosis, many men and women overwhelmed by
nervous symptoms would have been deemed weak-willed and deviant.
Now they were given a label that, as Barbara Sicherman has suggested,
"conferred many of the benefits—and fewest of the liabilities—associated with illness" on both patients and their doctors:[56] "The diagnosis
and its treatment helped physicians to justify a traditional role, threatened by the one-sided emphasis on science, of providing advice and comfort to patients and their families. In view of the impoverished state of
medical therapeutics in the late nineteenth century, this was by no means
an insignificant achievement."[57]

Beard had opened the door further to the incursion of medicine into
American society by insisting on the physician's prerogative to wield social power. Behaviors formerly designated as breeches of morality, such as
stealing and drunkenness, were to be replaced by the medical categories
of kleptomania and inebriety.[58] Apart from neurasthenia's importance as
a gateway to the broadening of medical influence, it also offers us a win-
dow on the early relationship between medical theory and practice and
popular opinion. Fears of the accelerated pace of middle-class life and the
symptoms that an "overcivilized" life might produce whetted a middle-
class populace's appetite for the kinds of stories and advice about people's
personal situations and relationships that found a home in such magazines as the *Ladies Home Journal*.[59]

Social Darwinist to the core, Beard believed that the culture was
evolving at a faster rate than the individual. He described neurasthenia
as a particularly American disease that owed its existence to a combination of urban living, the dry and cool climate of the American northeast,
and the competitive conditions of the American marketplace. In this representation neurasthenia represented the price paid by Americans for
progress—for the advancements of technology and the freedom to pur-
sue their own economic and religious course (freedoms that, of course,

were available primarily to white Anglo-Saxon men). It was a fashionable
—even a patriotic—disease, not only a credit to the sufferer, but to the
culture itself, reflecting the upward trajectory of American life.[60] Viewed
not only as medical theory but as social commentary, inconsistently jus-
tifying the social status quo at the same time as it "constituted an indictment of many of this society's failings, of premature industrialism, of materialism, and of the futile anxieties which this materialism fostered,"
neurasthenia can be interpreted as the expression of a characteristic
American ambivalence. On the one hand it conveyed optimism about the
nation's prospects for growth, while on the other it expressed a "chronic
[sense of] national insecurity."[61]

"Strength and vigor" were not merely descriptors of American civilization; they were terms that described what were thought to be the most
manly characteristics of America's male inhabitants. To Elaine Showalter,
Beard's metaphor for the neurasthenic man as "an engine with small
boiler-power, that is soon emptied of its steam"[62] mirrored men's fears
that overwork or mental strain would lead to impotence. The metaphor
of "nervous bankruptcy" employed by many medical men in their descriptions of neurasthenia also points up how the discourse of neurasthenia reflected not only the American love affair with capitalism but also
the discursive overlap of masculinity, earning, and owning.[63] Initially the
label of neurasthenia seems to have had its uses for men, for whom it was
impermissible to show any sort of debility.[64] Early in the 1880s when
some attributed the increase of neurasthenia among men to the feminization of American culture, Beard lauded that feminization as a marker of
cultural progress that was responsible for the refinement and sensitivity
of American men.[65] The model of the sensitive man did not hold over
time, however. Soon the conceptualization and treatment of neurasthenia
were to reestablish the gendered status quo.

Whether or not Beard's assessment that "nervousness" among Americans was on the rise was correct,[66] it had an enormous impact on his fellow physicians. The diagnosis awakened physicians to the possibility that
mental distress might lie outside the classification of organic illness or insanity.[67] Neurologists, who had been treating traumatic injuries of the
nervous system on the Civil War's fields of battle, soon adopted Beard's
new treatments and immediately following the war separated their discipline from general medicine and psychiatry, setting themselves up as specialists in the treatment of nervous disorders.[68] As the twentieth century
dawned, physicians were in general agreement that the key diagnostic

predictor of neurasthenia was emotional distress.[69] The *idea* of neurasthenia extended the trend in medicine toward individualized treatment of
psychological problems. As one physician put it: "The treatment [of
neurasthenia] resolves itself into an effort to treat the individual and not
the disease."[70]

Gender and Nervousness: Different Diseases, Different Cures

Despite the fact that the records of the day reveal that the number of male
and female neurasthenics was roughly equivalent and that men's and
women's symptoms were almost identical, it is clear from those same
records that physicians *perceived* numerous differences between men and
women related to the symptoms, causes, and treatment of neurasthenia
and strove to restore their patients to their appropriate gender roles.[71]
Beard even made a distinction between male "cerebrasthenia" and female
"myelasthenia." Cerebrasthenia was brought on by mental overload,
myelasthenia by physical or emotional shocks that today we would term
traumatic events. Thus, women were seen as the more easily traumatized
of the sexes, whether in the aftermath of such diverse events as a railway
accident or a jilting at the hands of a suitor. As we have discussed, the perceived causes of nervous disease in women reflected cultural views about
the sensitivity of women's nervous systems and the role of women in society. Neurasthenia in women was not usually traced to overwork; instead, the most frequent causes were thought to be biological, chiefly related to women's reproductive systems and the stress of childbirth. Symptoms were often thought to be induced via behaviors inappropriate to her
sex—seeking higher education, for example. The New Woman would do
better stay close to home and hearth as her mother had done if she were
not to expose herself to the possibility of nervous prostration.[72]

"Cures" for neurasthenia were tailored to existing gender arrangements. Silas Weir Mitchell's rest cure, consisting of six weeks or more of
confinement to the bed, fattening up with rich foods, and passive massage
and electrical "exercise," for example, was more often prescribed for
women than for men. Men could not generally be spared from their
worldly work for the long periods of time rest cure required, and restoring them to the masculine ideal might require building up their reserves
of energy through vigorous exercise.[73] From the case literature it is evident that physicians were more successful in their treatment of women

with neurasthenia than of men. Women were more malleable than men in physicians' hands, and, to borrow the metaphor of the physician Margaret Cleaves in 1886, physicians were dancing "chronic attendance" on their women patients like house flies.[74] Although some scholars have applauded the new dignity that Beard had introduced into the doctor/patient relationship, the denigration of women by physicians persisted.

Gender was by no means an incidental factor when it came to the consideration of whether to apply the diagnosis of hysteria versus that of neurasthenia to an individual. Hysteria was a "feminizing" label, clearly abjured by physicians when they were diagnosing men,[75] even though differences between neurasthenia and hysteria were often less than distinct. (Alice James, sister of the psychologist William James and the novelist Henry James, was given *both* diagnoses in her lifelong career as a patient.)[76] Distinctions were also frequently drawn along class lines, with the diagnosis of neurasthenia often reserved for the more "refined" middle- to upper-class patient. Neurasthenics were considered more cooperative patients, whereas hysterics were often viewed as evasive and even intentionally deceitful. One physician spoke for any number when he stated of the hysteric that "the sense of moral obligations is so generally defective as to render it difficult to determine whether the patient is mad or simply bad." The neurasthenic, on the other hand, was "just the kind of woman one likes to meet with—sensible, not over sensitive or emotional, exhibiting a proper amount of illness . . . and a willingness to perform their share of work quietly."[77]

Interest in neurasthenia peaked at the very beginning of the twentieth century, but by 1920, with lasting cures for neurasthenia hard to come by, the diagnosis gradually disappeared from the medical lexicon. However, the neurasthenic revolution vastly widened the scope of psychiatry in the first two decades of the twentieth century. Soon the disparate illnesses that comprised neurasthenia were being classified either as purely organic diseases or as disorders with a psychological basis.[78]

Psychoanalysis did not eliminate from the cultural landscape the phenomenon of stress-related disorders that Beard had introduced to the American consciousness, however. The sense that our own "advanced" civilization is the most psychologically punishing in history persists. We have appropriated the discourse of nerves—stress—to suit our cultural conditions, and medicine has continued to grapple with the particular "nervous diseases" that have become options available to Americans in coping with those conditions. Many of the symptoms people experience as they struggle with life's difficulties, symptoms that might once have been grouped under the aegis of neurasthenia, are subsumed today under the ambiguous category termed *stress*. And there are other commonalities between stress and neurasthenia, as F. G. Gosling suggests:

> The management of . . . "stress" has also defied scientific solution. Stress, in fact, has become a badge of professional achievement, much like neurasthenia a century ago. Stress is associated with white collar occupations, high-pressure jobs, and heavy responsibilities. . . . Like neurasthenia, stress is a non-life-threatening condition but one that nevertheless produces uncomfortable and disturbing symptoms in its victims. . . . It has generated a proliferation of counselors, therapists, and managers with fully as many unusual treatments as nineteenth-century physicians developed for neurasthenia, including exercise therapy, colonic therapy, vitamin therapy, and self-hypnosis, among other methods. . . . the continuing need for a varied approach to mental health care has produced new professions—clinical psychology, social work, child development—operating within the medical mainstream to provide counseling services to . . . anxious Americans.[79]

Gosling has argued that the "democratization of American nervousness" —the elimination of class and gender boundaries—occurred in the transition from Beard's theories to Freud's.[80] I would argue, however, that persistent class, gender, and racial differences in diagnosis and treatment belie the claim of increasing democratization. From the nineteenth century onward the discourse of stress has had different and more far-ranging implications for women than it has had for men.

In 1886 Dr. Cleaves, who believed that she herself had suffered from neurasthenia, waxed sympathetic toward the plight of women in changing times:

> In no country or time has there been so much would-be mental activity among women as in the here and now. *True* mental activity should not result [in] injury but good, [yet it does,] carried on as the struggle is, to keep up with the demands of the times, to fulfill the duties of wives, mothers, and homekeepers, with never ending social duties, and under unhygienic influences.

She lamented that women, unlike men, had received scant preparation for "certain work and distinctions."[81] Today, when stress is seen to result from women's attempts to juggle multiple roles, we can consider it, variously, as a medical problem to be treated by medical and therapeutic means; as a social problem with medical/therapeutic solutions; or as a social problem with social solutions. We will return in chapter 8 to a further exploration of the relationship between the discourse of stress and notions of women's "place."

5

Long Day's Journey
From Sentimental Power to Professional Expertise

The story of psychological woman and the feminization of the psychological professions unfolds in the religious and domestic spheres of nineteenth-century American middle-class life, and the history of this period offers a lesson on how the collective illusions[1] of gender underpin social existence. For the most part, when middle-class women *did* move beyond their place in the home it was to concern themselves with "feminine" matters—the material and emotional lives of individuals. Their concerns were not "psychological" in the sense they are today; nonetheless the domain of the psychological was soon to establish its primacy in women's lives. In a reconfiguration that dates back to the late eighteenth and early nineteenth centuries, a categorical distinction was made between male and female identities:

> For men, political individualism inaugurated a growing concern with self as agent and actor—self . . . as public man and accountable citizen. For women, who were barred from those public roles and identities, it also inaugurated a new concern with self and identity, but within the confines of a comprehensive discourse of domesticity. For men's accession to bourgeois individualism allotted women a newly defined role as "other."[2]

The early discourse of difference that cast the middle-class woman as moral center of the family has continued to regulate our understanding of women's psychological selves and women's roles in the affective and psychological terrain of family life, transmuted over time into a reification of middle-class white women's preoccupation with matters psychological.

The cultural importance of this preoccupation lies in the social need that bolstered and continued to support it.

Religion and Virtue

The term "virtue," which in the eighteenth century had had political implications, began in the early nineteenth century to become feminized, taking on moral and social meanings.[3] After 1800 the influence of women in the Christian church was strongly felt. At a time of few choices for women, religion offered them socially acceptable opportunities to exercise autonomy in the public world. Housewives read tales of a sinful world outside the home in magazines increasingly tailored to their interests, and these stories induced many women to venture from their homes in order to take up the socially sanctioned mission of combating the evils —alcoholism, prostitution, poverty—that threatened the safe haven of the family. Initiatives in charity and reform were coterminous with women's justifiable moral preoccupations.

Although male religious reformers and clerics had led the revivals of the Second Great Awakening (see chapter 3), what historians have since referred to as the feminization of religion occurred during this period as energetic women followers were encouraged to take on important roles in the movement, organizing prayer meetings and leaving their homes in order to carry their religious message into iniquitous cities. A number of women became missionaries and lay preachers.[4] Women revivalists shed many of the restraints formerly imposed on women's behavior and for a time posed an actual threat not only to the established role of women in the church, but to the role of women in the secular world as well. Although the antiritualism that characterized women's participation in the revivals did not endure beyond the 1850s, by which time tradition had reasserted itself in the form of established religion, it has much to say about what happens in the aftermath of challenges by women to existing societal gender arrangements.

According to Mary Douglas antiritualism functions as a rite of passage for societies in the process of social change.[5] It acts

> essentially as a conservative or restorative social instrument. Through the rite, social movement and change—and the elation and fear that accompany such movement—by being ritualized, become formalized and

controlled. In fact, societies use liminal rituals not only to contain the fragmenting and explosive emotions involved, but also to socialize the unformed individual, to train her to accept her new roles and responsibilities.[6]

The revivals of the Second Great Awakening, although permitting the enlargement of women's domain, also served to reassert the status quo through their containment of protest and their initiation of women into their new positions in Victorian society. Along with their encouragement of assertiveness on the part of individual women in the movement, male evangelicals' continuing emphasis on self-sacrifice was targeted more specifically at their female than their male congregants, instilling in the women an increasing sense of their own spiritual inadequacy that could easily be channeled into submission to men and into a new middle-class family form as the women's excitement about and interest in the movement flagged.

Because of women's cultural marginality they have historically been drawn to activities that have given them the ability to denounce the prevailing societal structure. However, extreme forms of antiritualism, such as those of the Second Great Awakening—or more recently the secular women's liberation movement of the 1960s and 1970s—do not sustain their appeal, showing themselves most compelling only when society itself is in a period of structural disorientation. As soon as a new social organization is embraced and women take their socially sanctioned positions within that structure, the lure of antiritualism dissipates for all but a few, and women's very rejection of antiritualism and acceptance of the new rituals that accompany the new social structure "become the symbol of stability within the new order."[7,8] As the nineteenth century progressed, not just the rituals, but the women themselves became symbols of stability. As I shall soon discuss, part of a middle-class white woman's job was to ensure that her husband, exposed daily to the harsh buffeting of the world outside the home, cleaved to the path of virtue. She was to be protectress of the moral domain and the touchstone for societal ideals.

Motherhood was seized upon as an ideal means of finding a place for women in the new social order. In motherhood was aggregated every female role and characteristic, from women's relationships with men to their identities, to their social roles; in the asexual identity of motherhood was found the "natural" destiny of women and the governing paradigm for a private self whose realization could be achieved through the devoted nurturance of husband and children. The fact that women were immured in a world that defined them through their attachment to men was concealed to some degree by an individualistic vernacular that, as Elizabeth Fox-Genovese points out, located women in "the realm of nature rather than the realm of history and politics, . . . struggle and progress."[9]

Oddly, the association between women and nature is at variance with the frequent depiction of the forces of nature as impersonal and violent— as "male." The civilized and *civilizing* nineteenth-century woman is in fact much closer to *culture* than she is to nature.[10] Nonetheless the distinction between the "female" private (natural) sphere, within which the needs of the body are fulfilled, and the "male" social (public) sphere, within which rationality and agency prevail in the determination of social affairs, *was* the perceived difference between female and male in the nineteenth century.[11]

By definition whatever is "natural" is also immutable, either unchangeable by human means or dangerous for humans to tinker with, and the determination that something is natural camouflages the degree to which patriarchy and industrial capitalism have, through ongoing human intercession, shaped the "natural."[12] For most women the cultural construction of motherhood as natural has become a controlling part of our own subjectivity; and yet, so is the notion that we can make and remake ourselves. Many white middle-class women hold, within our "selves," these contradictory notions: on the one hand, that motherhood is our natural destiny and, on the other, that we own and can refashion ourselves. As I shall discuss shortly, what we have internalized are the seemingly opposed notions of women's difference and women's equality.

"Self" Possession

The right to own, make, and remake themselves is a right for which some women have fought strenuously, if episodically, for more than a century. In the nineteenth century the model of individual autonomy that is one of the cornerstones of individualism, although often criticized as problematic for women today, held out great status and promise for those women whom it had previously excluded.[13] In her 1854 address to the New York Legislature, Elizabeth Cady Stanton's argument, typical of those in favor of women's rights, had its roots in the nineteenth-century political and bourgeois liberalism that were outgrowths of Enlightenment rationalism.[14] In this speech Stanton based her argument on the likeness of all humans:

> Here, gentlemen, is our difficulty: When we plead our cause before the lawmakers and savants of the republic, they can not take in the idea that men and women are alike; . . . we ask for all that you have asked for yourselves in the progress of your development, since the *Mayflower* cast anchor beside Plymouth rock; and simply on the ground that the rights of every human being are the same and identical.[15]

When she addressed the Senate Committee on Woman Suffrage in 1892, Stanton likewise invoked liberal democratic principles. In this case, however, the justification for women's emancipation rested not just upon the common humanity of men and women, but also upon the fact of women's ownership of *themselves*:

> The point I wish plainly to bring before you on this occasion is the individuality of each human soul—our Protestant idea, the right of individual conscience and judgment—our republican idea, individual citizenship. In discussing the rights of woman, we are to consider, first, what belongs to her as an individual, in a world of her own, the arbiter of her own destiny, an imaginary Robinson Crusoe with her woman Friday on a solitary island. Her rights under such circumstances are to use all her faculties for her own safety and happiness. . . . viewed as a woman, an equal factor in civilization, her rights and duties are still the same—individual happiness and development. . . . The strongest reason for giving woman . . . a complete emancipation from all forms of bondage, of custom, dependence, superstition; from all the crippling influences of fear . . . is because of her birthright to self-sovereignty; because, as an individual, she must rely on herself.[16]

The idea of possessive individualism referred to by Stanton argues for ownership as the determining factor in the achievement of actual freedom. With ownership, the ability to realize their full potentialities could be read into the nature of individual women as it had been for men.[17]

The Power to Civilize

> The man's power is active, progressive, defensive. He is eminently the doer, the creator, the discoverer, the defender. His intellect is for speculation and invention: his energy for adventure, for war, and for conquest. . . . But the woman's power is for rule, not for battle,—and her intellect is not for invention or creation, but for sweet ordering, arrangement, and decision. . . . By her office, and place, she is protected from all danger and temptation. . . . This is the true nature of home—it is the place of Peace; the shelter, not only from all injury, but from all terror, doubt, and division. . . . This, then, I believe to be,—will you not admit it to be, —the woman's true place and power? But do not you see that to fulfill this, she must—as far as one can use such terms of a human creature— be incapable of error? So far as she rules, all must be right, or nothing is. She must be enduringly, incorruptibly good; instinctively, infallibly wise —wise, not for self-development, but for self-renunciation.
>
> —John Ruskin

> In discussing the sphere of man we do not decide his rights as an individual, as a citizen, as a man, by his duties as a father, a husband, a brother or a son, some of which he may never undertake. Moreover, he would be better fitted for these very relations, and whatever special work he might choose to do . . . , by the complete development of all his faculties as an individual. . . . The talk of sheltering woman from the fierce storms of life is the sheerest mockery, for they beat on her from every point of the compass, just as they do on man, and with more fatal results, for he has been trained to protect himself, to resist, to conquer.
>
> —Elizabeth Cady Stanton

Although a market economy had been growing steadily for centuries, in the eighteenth century it had been primarily an artifact of the urban landscape. An agrarian order still prevailed in the United States as elsewhere. In the earlier tradition there had been no universal category of womanhood; rather, women were understood in relation to the men within their community.[18] But beginning in the late eighteenth century, femininity was newly defined in ways that made more emphatic the differences between men and women. In the transition from an agricultural to a market economy, two distinct, gendered spheres of activity emerged.[19] The household was no longer the sphere of production; it was the locus only of reproduction and its associated activities: eating, sex, sleeping, childcare, and the like.[20] Men went out to work; women, unless the family was impoverished, were expected to remain home with their children. Women's roles were circumscribed as the distance between home and work increased.[21] In the period after 1830 women suffered the loss of legal privileges, including the right to vote, and various professions were lost to them. If the "advances" of capitalist industrialization were freeing middle-class women from the burden of constant household drudgery, those same advances stripped them of their former roles as skilled contributors to the family enterprise. Although the middle-class Victorian woman was not thoroughly idle, it appeared that her "leisure, whether hypothetical or actual, was increasingly treated as the most interesting and significant thing about her; her function was obscured and intended to be so."[22]

In the nineteenth century, the ideology that defined the "cult of true womanhood,"[23] also referred to as the cult of domesticity, emerged from traditional European notions of women's inferiority. It was an amalgam of several complementary ideas: that woman and man inhabited different domains because of essential differences in their characters; that home was the natural province of woman; that woman was by her nature the moral superior of man; and that motherhood was a quasi-saintly function.[24] The characteristics of the cult of domesticity may have applied principally to white middle-class women; however, there is no question that its precepts strongly affected women outside this group as well. As morality increasingly came to be associated with a domestic sphere managed by women, and as society took an increasingly secular path, there was a widening gap between the economic world of men and the expressive, feeling-centered domestic domain.[25]

Domestic Individualism

This division of spheres was not a neutral demarcation.[26] Traditionally commerce had been denounced as dishonorable and crass;[27] now it was viewed as a civilized route to economic prosperity for both family and country, and private life was expected to provide all that the male world of rough competition could not. Home was the place where a man could be "himself," freed from the need to fashion a "workable" personality; home was a "haven in a heartless world" where individuals could feel cared for and valued. At its center, starched and smiling, stood the Victorian woman, the "angel of the hearth."[28]

Gillian Brown points out how, beyond Tocqueville's description of home as a "little society" to which individuals are bound through "feeling," and even beyond the vision of home as a sanctuary from the rigors of the marketplace, the values of domesticity can be viewed as *furthering* the development of capitalism in the nineteenth century. Viewed in this way all talk of women's difference from men and of women's moral domestic mission can be seen as obscuring the "cooperative, accommodating function of domesticity."[29] The domestic cult of true womanhood eased the pressures of a life lived at the mercy of the vicissitudes of a market economy by creating a personal realm insulated from its rigors. Just as the domestic world was woman's separate domain, so it was also the foundation of men's individuality. *Domestic* individualism, then, is a defining of the self—an "interiority"—that is rooted in domestic life. Domesticity (the civilizing hand of woman) and individualism (the autonomy/freedom of man) have long been viewed as adversaries (witness, as Brown suggests, the struggle of Huck Finn to escape from the "sivilizing" influence of the Widow Douglas) when they are in actuality related.[30]

Individualism was also divided along sexual lines *within* the domain of the domestic, resulting in a configuration that continues to regulate the interior lives of many contemporary men and women.[31] Both the gendering of the feminine "heart" and the belief that this heart existed on the "inside" of the outwardly aggressive man firmly buttressed the ideology of competitive individualism. A man could be free to engage in the new competitive world because, as Beryl Satter notes, "his worst excesses would be checked by both the feminine without (the influence of virtuous mothers and wives) and the feminine within (man's own gentle heart). Competitive individualism and sentimental selfhood were two sides of a coin." However, whereas man was minted whole, woman was only half (albeit the *better* half). While middle-class women's intuition and spirituality was of no help to them in the struggle to act independently, men could overcome their animalism by heeding the sensibilities of the feminine heart without and within.[32]

In the nineteenth century selfhood became associated with all that was female, and yet it was withheld from women.[33] I view the birth of "psychological woman" as taking place within this nineteenth-century gendered domestic arrangement. The requirement that they attain that "perfect" influence and "incorruptible" goodness and wisdom to which Ruskin had referred meant that women would increasingly need to understand both their own and their husbands' psychological "selves." We shall see in later chapters how middle-class women continue to struggle with societal messages that institutionalize, through the discourse of stress, the struggle between the interests of self-development and self-renunciation, and how the idea of domestic individualism is unwittingly incorporated by feminist psychologists into contemporary notions of women's "relational individualism."

The Good Fight

Even for nineteenth-century crusaders for women's rights who found little inspiration in the domestic ideal, the domestic delineation of the self had its uses. By employing a doctrine of womanly virtue to achieve social change, champions of women's rights posited a socially acceptable, "domesticated" model of selfhood.[34] For example, when Harriet Beecher Stowe maintained that it was only natural for women to take on the antislavery cause, she reasoned that it was because "God has given to women a deeper and more immovable knowledge in those holier feelings which are peculiar to womanhood, and which guard the family state."[35] As Lydia Huntley Sigourney had put it in her *Letters to Mothers* in 1838,

> How entire and perfect is this dominion over the unformed character of your infant. Write what you will upon the printless tablet with your wand of love. Hitherto your influence over your dearest friend, your most submissive servant, has known bounds and obstructions. Now you have over a new-born immortal almost that degree of power which the mind exercises over the body. . . . The period of this influence must indeed pass away; but while it lasts, make good use of it.[36]

But influence that "must . . . pass away" was not power in the material world, and this is what the activists sought. The contradictory notion that women could both embody transcendent ideals *and* serve as the mighty bulwarks of society could be easily exploited. Ideological separation of their spiritual, maternal essence from their corporeality proved problematic for women because a demand for power based in the metaphysical realm of self-abnegation and a higher morality failed to overturn conventional notions of female passivity.[37]

In the latter portion of the nineteenth century the group of public activists was rather small. Elizabeth Cady Stanton's assault on the cult of domesticity was far from the reigning perspective among women.[38] Thus, it was the merger of the domestic and public contingents that made success possible in the battle for women's rights. The fight could be mounted only by adopting an agenda on which all participants could agree. Stanton's objection to limiting feminism to one aim notwithstanding, the goal decided upon was the vote, and the new suffrage movement dramatically revised its strategy. In the past, the argument on behalf of women's suffrage had been made on the basis that women were the equals of men; now suffragists fell back on "domestic" arguments based on women's difference—that, if given the vote, women would bring their unique moral values into politics.[39] The commodification of women's unique qualities was used even to argue for their equality and their greater authority in the world.

Some women championed trying to enlarge woman's sphere without rocking the domestic boat. However, in historian Nancy Cott's view, it would be mistaken to call this group "protofeminist" or to assume that it shared a common ideology with the more radical activists.[40] *Domestic* feminism, which used the argument of woman's difference to insist that women, once given the vote, would bring a moral tone to politics, was quite different from a *public* feminism that argued for woman's rights.[41] The attempt to merge an activism that seeks social change with conventionally defined notions of womanhood is one that, I will argue in chapter 7, has eventuated in therapeutic notions of women's empowerment.

Domestic Commerce and Compensatory Power

Even before the turn of the nineteenth century the marketplace had offered magazines that counseled women on "domestic science" and other related matters. As literacy increased among women, and book production and distribution became more technologically advanced, women could buy books such as *The Frugal Housewife* (1829) or *Letters to Mothers* (1838),[42] which valorized the roles of mother and housewife. Those medical reformers who had endorsed the view that women were frigid were the same men who most energetically represented women to themselves as powerless domestic creatures: the first four chapters of William Alcott's *The Young Wife* (1837) are entitled "Domesticity," "Obedience," "Submission," and "Cheerfulness."[43]

But men were not alone in persuading women of their domestic role. Not only did women exert a potent influence on the popular authors of the day, but many of their number, writers and magazine editors, exercised their own brand of "domestic" influence over other women—a "Pink and White Tyranny," as Harriet Beecher Stowe called it. Ann Douglas, in her book *The Feminization of American Culture,* has argued that domestic ideology was sustained through women's use of their socially sanctioned "feminine identity" to influence others in the direction they believed to be morally right; their finer sensibilities endowed women with "compensatory power."[44]

By the late nineteenth century, at the time when home became increasingly identified as woman's realm and white middle-class women were freed by servants from the most backbreaking domestic labors, these same women were being targeted as consumers by the new American culture of commerce. Advertisers quickly came to appreciate the fact that women were their natural audience: "One could say that the late nineteenth-century advertiser was as ready as Freud, if for different reasons, to posit and explore the unconscious." The advertisers knew that "women would operate as the subconscious of capitalist culture which they must tap, that the feminine occupation of shopping would constitute the dream-life of a nation."[45] Women were the ones who made the household purchases; it was they who read advertisements and could be swayed by their emotions.[46] As the twentieth century progressed, shopping would "consume" more and more of women's time: in 1920 the average housewife spent about two hours a week in this pursuit; by 1950 as much as a full working day might be required.[47] We have already discussed how women were the principal clients of mind curists; now they were the primary targets of a different sort of therapeutic message.

After 1885 cheap magazines became the vehicles through which advertising and market research gained ground, and the experts—including those in the psychological professions—were able to reach a large popular audience. Magazines like *Ladies Home Journal* eschewed their older sentimental message of motherly virtue in favor of an emphasis on domestic practicality and civic contribution. Even newer, however, was the personal voice in which the magazine pieces were written—direct and conversational, intended to inspire trust and a sense of shared enterprise. Magazine editors invited readers to send in letters, furthering a sense of intimacy calculated to encourage faith in the magazine's ability to present only the most trustworthy advertisers and the best products.[48] Through these and other means, leaders of the new culture of consumerism set the stage for the ongoing, reciprocal interplay between individuals' emotional and psychological needs and advertisers' tactics.[49]

As early as the 1890s some advertisements were speaking to people's yearnings for a more dazzling personality and a more satisfying life.[50] As advertisers and their psychological consultants entered the domestic sphere, the most common message given to women was that love, marriage, and a stable and happy home life could be theirs if only they would purchase the *right* consumer goods. Women's sexuality became the basis for newly defined male-female differences, and the "sexy saleslady" offered women both sexual *and* consumer satisfaction. She sold the importance of finding a mate, and this imperative engendered competition among women for men's attentions, again cutting off women's lifeline to the outer world. This time women were not chained to the hearth, but to another type of cloistered existence characterized by the "privatized sphere of heterosexual relations."[51]

Jackson Lears argues that as the "therapeutic ethos" took hold of the dominant culture (and consumer culture was just one of the domains affected by this transformation) women were newly victimized. The "therapeutic imperatives" to achieve "self-realization through emotional fulfillment, [and] the need to construct a pleasing 'self' by purchasing consumer goods . . . helped domesticate the drive toward female emancipation. With great fanfare, advertisers offered women the freedom to smoke Lucky Strikes or buy 'natural' corsets."[52] One woman, in a 1906 letter to *The Atlantic* magazine, complained of the cruel optimism of its Woman's Page:

> The Woman's Page . . . pursues me, weighs me, and finds me wanting, without my invitation. . . . Quite against my will, I am spurred to the performance of imperative duties galore. . . . It is without my real privity and consent that I am prodded with precept and stirred to teasing ambition . . . , and am made uneasily aware of the latest collar and the newest style of hair-dressing—destined to change ere I can make them mine.[53]

As I will discuss further in chapter 8, because in women's magazines today a premium is often placed on what women owe to themselves rather than on what they owe in service to others, one might be led to conclude that the advice therein is merely encouraging narcissism.[54] However, contemporary "self-service" messages frequently cloak—and scantily—the underlying message that women must take care of themselves *so that* they can manage the "stress" of their jobs, parent their children better, or be more appealing objects for the gaze of men. There are many products that naturally can assist them in these endeavors, from medications to nail polish to psychological advice and psychotherapy.

A Long Day's Journey: Women and Emotion Work

"Dark Hidden Things"[55]

The 1920s saw a wave of intense interest in personal, revelatory narratives, and advice columns for the lovelorn proliferated, along with such magazines as *True Confessions*. Fascination with the personal problems of other people promoted the popularization of psychoanalysis. Through these confessional accounts readers, peering at the guilty secrets or deviant behavior of others, could see themselves. And even more alluring than the true confessions were the case reports that proliferated in the literature of the "new psychology" of the 1920s. Soon psychoanalytic ideas were being incorporated by novelists and playwrights into their characterizations and their depictions of family life.[56]

The idea that it is of utmost importance for each of us to uncover our "hidden self," a "real self deep inside" that might be full of possibilities as yet unknown to the mundane self, was an artifact of early popular interpretations of psychoanalysis.[57] To observe hidden motives in order to expose one's "real self" was one way of using psychoanalysis in the search for authenticity; another was to "gain objectivity" by trying to break free of obstacles that stood in the way of perceiving the truth. However, there was something to be feared from this exercise since the unconscious could turn out to have a frightening primitive force. Unwittingly, Walter Lippman used the language of male-female difference to describe this concern when he wrote, "We draw the hidden into the light of consciousness . . . , and we find that our conscious life is no longer a trivial iridescence, but a progressively powerful way of *domesticating* the brute" (my italics).[58] Here the conscious business of working on oneself is conceptualized as a process of feminization, signifying an extension of domestic individualism into the "liberated" post-Freudian environment.

The More Things Change . . .

The demise of the idealized Victorian mother is expressed grandly and tragically through the character of Mary Tyrone in Eugene O'Neill's semiautobiographical play *Long Day's Journey into Night*. The play, set in 1912 in the summer home of the Tyrone family and written by O'Neill in 1941, pays obeisance to an older era while at the same time opening up family life to the Freudian searchlight of America's first truly "psychological" playwright. As astutely as O'Neill gives voice to some elements of women's entrapment in bourgeois American family life, his willingness to subscribe to the modern discourse of a claustrophobic "psychological and familial determinism," wherein everything we do seems to be limited by interior motives and parental neuroses, denies the sociohistorical context of family life.[59]

In *Long Day's Journey*, O'Neill depicts a single day and night as experienced by the Tyrones. It is clear from early on that all is not well in the family. Mary, fifty-four, having been given morphine for pain after Edmund's birth, has battled an addiction for years and has just entered a period of remission at the time we meet her; Edmund, twenty-three, does not look well, and there is concern that he may have more than a summer cold; his older brother, Jamie, thirty-three, has yet to settle on a solid career and spends what little money he makes or his father gives him on booze and whores; James, sixty-five, in the late stages of his successful acting career is nursing some regret that, as a young actor, the irresistible lure of a large, steady income had caused him to settle for the sinecure of a melodramatic role in which he toured the country for decades. Mary is described as nervous by O'Neill, and her son, Edmund, is described as having his mother's "hypersensitiveness" (I:19); her husband, James, "has no nerves" (I:13). When we meet them the Tyrones have experienced their losses, collectively and individually; an infant son lost to measles contracted from the young Jamie when Mary was on tour with her husband; Jamie's illusions of youth gone; Edmund's health rapidly deteriorating; the bourgeois ideal of a bustling, cheery mother around whom the family can gather, despoiled.

Mary is a compelling figure, both for what she is and what she has not yet quite become. Through her are played out many of the tensions and contradictions of American middle-class womanhood on the verge of the age of the "New Woman." Mary's two youthful aspirations—to be a nun or a concert pianist—can be interpreted as the private-to-public transformation of middle-class women's lives over the early decades of the twentieth century. The theme of innocence and purity lost is regularly sounded in the play. When she met James, Mary was a convent girl. To have become a nun would have been to embody every chaste notion of

Victorian womanhood, taking her farther from the world; the career of concert pianist would have pushed her out into it.[60] And yet as Mary describes it, when as a girl she met James Tyrone, the matinee idol, "all I wanted was to be his wife." She is only marginally aware of how her choices have been shaped by the mass-produced, gendered mythology of Prince Charming.[61]

The play offers a canvas on which can be etched the lineaments of women's place in a newly psychologized and scrutinized family life. If gender is a principal means of indicating power relations rooted in the perception of differences between men and women,[62] we can view the meaning of Mary's actions in terms of those perceived differences. It would be easy, as the "long day" progresses and Mary, apparently struggling with her private demons, relapses into her addiction, to view her story primarily in terms of a departure from reality and a descent into morphine-tinctured memory, remorse, and fantasy. But Mary's story is more complex than this. Viewed from a sociocultural perspective the character of Mary embodies the fragility of the ideal of nineteenth-century domestic individualism, according to the mythos of which Mary should have been the keeper of hearth and heart. Early in the play, before the morphine has reclaimed her, James tells her, "I can't tell you the deep happiness it gives me, darling, to see you as you've been since you came back to us, your dear old self again" (I:17). What becomes clear as the drama unfolds is that all the men in her life urgently want Mary to take up that work of her "old self" once more.

Her husband and sons feel that they should protect her from anything that might distress her, but her wifely and motherly role—and their desire—dictate, to the contrary, that she protect *them*. At one point Edmund admonishes his mother when she worries over him. "Never mind me. You take care of yourself. That's all that counts" (I:44). But later on, his tone alters distinctly:

> Listen, Mama! You're not so far gone yet you've forgotten everything. You haven't asked me what I found out this afternoon. Don't you care a damn? . . . And why are you so against my going away [to the sanitarium] now? I've been away a lot, and I've never noticed it broke your heart. . . . All this talk about loving me—and you won't even listen when I try to tell you how sick—. (III:120–122)

In the evening, after a few drinks, Edmund wails

The hardest thing to take is the blank wall she builds around her. Or it's more like a bank of fog in which she hides and loses herself. Deliberately, that's the hell of it! You know something in her does it deliberately —to get beyond our reach, to be rid of us, to forget we're alive! It's as if, in spite of loving us, she hated us! (IV:142)

Her husband and sons want Mary to return to her true "self," to *be* herself, but that self is not necessarily the one she has lost or the one to which she desires to return. When she is not "herself" they leave her and go out to the bars. One falls more ill; one drinks to the point of forgetting. But they never perceive *themselves* as leaving *her*. James Tyrone answers Mary's plea that he not go out and leave her alone "*with bitter sadness*: 'It's you who are leaving us, Mary'" (II:86).[63]

Mary's abandonment of the family is by no means total. As her job description would seem to dictate, she continually rises to defend her sons and her husband from attacks, each by the other: "Now don't start on poor Jamie, dear" (I:18). She knows her motherly role and pushes herself to "act" it in order to restore family normalcy. In O'Neill's stage directions:

He [Jamie] goes out on the porch. She waits rigidly until he disappears down the steps. Then she sinks down in the chair he had occupied, her face betraying a frightened, furtive desperation, her hands roving over the table top, aimlessly moving objects around. She hears Edmund descending the stairs in the front hall. As he nears the bottom he has a fit of coughing. She springs to her feet, as if she wanted to run away from the sound, and goes quickly to the windows at right. She is looking out, apparently calm, as he enters. . . . She turns to him, her lips set in a welcoming, motherly smile. (I:43)

A minute later, arranging a pillow behind Edmund's head, she tells him, "All you need is your mother to nurse you. Big as you are, you're still the baby of the family to me, you know." Later, O'Neill describes her as emerging from sobbing on Edmund's shoulder: "*her manner is again one of detached motherly solicitude*" (II:94). What is never clear is to what extent Mary has ever relished her maternal role, although she realizes that she has frequently abdicated it and struggles to regain it.

When Mary describes to Cathleen, the servant, how she loves the fog ("It hides you from the world and world from you. . . . No one can find or touch you any more. . . . It's the foghorn I hate. It won't let you alone.

It keeps . . . calling you back" [III:100, 101]) there is a deliberate ambiguity concerning from what and from whom she is hiding; her inner and outer realities are consistently melded. She is hiding both from her "self" and from those who would demand of her what she cannot give. And yet it is when she becomes unavailable to the men, when she hides from herself, that she receives maximal attention from them as a separate person; when she is not in a fog, when she is available to them, they absorb, unthinking, what she has to give them.

While it is true that when Mary, with the help of morphine, "leaves" her family she wields her greatest power over them, she is not making a powerful choice in refusing to play the role of keeper of the hearth and heart, as some interpreters have claimed,[64] any more than the nineteenth-century hysteric, through her symptoms, was intentionally launching a feminist protest against her domestic role.[65] Mary leaves the family by becoming symptomatic, not through any choice. And as she slips into the "fog," the men, without her in their midst, seem at first rudderless, lost. But as the long day progresses and it is clear that Mary is becoming more and more detached and isolative, the men begin talk to each other—with the help of alcohol—about some of the emotion-laden subjects she has raised, and others as well. In her absence they must make a stab at communicating with and taking care of each other. And through her absence we begin to see what functions Mary has performed; why their need for her is so intense.

The men watch her; they wait to see what she will do; they despair, they rail; they disagree about the deliberateness of her betrayal; they try to forgive her; they are preoccupied with her. They speculate about her mental state: "She has control of her nerves—or at least she had until Edmund got sick. Now you can feel her growing tense and frightened underneath" (I:37). Mary is aware of the constant scrutiny and is continually putting her hands to her hair, worrying that it might be disarranged. She knows that she is being watched for signs that she is taking the drug, but monitoring her physical appearance is nothing new. As is the case today, the physical becomes the symbol of the psychological; looking good (e.g., fit, "pulled together") on the outside is thought to convey something of the inner life.[66] As John Berger, the art historian, writes, a woman

is almost continually accompanied by her own image of herself. Whilst she is walking across a room or whilst she is weeping at the death of her father, she can scarcely avoid watching herself walking or weeping. From earliest childhood she has been taught and persuaded to survey herself continually.

And so she comes to consider the *surveyor* and the *surveyed* within her as the two constituent yet always distinct elements of her identity as a woman.[67]

As Joel Pfister suggests, Mary is psychologically confined "in a culturally produced body. . . . Desire and depth take on particular configurations for women because they are squeezed, patterned, molded, and formed by the social pathology of constructs like beauty, aura, presence."[68]

Sex and Sales

When psychiatry finally acknowledged women's sexuality or, to borrow psychoanalysis's own term, when psychiatry "fixated" on it, sexuality became a way to explain the New Woman question—the question of women's greater visibility in the public arena,[69] just as the romantic idealization of woman had served this function when the original Woman Question had been raised decades earlier. But the acknowledgment of women's sexuality did not come without a price. Powerlessness was once again redefined as power—not, this time, as moral influence, but as seductiveness.

By the 1940s when Helene Deutsch published her multivolume work *The Psychology of Women: A Psychoanalytic Interpretation,* the popular delineation of male-female differences had reached new extremes of pathology.[70] Women's power was portrayed as the "power of sexual surrender," an ability to take joy in her passivity, a form of masochism. If her gratification derived from her sexual submission, her sexual desire was predicated on her power to attract, pathologized as a form of narcissism. In the most pervasive popular rendering of the psychology of women, then, the stereotype of the angel of the hearth was recast. This time around, women were rewarded for their passivity and patience with "promises of sexual fulfillment" in a celebration of "a domesticated version of female sexuality."[71] Masochism and narcissism were distilled in the agonies of childbirth and ecstasies of motherhood, respectively. At the same time the discourse of seduction, of "feminine wiles masquerading as feminine submission," supported the broadly held illusion that women had the power when it came to heterosexual dealings, when in fact the reverse was true.[72] By the 1950s the psychoanalytic send-up of sex had shooed middle-class white women straight back to their separate sphere —now to their suburban coffee klatches, PTA meetings, and, for some, to their psychotherapy appointments. Just as in the nineteenth century, troubled women seemed to require the ministrations of doctors to help them manage their distress, although, this time, rather than rest cure, Valium became the panacea.

Psychological Family as Woman's Burden

As Mary points out to James, unlike her, he at least has an "excuse" for *his* drinking: *she* is the excuse. Family blame is dished out along gender lines. Whereas James is blamed by Mary and his sons for his cheapness and his failure to provide a real home for Mary or a good doctor (it is the "quack" that James hired to treat her who is blamed for Mary's morphine addiction), the blame leveled at Mary is qualitatively different. Hers is perceived as a distinct kind of failure, a failure to provide emotional nourishment for the family.

Much of the guilt that torments Mary relates to her belief that had she not left the infant Eugene to go on tour once again with her husband, the baby would not have fallen ill and died. In being a loyal companion to her husband she has failed as a mother:

> I knew from experience by then that children should have homes to be born in, if they are to be good children, and women need homes, if they are to be good mothers. I was afraid all the time I carried Edmund. I know something terrible would happen. I know I'd proved by the way I'd left Eugene that I wasn't worthy to have another baby, and that God would punish me if I did. (II:90–91)

If we interpret Mary's use of the word "home" to signify *psychological environment,* the meaning O'Neill most likely would have ascribed to it in 1941, it is clear how much responsibility Mary takes for her children's welfare. She blames her husband for never having provided a stable home for her, in Joel Pfister's words, "the sentimental home [that] was supposed to provide 'mother' with psychological compensation for not attending to her own needs."[73] And yet, at the same time, Mary seems to see that her idea of home requires a form of partnership that does not exist:

> *With increasing excitement.* [Mary speaks to her James]: Oh, I'm so sick and tired of pretending this is a home! You won't help me! You won't put yourself out the least bit! You don't know how to act in a home! You don't really want one! You never have wanted one . . . You should have remained a bachelor and lived in second-rate hotels and entertained your friends in barrooms! (II:69)

By the time O'Neill wrote *Long Day's Journey,* a shift in marital expectations had occurred, ushering in our modern form of companionate marriage. Now marriage was expected to be a relationship of emotional and sexual intimacy rather than an association based on the exchange of goods and services. However it was women who had received a more thorough schooling than men in the ways of emotional partnership, and it was women who accepted more of its burdens. Popular magazines from the 1920s on trumpeted the psychology of heterosexual relations. Most of the relational propaganda was for women's ears: how to become popular with the boys, how to win a man, how to keep him.[74]

The "psychologization" of the family, fostered by a mental hygiene movement that had established that the family's primary function was to provide a healthy environment for children, had carried with it the message of maternal responsibility for the psychological fate of children. As motherhood began to be divorced from instinct and considered a job for which education and even expert assistance were necessary,[75] maternal blame and maternal guilt could only be heightened. Although the message of responsibility was constant, cultural preoccupations varied from one era to the next: not so many years after *Long Day's Journey* was published, middle-class white women who had only recently been encouraged to shiver over their children's development were being accused of a psychologically corrupting overinvolvement with their children, particularly their sons.[76]

With respect to women's own self-representations, popular renditions of psychoanalytic theory, far from "empowering" women, helped them ascribe to themselves a gendered identity with a basis in the notion of a "naturally" feminine inner self. That identity is firmly embedded in the social structure. As Joan Scott contends, it is "part of the meaning of power itself" and cannot be altered without creating a profound threat to social stability.[77] When Mary says, "I've become such a liar. I never lied about anything once upon a time. Now I have to lie, especially to myself" (II:96), the self to whom Mary says she lies is a "self" fashioned in gendered ways; it is not the same self that her husband might reveal or conceal. In fact, the injunction to locate an "authentic," unsullied self is clearly stronger for her than for her husband. James, as his family can plainly see, is better than Mary at concealing his shortcomings from himself. As we have seen, Mary may blame James for never giving her the home in which all good mothers should operate and all children deserve to be raised, and he may blame himself for this; but for the failures of the family she—like James—blames herself. Self-blame and mother-blame have persisted well beyond the time of O'Neill's playwriting.[78] As Wendy Simonds points out, contemporary self-help literature is rife with mother-blaming in which

> individual mothers are held responsible for the individual men (the commitmentphobes, the misogynists, the drunkards, the lovers-and-leavers) who will become problematic in relationships with other women's individual daughters. And individual mothers are seen as creators of individual women (the clingers, . . . the passive-aggressives . . .) who will become problematic in relationships with other women's individual sons.[79]

A Message in Her Madness: Symptom as Communication

It is easy for her husband and sons to write off Mary's bitterness, accusations, and visits to the past as products of "nerves" or the "poison" she injects to combat them, as James does ("it's the poison talking" [IV:144]). The very melodrama of Mary's drug-induced monologues, themselves a play within a play, makes them—and her—easy for the men in the family to dismiss. Like women before and after her, Mary has had no training in directness or assertiveness; she resorts either to coy, girlish flirtation, or to what one of her sons uncharitably refers to as her "Mad Scene." However, what the men in the family might see as an "act" is, in fact, the only way she knows to make herself heard.

It is not when her evocation of her convent girlhood evokes Rebecca of Sunnybrook Farm or when her "ravings" recall Ophelia, but when she plays a third role, her motherly role—when, as O'Neill puts it, *"her lips [are] set in a welcoming, motherly smile"*—that she is thought to be conveying her *authentic* self, the self her family so desperately wants her to reclaim. And yet as removed from reality as her family perceives her to be, it is when Mary speaks through the "fog" of the morphine that she touches upon the emotion-saturated themes of family life. It is *she* who recalls and recounts the losses, the loneliness, the memories of more innocent or more joyous times. Mary may be drugged, but she does not forget; she holds the emotion for all the men. Indeed one has the sense that were Mary not in the "fog" that has metaphorical as well as literal significance in the play—the fog that shrouds emotion—she and everyone else might be overcome with feeling. As has been the case for decades, women's symptoms and men's perception of women's hyperemotionality obscure the psychological functions of that emotion—of the "emotion work" women perform. At one point, when she is running on and Edmund begs her to stop talking, Mary replies, smiling, as O'Neill writes, "*with an ironical amusement to herself*: 'Yes, it is inconsiderate of me to dig up the past, when I know your father and Jamie must be hungry'" (II:70), and later, to James, "I'm sorry I remembered out loud" (III:116). When James implores her to let go of the past, she answers "*with strange objective calm,* 'Why? How can I? The past is the present, isn't it? It's the future, too. We all try to lie out of that but life won't let us'" (II:90). Here Mary is the spokeswoman for the new realm of the psychological in which what is past is incorporated into the present as psychological "truth."

Social science had transformed the family from a sentimental to a psychological entity, isolating both the self and the family from the social surround in such a way that the family came to be largely understood as the stage upon which humans played out their individual dramas. The family became the darkly puzzling location for the authentic self—or its burial ground.[80] Mary's statement that "None of us can help the things life has done to us. They're done before you realize it, and once they're done they make you do other things until at last everything comes between you and what you'd like to be, and you've lost your true self forever" (II:63) reveals O'Neill's distaste for the American faith in the power of Emersonian self-reliance. O'Neill, who in 1946 spoke disparagingly of "that everlasting game of trying to possess your own soul by the possession of something or someone outside it,"[81] provided no bootstrap for the new Everyman or Everywoman to grasp. In a turn on the Romantic, aesthetic tradition, O'Neill expressed a fervent belief in art and the inner life, but without Romanticism's thoroughgoing confidence in the redemptive power of either.

Although the theatergoing public might embrace his tragic vision for a night, tradition did not favor viewing the struggle to reclaim the true self as a mug's game—not in the face of so strong a cultural romance with the notion of human perfectibility, and not when there were so many professionals prepared to help individuals examine the hidden self and repair it. And whereas it might be assumed that women's participation in the helping professions would be of great benefit to women, as it turned out, and as we shall discuss in the chapters that follow, this development was not an unalloyed good.

Emotionalism vs. Professionalism

The story of the professionalization of social work after the turn of the century is a cautionary tale about what can occur in the attempt to make helping human beings an expert activity. Social work was from the beginning a female-dominated profession whose low pay and low status has been strongly associated with its gendered identity. It was viewed as a field best left to women, who were not only more apt than men to accept its difficult conditions, but who, it was thought, were well-suited to it by virtue of its call for "feminine instinct" over expertise.[82]

As unpaid "friendly visitors," middle-class women had not only given material relief to the "worthy poor" but also favored them with moral nostrums aimed at helping the indigent build better habits and character. This volunteer system of ladies bountiful and charity organizations, however, could not sustain a new social psychiatry whose cornerstone was the belief that a knowledge of the patient's social environment was as important as an understanding of his or her mental and physical functioning. The mental hygiene movement's insistence that attention be paid to the environmental determinants of mental illness heightened psychiatry's need for workers with experience in the social domain.[83] The paid, college-educated women hired at the request of psychiatrists repudiated the old association between sentiment and women's work, insisting on their professional status as specialists in casework based on "scientific conceptions of the nature of social maladjustment" rather than on moralism.[84] Mary C. Jarrett, chief of social service at the Boston Psychopathic

Hospital in the early 1900s, insisted that the only route to achieving professional respect would lie in the embrace of "defined and systematized principles" and "communicable technique" that would transcend the "personal qualities in the social worker." However, she reassured the caseworkers, professionalism would not erase those qualities: "to be scientific is not to be less humane; to be thoughtful is not to be unfeeling."[85]

The relationship between psychiatrists and social workers in the early twentieth century tells us something about the tensions implicit in the gendered distinctions between the domestic (feeling) and the professional (science) that have come to characterize today's therapeutic culture. These distinctions were accepted as natural from the first, given the extent to which they reflected societal norms.[86] When male psychiatrists sought to enter the world of the everyday, they faced a conundrum: they were actually intruding in a domestic arena long associated with women and their activities. A great deal of the expertise to which the psychiatrists laid claim, Elizabeth Lunbeck tells us, "was not medical but social, not esoteric but common, not scientific but domestic—risky ground from which to advance claims for special expertise."[87] But where there was only one knowledge base there could be only one profession. Psychiatry's entanglement with social work

> threatened to expose how much of the apparent inevitability of their domination was premised on their prerogatives as men. . . . Their argument was straightforward: Psychiatry was science, and science was masculine; social work was sentiment, and sentiment was feminine. Forced, by their own ambitions, to abjure hierarchical claims vis-à-vis social workers based primarily on expertise, [they] simply redefined as "scientific" that to which the term referred.[88]

Determined to rise above their status as psychiatric handmaidens, caseworkers embraced psychoanalytic theory in the 1920s, and many fashioned themselves into psychotherapists.[89] Social work has ever been on the defensive about its status, looking to how to render the profession more "scientific" through defining a base of knowledge that distinguishes it from psychiatry and psychology, and many observers have made the case that its efforts to professionalize have marginalized those reform activities (e.g., advocacy, community organizing) that are the essence of "social" work.[90] The very need, then, to separate themselves from the "unprofessional" realm of feeling that was traditionally women's domain caused social workers to embrace scientism and to develop expertise in psychotherapy.

Women Observe Women: Mixed Blessings

> The position of the case worker is at once the most thrilling and the most terrifying in the whole gamut of scientific or semi-scientific undertakings which seek to gain social control in terms of the behavior of the human organism. There is no turning back. The choice lies not between doing or not doing, but between doing on a more or less sentimental and subjective level, which leaves the results to Providence or doing as courageously and consciously as possible whatever is done, however inadequate the equipment, struggling for a greater and greater scientific understanding and reduction of the intuitive field to a minimum.
> —Jessie Taft, "The Social Worker's Opportunity" (1922)

In the name of bringing scientific understanding to human problems, and at the behest of psychiatrists, social workers traveled from the state hospital into the home to assess what might be interfering with a patient's "social adjustment." Naturally this breach of the boundary between public and private life for the purpose of collecting "domestic knowledge"[91] brought social psychiatry—and social workers—squarely into women's sphere. At the same time, professionalism was to place social workers, the first women to examine the social and emotional environments of their fellow citizens, increasingly at a remove from the women whose families they sought to understand. Social workers' commitment to the family's—rather than the woman's—interests, paired with unrealistically optimistic notions about the virtues of domesticity, frequently led them to overlook the very difficult conditions of some women's married lives and guided their frequent attempts to keep marriages together at all costs.[92]

Even when, in the 1920s, the clinic, rather than the home, became the locus of the "hygienic socialization of the community," incursions into women's domain proceeded unabated.[93] In child guidance clinics, in many cases, a psychiatrist took charge of a child's psychotherapy while a psychiatric social worker interviewed the child's mother. The social worker's function did not end with gathering information about the family, but involved obtaining the mother's cooperation so that work with the child could proceed. This might include explaining the work of the clinic so that mothers would not worry about having their authority usurped and would not pose a threat to the work with the child. Such concerns about maternal sabotage are reminiscent of the warnings issued to structural family therapists in the 1970s and early 1980s, when therapists viewed the middle-class family as taking the form of a symptomatic child, a distant father who needed to become more engaged in family life, and an overinvolved mother whose grip on the child needed loosening.[94] Of course, women clinicians no longer operate as tools of a male psychiatric establishment. But even as they deplore the weight of family burden that devolves on women, some therapists have continued to blame women for and trade on their sense of responsibility for the family's psychological well-being.[95] In the chapters to follow we will explore how feminist theorists and therapists have sought to stem that tide and what they have made of psychological woman.

Interlude

Feminism and the Ongoing Dialectic of Equality versus Difference

For decades, equality and difference have defined the poles between which feminism has slipped and slid. In feminist terms, difference speaks to those qualitative distinctions between women and men that determine their roles, prerogatives, and identities; equality, on the other hand, speaks to the common humanity of women and men that entitles them to common rights.[1] From the time—around 1913—when the use of the term *feminism* was regularly employed, equality and difference have been debated; at times, despite the apparent contradiction, both have been used simultaneously to challenge patriarchy. Arguments over equality and difference have caused deep divisions among women who identify themselves as feminists. As Nancy Cott has suggested, in the 1910s and 1920s paradoxes were revealed that came to define twentieth-century feminism:

> Feminism asks for sexual equality that includes sexual difference. It aims for individual freedoms by mobilizing sex solidarity. It posits that women recognize their unity while it stands for diversity among women. It requires gender consciousness for its basis yet calls for the elimination of prescribed gender roles. . . .
>
> That feminism is a theory about equality appears most visibly in its goal; as many have argued, feminism can be seen as a demand to extend to women the individualistic premises of the political theory of liberalism. . . . Yet feminism is also a theory about sexual difference, as can be seen in its method of mobilization, for it posits that women, as *women,* will feel the collective grievances to push forward toward equality.[2]

The historian Joan Scott makes the point that the dichotomization of equality and difference creates unnecessary difficulties for feminism and feminist politics. To place equality and difference in opposition to each other fails to capture their interdependent relationship, when in fact equality takes for granted a social pact to consider very different individuals as similar for a particular purpose. Thus the idea of equality implies a dependence on *difference,* and implicit in demands for equality are the differences among the individuals and groups that are making such demands; indeed, if we "were identical . . . there would be no need to ask for equality." In this sense, equality can be considered a conscious *inattention* to designated differences. And although differences may appear obvious or overriding, they are not. A central question that must be asked with respect to difference should be, "How is the meaning of difference constructed?"[3]

In the 1910s, giving greater prominence to a theme established in the previous century, feminist leaders invoked the need to develop the self as a means of helping many women emerge from the stifling environment of domestic responsibility. The model of the New Woman of the first two decades of the twentieth century who not only chose her way of living but also her way of *making* a living "stood for self-development as contrasted to self-sacrifice or submergence in the family." But although the phenomenon of the New Woman represented a coming of age for women's individualism, Cott maintains that

> self-proclaimed Feminists held individualism in dynamic tension with their political and social identification as women. . . . They moved toward a definition of women's common political task and consciousness that relied less on that staple of the nineteenth-century woman movement, the uniting theme of motherhood, than on the themes of deprivations and rebellions felt in common by women of various sorts.[4,5]

This agenda continued to resonate well with the prevailing ideology of individualism over subsequent decades. However, by the mid-twentieth century it was not clear how equality of opportunity was to be achieved, given that the individualistic premises upon which the demands for equality were based—the will toward self-actualization and individual achievement; the valorization of diverse group interests—militated against the coalescing of forces necessary to mount a common women's movement to achieve these ends. The twin "illusions" of feminism, as Elizabeth Fox-

Genovese sees them, are on the one hand the idea that "the abstract possibilities of 'autonomous' individualism could ever be fully realized for women (if indeed they have been or could be for men)" and on the other the "illusion that the individualist view of woman-as-other can . . . be converted into a general and 'feminist' law of female experience."[6]

To the extent that feminism reified the individual woman through its challenges both to limitations on freedom imposed by sex and its opposition to the historical imperative to nurture others, undiluted individualism neutralized feminism by eliminating the very foundation for any action women might take collectively.[7] However, if differences among women made new problems for feminism, the tradition of associating differences between women and men with women's inferiority meant that exploring differences "always risked reconfirming rather than subverting gender hierarchy," plunging women into a backwater of old stereotypes that seemed to take on new guises in each era. Feminist leaders became caught up in an unacknowledged gendered discourse in which extreme sex differences that were believed to influence men and women in private were to be ignored in the public domain, where it was assumed that women, as individuals, were to have power equal to that of men.[8] Domestic individualism, protected from the public discourse of equality that surrounded it, has indeed survived.

Conservative Feminism: Another Oxymoron?

A capsule reprise of the history of feminism in the latter half of the twentieth century illustrates a dramatic shift in feminism's agenda. From the period of the 1960s and 1970s, commonly called the "second wave" of feminism, when the needs of women were highlighted and a commitment made to forcing an end to gender inequalities and women's subordination to men, to the 1980s' grappling with differences among women as well as differences among feminist factions, to the 1990s' poststructuralist analyses of identities, the overall direction of change has been from the political to the personal. As Lynne Segal has maintained, the resurgence of interest in psychoanalysis in the early 1970s that moved feminism toward psychoanalysis and away from the early liberationist goal of social transformation is attributable to "women's own subjective resistance to change": "It was never going to be easy to persuade individual men to change, but it was going to be far harder to undermine the interconnecting worlds of home, jobs and cultural and public life which overwhelmingly reflect the principle of male authority."[9] Michelle Fine and Pat MacPherson in their interviews of economically privileged women found these women to have an "obsessive commitment" to both privacy of thought and of body, a need to "work out" their problems privately. For these women, achievement was the measure of their singularity, an outlook that hearkens back to the earlier decades of the twentieth century.[10] The media carry the message of the need for individual management of individual lives, and psychotherapy reproduces that message in a variety of ways.

As we have seen, in the United States individualism has necessarily had to serve as the ideological bulwark for women's demand for equality since, if any such claim is to have any chance of making cultural "sense" and succeeding politically, it must be articulated in the terms of the prevailing ideology. As Patrice DiQuinzio suggests, "If feminism cannot show that women are subjects as individualism defines subjectivity (i.e., identity), then it cannot argue for women's equal political agency and entitlement." At the same time, however, feminism has struggled against the premises of individualism. But even what an ideology attempts to rule out or manage may still be at work within it. The interlaced ideas of identity and difference depend upon individualism for their expression. As a result, "the concept of difference persists—even in its disavowal—in feminism's identity-based challenge to sexism and male dominance, and the concept of identity persists—even as it is challenged—in feminism's difference-based challenge to individualism." Because of the inseparability of identity and difference within the paradigm of individualism, feminism is saddled with the problem of difference, and feminist theory must come to terms with the persistence of theoretical puzzles and paradoxes, no matter whether identity or difference is embraced, or whether a given theory appears to depend on or reject the premises of individualism.[11]

The "Power" of the All-Natural Woman

We are forced, when we ask the question of woman, to question the extent to which we make ourselves the riddle, establishing among us a new set of experts who will speak the truth of ourselves and our sex in categorical terms; . . . the extent to which we close our struggle around certain privileged meanings, naturalizing the construct woman once again.

Is it possible to ask and not answer, or to avoid the certainties and limitations with which the question has been answered by those who would
consolidate their power around their privileged position with respect to
knowledge?[12]

I would like to believe that, as Biddy Martin suggests (above), we could
indeed be content to "ask and not answer." In the decades since the 1970s
the distance between academic feminists and feminist activists has been
on the increase. Many of the former, as they immerse themselves in parsing language, are detached from the day-to-day dilemmas of women;
many of the latter, a group that includes some feminist psychologists and
psychotherapists, are, as we shall see in the following chapters, busy "an-
swering," emphasizing differences between men's violence and appetite
for power as contrasted with women's relationality and essential capacity
for nurturing.[13]

6

Psychological Woman and the Paradox of Relational Individualism

"Career Women Feeling the Pinch of Fertility Issues," trumpeted a headline in the *Philadelphia Inquirer.* Under discussion was Sylvia Ann Hewlett's book *Creating a Life: Professional Women and the Quest for Children,* in which Hewlett drew the nation's attention—in particular the attention of middle-class women in their thirties and forties—to the fact that many women who put all their energies into career advancement, believing that motherhood will come later, are failing to take account of a winding down of their biological clocks that might foreclose permanently on the possibility of motherhood.[1] *Time* magazine took up this theme as the cover story for its April 2002 issue.[2] Inside the magazine a photograph of a woman in a business suit cradling an attaché case, as one might a baby, was splashed across the centerfold. Both the *Inquirer* and the *Time* stories underscored the importance for women of making wise choices about career and motherhood; in fact the word "choices" was a constant fixture in the *Time* feature. Despite her self-identification as a feminist, Hewlett criticized feminists for overfocusing on reproductive choice at the expense of the needs of those who decide to become mothers. Jane Eisner, the author of the *Inquirer* editorial, urging women to "stop whining and start telling our daughters the truth about the hard and wonderful choices they will be lucky enough to make," echoed Hewlett's advice to young women: "Be as intentional about finding love, marriage and children as you are in building your career." In a *New York Times* piece Lisa Belkin chronicled the troubles Hewlett herself had had in trying to blend motherhood and career: a bid for academic tenure defeated, and the defeat attributed by one member of her appointments committee to the fact that she "had allowed child-bearing to dilute [her] focus"; a resignation at age thirty-nine from a "plum" executive job because she felt she could not contribute enough to both job and family.[3]

Just as Hewlett's book was published, the demise of Fox's television comedy *Ally McBeal* was announced, evoking memories of how its heroine, a young, Harvard-educated lawyer who, with her teeny-tiny skirts and neurotic ways, had become a symbol in the late 1990s of "the nation's collective fatigue" with the concerns of 1960s and 1970s feminism (early on, Ally had been featured on the cover of *Time* above the caption "Is Feminism Dead?").[4] On NBC's *Today* show "relationship expert" Regena Thomashauer, known as Mama Gena, author of *Mama Gena's School of Womanly Arts: How to Use the Power of Pleasure,* exhorted women to accept the principle of self-indulgence as the gateway to self-empowerment. Mama Gena's book, excerpted on *Today*'s Web site, revealed all: how the "womanly arts," as she identified them—tapping into your "innate understanding of [sensual] pleasure"; flirting; "befriending your inner bitch"; and "owning and operating men," among others— would bring women absolute fulfillment. Mama Gena insisted that adopting a "positive point of view" rather than "whining about the past" was imperative if one were to grasp the womanly arts, and that "what might surprise you most is that true selfishness can be the path to real generosity."

A *New York Times* feature published on Mother's Day, 2002, offered up a discussion of what its author identified as a recent increase in the expression of maternal ambivalence among women:

> After two decades in which [baby] boomers managed to make children the raison d'être not only of their lives but of the culture at large, another version of motherhood is beginning to seep out, with some mothers speaking up in the impassioned tones of those breaking a taboo— about the drudgery of child care, the isolation of the playground and their loss of identity.[5]

The article, printed in the Sunday "Styles" section, is typical of many other such pieces that focus on women's feelings to the almost total exclusion of the social, historical, and political contexts in which motherhood and the feelings about it are embedded. There is no mention of the origins of the social pressures that create the rigid taboo against the articulation of that other, ambivalent version of motherhood. The mothers under discussion in the article were white professional women, and men were not once mentioned.

Coproducers of a documentary on motherhood for the women's cable network Oxygen were quoted in the article as saying, "Why aren't we allowed to talk about hating the park? You feel alone and think you're crazy. . . . It's boring, lonely, not valued and not paid. It's mindless and repetitive and no one ever says to you, 'It looks like you're having a tough day, go for a cup of coffee' like they do at the office." The coproducers' stated aim in making the documentary was to offer mothers personal reassurance that what they are feeling is "normal" (i.e., not "crazy") and that it is "O.K. to dislike *parts* of being a mother" (my italics). One reasonably might assume that it would be truly crazy to dislike more than *some* components of motherhood, and one is tempted to ask whether coffee and sympathy are, indeed, all that would be required to boost these middle-class mothers' morale, as the producers suggested. If so, who would offer the boost—a husband? Friends? Even if she received that infusion of support with her caffeine, would not a mother be expected—or expect herself—to get right back to the job after the last sip? After all, childrearing in our society is *her* job.

From the look of things, women are being cautioned not to "whine" about their problems; not, in the vernacular, to have a "pity party." The goal of the documentary was to validate women's feelings, not to arouse anger about historically gendered social arrangements that make it women's lot to work, unpaid, in a societally devalued job that can at times be boring and lonely or to spur women to take social and political action to alter these arrangements. In fact some of those interviewed for the *Times* piece held the women's movement responsible for women's discontents: as its author remarked, "one of the paradoxes of the feminist movement is that after opening the workplace to women, offering them independence and professional fulfillment, it sometimes made childrearing feel like a letdown." In this rendering, the "movement" that was credited with creating opportunities was held equally responsible for the "letdown." The political power of the movement is not evident in the memory of it, nor is women's power—apart from the power to express feelings —assumed here.

If the themes that pervade these media representations of women and women's dilemmas seem familiar to us, it is because ever since women have set foot outside the domestic circle they have been cautioned against the perils that might befall them. They have been reminded of their "imperative to nurture," taught the womanly arts, and told what form their complaints should—or should not—take.[6] More recently, women have been told that they are free to make the choices that suit them, but many women have found themselves constrained in making those choices—by race, class, sexual orientation, and by age as well as by gender. The legacy of the nineteenth century is not only readily apparent in the increasing medicalization of women's problems, but in the psychologization of those problems.

The domain of the therapeutic offers a kinder, gentler forum for tackling female complaints than the picket line or the halls of the U.S. Congress, and some fear feminism itself devolving into a movement that champions mental health rather than social change.[7] It may be, as Celia Kitzinger and Rachel Perkins maintain, that these days, "psychology is part of what passes for feminism," having "replaced feminism as a way of understanding the world."[8] In this and the chapters to follow we will examine the nexus between feminism and the therapeutic as it is associated with the legacy of individualism, as well as notions of the self and the self's agency as they are related to ideas about power. We begin with an analysis of the sense of relationality presumed to be the essence of psychological woman.

Maternal Revivalism

In feminism's second wave there had been a determination to make changes in men, to push for their greater participation in childrearing and domestic work. In the decades since, the prevailing view among radical feminists—that the disease of male domination is "inevitable and incurable"—has been considerably less sanguine. Although it has been important to help women feel their own "powers" and to experience anger toward the oppressive atmosphere created by male supremacy, the influential and commercially successful efforts to celebrate womanly strengths can be viewed as dismissive of the important work of second-wave women's liberation. An overemphasis on the dangers that men pose to women as well as on basic differences in the way men and women experience the world and internalize that experience does not leave much room for transforming relationships between men and women.[9]

"Women," as Michelle Fine and Susan Gordon contend, "are nestled not only inside relationships but precisely inside the most contradictory moments of social arrangements. Indeed, it is often women's work to be stuffed inside such spots and to testify that no contradiction exists."[10] Since social change relies upon our ability to delineate the strains and contradictions that inhere in male-female relationships,[11] whatever obscures them does not favor social change.

The valorization of mothering as a vehicle for women's empowerment began in the 1970s with the advent of the second wave of feminism. This time around it was not medical men who argued for male-female difference on the basis of biology and anatomy, but psychoanalytically oriented feminists, who based their arguments for difference on the "seemingly invariable processes of early development."[12] Although it was not the aim of these feminists to stop the clock in the late nineteenth century, the promulgation of sex differences and "traditional" values has led to a host of conservative social agendas supported in such discourses as that of "restoring" the family and in warnings to women about the ticking of the biological clock.[13] These worries, amply chronicled in the media, buttress men's power and reinforce the value of separate spheres in the public mind. As we have previously discussed, the qualities we find so compelling in women are not necessarily those that garner most respect in the culture at large.[14] What we must remember is that *women's* own valuation of their "essential" attributes is given its form by the *same social forces that have made men dominant.* As Lynne Segal maintains,

> Women value nurturance, warmth and security, or at least we believe we ought to, precisely because of, not in spite of, the meanings, culture and social relations of a world where men are more powerful than women. Women's and men's experiences and values are shaped by the same ideologies and the same meanings handed down to us from the past, though we are placed differently in relation to them. These are also shaped by the changing social practices and circumstances of our lives in the present. . . . It is only when we abandon all hope of any real change in the lives of women that we may console ourselves with the reassuring, complacent belief in women's essential superiority.[15]

If we truly consider relationality an important quality for humans to possess, then removing it from the intrapsychic realm and placing it in context will alter how we think about change, inducing us to create environments that evoke "doing" relationality rather than applauding relationality as a feminine attribute.[16]

In the decades following the heyday of second-wave feminism, the celebration of mothering may also have been spurred by the disappointment experienced by many feminists over the fact that the multiple goals of engaging in valuable work, achieving social change, and building networks of friends—all while caring for children—"have proved so often difficult, stressful or transitory" to attain.[17] From Segal's perspective,

> It is these difficulties which make the supposedly "private" world of family life a more optimistic terrain for feminist theorizing (especially for middle class feminists with the time and financial backing to create reasonable conditions for their own mothering). And that is at least partly why [theorizing that focuses on the maternal has] become so popular in American feminism. It is also popular precisely because it has enabled the return and re-emphasis of the familiar certainties of "common sense": the return to conventional ideas of fundamental and comprehensive cognitive, emotional and moral difference between women and men.[18]

The irony of the present time, Segal maintains, is that the more entrenched women's presence in the workplace has become and the less entrenched gender differences are in daily life, the stronger the validation of the unique connection between women and the domain of the personal.[19] For the women's movement of the 1970s the discourse of women's equality trumped the discourse of male-female differences. As a result, second-wave feminism made little of women's strengths, an omission that left a gap that later radical and cultural feminists sought to fill, and, ever since, their theoretical formulations have had a profound influence upon academic psychology, feminist psychotherapy, and the popular sphere.

One theorist who has contributed, even over her own protests, to the validation of women's special affiliation to personal life is Nancy Chodorow. Taking as the basis for her ideas psychoanalytic object relations theories that focused on the dynamics of separation and attachment, Chodorow, a sociologist, fashioned a new theory of female development.[20] Her book *The Reproduction of Mothering: Psychoanalysis and the Sociology of Gender* (1978) achieved popularity beyond the author's wildest imaginings. Both Chodorow's ideas and the misconstruals of them continue to have a sweeping impact on feminist thinking and on the conduct of feminist psychotherapy. Chodorow and Dorothy Dinnerstein, author of the influential 1976 book *The Mermaid and the Minotaur:*

Sexual Arrangements and the Human Malaise approached development as other post-Freudians had not, viewing in the relationship of self and other not only the origins of gender identity but also the roots of women's subordination. Each sought to explain how differences in the early relationship between mother and male or female infant came to produce "masculine" and "feminine" personality traits.[21]

Chodorow believed that femininity was to be found in the infant's primary love of mother. In her theoretical formulation, girls, raised primarily by their mothers, face a different developmental challenge in their early years than do boys.[22] They must identify with and at same time differentiate themselves from their mothers. This process of identification renders separation more difficult and less complete. As adults, women attempt to recreate the early relationship with their mothers and, finding men not up to the task (for a variety of reasons that Chodorow specifies), they partner with men, not so much to satisfy their needs for emotional closeness, but to reproduce this early mother love through having their own children. For Chodorow, motherhood is an organic part of the psychological makeup of women. Women's less than complete separation from their own mothers produces permeable boundaries between self and other that nourish women's capacities for empathy as well as their ability to think in the sort of relational terms that create a predisposition for connection with others.[23] A boy in Western society also faces the task of separation from his mother, but he cannot identify with her as girls can; rather, he must identify with a father with whom he has significantly less contact. Difficulties in forming an identification with a peripheral father leave a boy the alternative of devaluing and rejecting his mother, whose identity is not-masculine, or "other." Thus the boy must continue to reaffirm his shaky identity through defining what is feminine as different and lesser. As a result men view all women as objects they can dominate.

According to Chodorow this process of separation aptly prepares men and women for acceptance of their masculine and feminine fates. For men it yields such traits such as competitiveness, useful in the sphere of production. Women, on the other hand, develop traits that equip them for the domain of reproduction—motherhood. Chodorow by no means viewed these as necessary developmental outcomes; in fact, she believed that they were deleterious both for women and for civilization as a whole. Her aim was to see childrearing shared equally by mothers and fathers, a result that she believed would achieve concord between men and women as well as much-needed transformations in the capitalist order.

For decades prior to the publication of Chodorow's book, feminists had dwelled negatively on motherhood in general and the mother-daughter relationship in particular. This new work offered the possibility of giving women—especially mothers—their due. Despite Chodorow's insistence that the cultural mandate to give themselves over completely to raising their children had had the adverse effect of compelling many mothers to look to their children to meet their emotional needs, readers overlooked this message in favor of celebrating *The Reproduction of Mothering* as a hymn to mother love. Reproduction itself was again reified, and what *was* taken from Chodorow's work—a glorification of motherhood and the self-in-relation, or as critics such as Janice Doane and Devon Hodges have put it, "an oppressive identification of the 'feminine' with the 'maternal' "[24]—has been relied upon by many feminist theorists and clinicians. What they took from Chodorow's work was the notion of a feminine identity, more complex, more caring, and in every way superior to the masculine identity associated with violence, intolerance, and callousness. Furthermore, female superiority was assumed to have universality, given its historical and cross-cultural foundation in mothering.[25]

Chodorow herself has inveighed against interpreting "ideologies of [male-female] difference" as anything other than socially constructed.[26] Nonetheless, Chodorow *does* believe that men and women have different gender identities, essential and unvarying, albeit historically constructed and amenable to change; she *does* locate the roots of male supremacy in personality structures built by a centuries-old universal model of child rearing. Despite the fact that many contemporary American men are more sensitive than their fathers and grandfathers, power relations between men and women remain problematic. Because, as Segal points out, Chodorow's theory "pays only lip service to the actual variations, complexities, dialectics and history of social relations," her work, for all her declarations to the contrary, was doomed to be read as a celebration of women's difference.[27] A knowledge of mother-child attachment and separation is necessary but not sufficient for the project of understanding our ideas about the self. The materialization of "an original or genuine femininity," even when inadvertent, constitutes a "before," in Judith Butler's terms, a nostalgic rendering of the past that contributes to cultural conservatism in the present.[28] Elizabeth Spelman has taken Chodorow to task for making it appear "as if a woman's mothering takes place in a social context that is simply sexist (leaving unexamined and unexaminable how the existence of racism and classism affect a mother's endangerment of her children)."[29]

The valorization of woman-ness that defines what theorists term *cultural feminism* reached its pinnacle in the 1980s with the publication of a book by psychologist Carol Gilligan that emphasized differences between women's and men's moral development, *In a Different Voice: Psychological Theory and Women's Development* (1982) (a related work that made a big splash, *Women's Ways of Knowing: The Development of Self, Voice, and Mind*, a study of women's cognitive development, was published in 1986 by Mary Belenky, a student of Gilligan, and her colleagues). Gilligan, a psychologist, and Jean Baker Miller, a psychiatrist and psychoanalyst whose ideas were initially put forward in her 1976 book *Toward a New Psychology of Women*, were to become increasingly influential. Both argued against the reification of autonomy in developmental theories, importantly critiquing androcentric theories of development, such as those of Erik Erikson, which placed the achievement of autonomy rather than the development of relational capacities at the apex of human development.[30] Gilligan, in her study of moral development, sought to demonstrate that many women develop a personal, relational moral sense—an "ethic of care"—that is less tied to abstract moral principles than is the male "ethic of rights," which equates morality with impersonal ideas about justice. Whether or not Gilligan actually elevated the ethic of responsibility that she attributed to women over men's presumably more abstract conceptualization of justice continues to be a subject of debate (Gilligan herself opposes any suggestion that she intended "different" to mean "better").[31] In contrast, Miller's point of view was boldly unconcealed: "it is the woman who is motivated to make the just society come about. It is she who is hurting and who deeply feels the need for change; for her it is not merely an intellectual theory about justice."[32]

In addition to the widespread appreciation of what was taken to be their celebration of women's unique capacities for caring and relationship, sharp criticism was leveled at both Gilligan and Miller for failing to address the historical context of women's subordination. Gilligan, it was argued, unwittingly engaged in the historical discourse of separate spheres, rendering women's caretaking and tendency toward self-abnegation as the outgrowths of a personality that was a product of women's unique psychological development rather than the consequence of overt socialization practices.[33] History made clear, critics maintained, that women's need for connection and their capacity for affiliation were not innate, as Miller implied. The "different" (female) moral voice that Gilligan had discovered in her studies of women and girls might well derive from a sense of powerlessness that makes women's place in the social order more tentative than men's. An ethic of care is characteristic of minority groups that bear a major responsibility for the well-being of others. From this perspective, caring is a way of bargaining from a weak position,[34] and altruism can spring from a fear of others' power or their anger, fear of abandonment, or fear of one's own aggressiveness.[35]

Gilligan's ideas were soon ubiquitous in feminist circles, often entangled and confused with Chodorow's, much to Chodorow's dismay.[36] What had begun as an attempt by Chodorow and Dinnerstein to argue for a diminution of gender differences in subsequent generations through the partnering of men and women in household and parenting tasks evolved into a further dichotomization of feminine connectedness and masculine autonomy on the basis of fundamental differences in men's and women's natures and, in some interpretations, an effort to valorize the former while condemning the latter.[37] The fact that misreadings of Chodorow's book launched at least a thousand cultural feminist ships demonstrates how strong the current of public sentiment ran for a theory that would support the notion of a superior feminine nature.[38] Here was an argument for "a distinctively feminine ethos of love, altruism, and cooperation" that formed "the basis of a new essentialism."[39]

Like Dinnerstein and Chodorow, Miller perceived a greater emotional attunement between mother and daughter than between mother and son. According to Miller, a difference in empathic attunement provokes differential responses in boys and girls—with the result that girls acquire a greater desire and capacity for relational sensitivity and intimacy.[40] Unlike Dinnerstein and Chodorow, however, Miller did not call for a restructuring of gender arrangements; rather, she called for women to embrace their relational capacities as strengths. In her view, female subordination derived, not from mothering performed exclusively by women, as Chodorow and Dinnerstein had suggested, but from a societal devaluation of mothering.[41] Women should validate their skills and desires: "Women are better geared than men to first recognize others' needs and then to believe strongly that others' needs can be served—that they can respond to others' needs without feeling this as a detraction from their sense of identity."[42] Although Miller expressed a wish that "as women refuse to become the carriers of some of the central unsolved problems of male-led society" a climate would be created in which "men will face the challenge of grappling with their own issues in their own way," thus "reclaim[ing] the very parts of their own experience that they have delegated to women," she did not delineate how this shift would occur. This omission is particularly salient in the face of her insistence that women celebrate their "natural" propensities for caregiving.[43] One cannot help but hear the delicate footfalls of her nineteenth-century sisters marching close behind, singing the gospel of universal salvation through feminine virtue in the following statement by Miller's colleague Janet Surrey on the subject of the "self-in-relation": "[the] abundance of women's psychological strengths exists but cannot flourish or come forward fully into a world that sorely needs precisely these kinds of strengths."[44]

Even though Gilligan and other feminist psychologists have paid considerable attention to social context, a consistent emphasis on the internalization of gender, whether in the form of sex roles, dominant discourses, or the differential effects of mothering upon boys and girls, has replaced older forms of biological reductionism with new types of what Lynne Segal calls *cultural* reductionism. Contemporary theorizing has not deepened our understanding of how the social affects the subjective in a way that might furnish an antidote to the stale dichotomization of the biological and the social.[45]

The psychological study of gender has, overall, constructed gender as difference, and psychological theories of gender tend to be biased either in terms of their exaggeration of male-female differences or in their attempts to de-emphasize those differences.[46] There is a "dynamic tension" that exists between an essentialist explanation of gender and a social constructivist position (i.e., one that defines all ideas about gender and gendered behaviors as socially constructed).[47] However, the bias in feminist psychology tilts sharply in the direction of essentialism.[48]

Researchers under the Influence (of Essentialist Theories)

A sampling of recent articles in the *Psychology of Women Quarterly* (house organ of the American Psychological Association's women's division) and the journal *Women & Therapy* tells the story of the far-reaching influence of essentialist ideas upon the direction of research and theory on women's mental health. A fairly typical example of a common genre is an article entitled "Women's Voices: A Guide for Listening to

Chemically Dependent Women," in which the author uses ideas about "women's ways of knowing" to inform treatment with addicted women, citing Belenky, Gilligan, and Miller in the process.[49]

If any doubt lingers that the theories of Chodorow, Miller, and Gilligan are blandly conflated and distilled, shorn of any historical or social implications, and interpreted to imply a female relational identity, the authors of "Depression in Women as Related to Anger and Mutuality in Relationships" sweep it away with the following assertion: "The link between women's depression and the nature of their relationships has been provided by female developmental theorists such as Chodorow (1978), Gilligan (1982, 1990), and Miller (1976, 1988, 1991) who emphasized the *importance of having relationships as a key element in women's identity development* and healthy psychological growth [my italics]."[50] The authors hypothesize an association, based on the "self-in-relation" model, between depression and the lack of mutuality in relationships. The study, its authors tell us, is "a quantitative attempt to investigate the construct of mutuality as it relates to both depression in women and anger issues for women."[51] Neither the research question nor its methodology has any grounding in the sociocultural domain, and the authors' conclusion, bare of any discussion of its ramifications, is that "consistent with the self-in-relation theory . . . and recent research . . . , our findings support the idea that the relationship between mutuality and depression is direct, with higher levels of mutuality predicting greater psychological benefits for women."[52]

The authors of a research article entitled "Marriage and Depressive Symptoms: The Role and Bases of Self-Esteem Differ by Gender" move swiftly through a series of linked assumptions that amplifies male-female differences and eventuates in a recommendation for gender-specific clinical interventions. The researchers initially delineate differences between the "self-schemas" of women (more relational, as fate and theory would have it) and men (more "individualistic or autonomous").[53] Socialization, they opine, accounts for these self-schemas. Self-esteem "may derive from fulfilling gender-appropriate norms"—for women, sensitivity to and connection with others; for men, "being independent, separate, and better than others." In the study, the authors' hypothesis that "for women, marital quality would be related to depression, but that this relationship would be mediated by self-esteem," was borne out: "Consistent with socialization explanations, women may take responsibility for relationships as part of fulfilling their gender roles. When they are in poor relationships . . . their self-esteem may become eroded, which in turn may increase their level of depressive symptomatology."[54]

How, then, do the researchers suggest clinicians intervene? Do they propose alterations in societal conditions that address the social expectations for women's relational responsibility? They do not. Instead, they recommend that interventions for individuals who are depressed and whose marriages are full of conflict be tailored to men and women differentially. For women they recommend "a focus on increasing intimate disclosure"; for men, since their self-esteem is not wholly dependent on relationships, they suggest additional "interventions designed to increase men's self-esteem in areas external to the marriage" because "high self-esteem may act as a protective factor in buffering the relationship between lack of intimacy and companionship and depressive symptomatology."[55] According to the authors, it would seem, a focus on a man's expertise as a fly-fisherman may be able to keep him from the maw of depression when his marriage is in trouble. For the woman it is not so easy. A tense marriage will depress her, and her only way out, it would appear, is through "self-disclosure." But to whom? One assumes that her husband will be the recipient of her confidences. Given the male-female differences consistently emphasized by the authors, however, one can only wonder whether he will be able to hear her as she needs to be heard. Marital therapy is in order, and the woman unhappy in her marriage may need it more desperately than the man unhappy in his; Mars goes fly-fishing and Venus goes to therapy. For the authors of the study under discussion, to assume male-female differences is not only to find them, but to use them to shape therapeutic interventions that further enhance them. Here the difference paradigm does not lead us out of the wilderness of male-female relations but straight into the thicket.[56]

Self-in-Relation Theory

There has been a complex interplay between feminist theory and feminist therapy since the 1970s, leading to a variety of models, methods, and aims over more than three decades.[57] Feminist therapy, however, is not a unitary phenomenon. It has never cleaved to a particular "school," but has been defined by an underlying set of principles that constitute an ideology.[58] If there is one theory, however, that can be said to have had a profound effect on our view of psychological woman over the past twenty years or so it is "self-in-relation"[59] theory. Now prominently associated with writings that have emanated from the Stone Center for Developmental Services and Studies at Wellesley College, of which Jean Baker Miller was the first director, this theory, which posits women's relational capacities as central to women's identities, has formed the theoretical backbone for much feminist psychotherapy today, possessing an intuitive appeal for therapists and clients alike.[60] Because of its continuing and pervasive influence on the societal representation of women and upon therapists who identify themselves as feminists, it seems important to explicate and analyze it in some detail.

Taking Care of Relationships

In our culture, caring and affiliation continue to be motivated by gendered expectations. In self-in-relation theory, women's power to make choices seems to be a personal power generated through the waging and winning of an internal battle—what Gloria Steinem has called in *The Revolution from Within* the battle for self-esteem.[61] A significant factor in the development of girls, according to self-in-relation theory, is "a mutual process in which both mothers and daughters become highly responsive to the feeling states of each other. . . . they care for and *take care of the relationship* between them. This is the motivational dynamic of mutual empowerment, the inherent energizing force of real relationship."[62] A girl's sense of self-esteem is closely tied to the achievement of this mutual empathy in relationships with others and is "based in feeling that she is part of relationships and is taking care of those relationships."[63] In this model, the young girl is exquisitely attuned to the nuances of relationships, particularly the relationship with her own mother.

In their discussions of "mutual empathy" as the cornerstone of that relationship, the Stone Center psychologists indicate that there is a natural need on the part of mothers for their daughters' understanding and care. The difficulty here is that the mother-daughter relationship is not a relationship of equals. As Marcia Westkott points out, what a mother seeks from her daughter and what her daughter offers "are not expressions of an essentially human, relational self, but the protective devices of one who feels she must display these behaviors in order to gain her mother's love and acceptance." While a mother who looks to her daughter for empathy and care is not reprehensible, she *is* acting on a widely held societal belief that empathy and care can only be provided by women—a belief that results from the very cultural devaluation of women and care that Jean Baker Miller decried in her earliest work, *Toward a New Psychology of Women*. And the daughter's responsiveness, the empathy so greatly valued by the Stone Center theorists, may be thought of as contributing to a defensive personality organization.[64]

For Miller, "being in relationship . . . is a *goal*, not a detraction or a means to some other end, such as one's own self-development. Thus it forms a *motivation*" [Miller's italics].[65] If this is so, relationship exists both as the context for development of the self and as the goal it seeks to achieve.[66] I find it particularly worrisome that throughout the being-in-relation literature there is little discussion about how to get the other to attend to oneself. Hannah Lerman, who has inveighed against the rehabilitation of psychoanalytic theory in all its forms, has contended that to view all "pairing relationships" of women as rooted in the mother-daughter relationship—to look at relationships only through the prism of the nuclear family—is to fail to depict accurately the complex dynamics of other adult-adult relationships.[67] In descriptions of self-in-relation theory, relationships with men rarely achieve the mutuality prevalent in female-female relationships. However, the assumption of the ease with which women achieve mutuality in relationships between and among each other presupposes a greater equality among women than existing social divisions with respect to race, class, age, and sexual orientation would warrant.

Removing the relationship between mother and daughter from the social context in which it resides and then, as Marcia Westkott contends, viewing it "as if the idealized qualities of care and relationality were not themselves informed by patriarchal meanings and purposes" locates woman's psyche in some patriarchy-free zone. In fact the cultural expectation of women's caring and empathy grows from a pervasive sense that men's needs are more important women's.[68] In addition, if woman's self-esteem is derived from being part of and "taking care" of relationships, as Jean Baker Miller herself argued so persuasively in her 1976 book, then her interest will continue to lie in holding the feminine "heart" for men. For many women this involves taking a large share of emotional responsibility—performing the "emotional labor"—in heterosexual relationships.[69] Many women embark on what Thelma Jean Goodrich calls a "career of protectiveness," that is, "guarding and supporting another's personhood" at the expense of their own.[70]

Women, as Jacques Lacan would have it

reflect . . . masculine power and everywhere reassure that power of the reality of its illusory autonomy. This task is confounded . . . when the demand that women reflect the autonomous power of the masculine subject . . . becomes essential to the construction of that autonomy and, thus, becomes the basis of a radical dependency that . . . undercuts the function it serves.[71]

It is questionable whether any psychodynamic theory, no matter how "relational," could have ushered in the structural changes needed to transform domestic labor arrangements and equalize male-female wage-earning in the workplace. However, the place to which self-in-relation theory has brought feminism seems perilously close to the territory of the Gilman-Key debates of 1909 (see the Interlude, note 2). As we shall discuss in the chapter to follow, this does not bode well for women's empowerment within the context of relationships, given the fact that many relationships they enter are power-unequal.

One might well conclude from the Stone Center critique of American caretaking that in our culture "women care and men take," or, more broadly, men "care about" (the public universe) and women "care for" (personal relationships).[72] The dichotomization of public and private spheres is still with us, to the extent that we persist in formulating a vision of caring as confined only to those who, metaphorically, stand close to the hearth.[73] As we have seen, this was Tocqueville's worried vision: a "little society" of domestic life to which individuals were drawn through "feeling," potentially at the expense of their participation in the activities of citizenship.[74]

One way of grappling with the societal devaluation of caring is to teach women and men how to value themselves on the basis of their ability to care and to practice caring well, a "feminine" approach to caring, from which perspective, as Joan Tronto maintains, "caring will always remain as a corrective to morality, . . . neither suggesting nor requiring a fundamental rethinking of moral categories." Another, and infinitely less gendered way to view caring, is to consider "the social world in terms of caring for others." This vision would result in a less self-interested form of caring that combines "caring for" and "caring about," moving us away from the privatization of caring that keeps it beneath our societal radar.[75] It would offer a corrective to a theoretical framework such as self-in-relation theory that, in Westkott's terms, prepares the ground for "compulsory femininity" to be "compulsively pursued" rather than radically revising our constructions of both gender and care.[76] Lykes decries the "lopsided focus on attachment" inherent in self-in-relation theory that grounds the theory in "individual, interpersonal experiences" rather than viewing both individuality and relationship as rooted in collective experiences:

> An elaboration of experiences of "community" and "collectivity" in our society and of the ways in which these experiences are constrained by differential access to power and resources (i.e., the material fabric of these experiences) provides a critical base for developing a notion of the self as social.[77]

Individualism Misinterpreted

The "relational self" or "relational individualism" was conceived by Miller and the other self-in-relation theorists working out of the Stone Center as a corrective to a centuries-long history of the cultural dominance of a male-modeled self that has embraced autonomy while denying male dependency.[78] There is no doubt that propounding a "deepening capacity for relationship and relational competence" deriving from a mutually empathic mother-daughter relationship as a fundamental developmental goal posed an effective challenge to an earlier model of development that stressed the goals of separateness and autonomy. A focus on mutuality clearly makes an important transformation in the binary of self and other, and through their conceptualization of mutuality in relationships, relational theorists expose the reality of the interdependence of individuals that the ideology of individualism obscures.[79] Nonetheless, the old individualism continues to serve as the container for the "new" relational self.

Self-in-relation theorists reveal the kinds of confusions about individualism—the term, its roots and rootedness in the culture—that are endemic to the feminist psychological literature. For example, Surrey states that Margaret Mahler's and Erik Erikson's theories of development placed a high premium on

> autonomy, self-reliance, independence, self-actualization, "listening to and following" one's own unique dream, destiny, and fulfillment. . . . Our [self-in-relation] theory suggests, instead, that for women a different—and relational—pathway is primary and continuous, although its

centrality may have been "hidden" and unacknowledged. . . . The values of individuation have permeated our cultural ideas as well as our clinical theories and practices.[80]

Here, Surrey includes notions of autonomy and independence with other values that have long been related to them (i.e., self-fulfillment, following one's dreams), seeming to imply that the valuing of "relationship" as paramount precludes tne holding of other deeply ingrained individualistic American ideals.[81] This appears to suggest that women who become relationally "competent"—as a result of therapy or otherwise—are able to separate themselves completely from the cultural climate in which those ideals have flourished. What Surrey and her colleagues fail to realize is that interior "growth and development" exist as a part of the heritage of individualism, whether they are believed to be achieved relationally or otherwise.

Others who decry the grip of individualism on psychological theory likewise confuse its meanings and fail to perceive their indebtedness to its teachings. In a critique of the Stone Center's tendency to generalize on the basis of white middle-class women's experience, Joan Griscom has discussed how a psychology that fully embraces "racial and other" differences cannot "be individualistic, for it takes at least two persons to establish a difference."[82] The meaning of "individualistic" in this context is less than clear. What Griscom seems to mean is that when differences are taken into account, no one group can dictate norms. That selfsame psychology, however, can and does embrace differences while continuing to concern itself with the subjectivities of individuals, even the subjectivities of individuals within groups.

Surrey's statement that "the values of individuation have permeated our cultural ideals as well as our clinical theories and practice" implies a more than semantic confusion between the concepts of individuation and individualism. Theories of psychological development such as Mahler's or Erikson's, which Surrey disparages, emphasize psychological differentiation (individuation). These theories are embedded in our culture of individualism—*but so is self-in-relation theory.* A concept such as "self-esteem," now equated by Surrey and her colleagues with "emotional sharing, openness, and shared sense of understanding and regard," is steeped in the ideology of individualism. As we have seen in chapter 1, a social focus on self-esteem is a technology of the self, a vehicle for self-monitoring or self-governance through subjectivity. In order to feel worthy, one must have a deeply ingrained sense of a separate self, whether one only feels worthy when one succeeds at empathizing well—the apotheosis of self-esteem, in Surrey's view—or whether one feels worthy primarily when one achieves success in the workplace. The discussion of growth itself, even growth *within* relationship, which, to the Stone Center theorists, is the most important kind of growth, carries with it the freight of our American notions of progress through individual self-fulfillment. A relational self is still a self, after all.

Although criticism of self-in-relation theory has been commonly aimed at its valorization of women's difference, the theory's deep entrenchment in the tradition of Western individualism is not often addressed, perhaps because its proponents so adamantly insist that the theory rejects that ideology. But what the theory's adherents appear to be rejecting is individualism as *they understand it,* that is, either in an ahistorical meaning close to "individuation" (recall Surrey's statement, about "the values of individuation") or a type of "every man for himself" utilitarian individualism.

The conclusion to which the naive reader must subscribe is that it is not so much the sense of self as agent that is problematic for the self-in-relation theorists (although they do expend quite a bit of energy decrying Western notions of agency), but the notion of being *out for oneself,* to which they refer as having "power-over." By no means, however, are the self-in-relation theorists going against the grain of liberal individualism. As I mentioned in chapter 1, they seem to be identifying it only with its excesses, particularly Bentham's "narrowly selfish, narrowly rationalist, version of it" in which man was seen purely as a "calculator of his own interests." The heritage of liberal individualism, however, was never purely utilitarian; it was leavened at least to some extent by Puritan and Lockean strains.[83] Referring only to the utilitarian form of individualism, the self-in-relation theorists appear to be setting up a straw "man" to knock down in the name of countering our individualist legacy. Elimination of the word "self" from the Stone Center vocabulary (of late self-in-relation theory has been renamed "being-in-relation theory") cannot obscure the debt of their theory to that tradition.

Acceptance of differences in types of individualism would enable the self-in-relation theorists to locate relationality where it rightfully belongs —inside the cultural surround of American individualism, making it possible for them not to have to throw out the bathwater with the baby. Adrie Kusserow, decrying anthropologists' consistent dichotomization of these terms, has pointed out that individualism and sociocentrism are not mutually exclusive. Societies or communities can encourage sociocentrism and yet prize independence and agency.[84] In studying the socialization practices of Long Island mothers from three different communities with a view to understanding what types of individualism they might espouse, she distinguished among three types of individualism.[85] Lower-working-class mothers from South Rockaway, espousing a "hard defensive" individualism, encouraged a tough-minded, cautious approach to social relations that emphasized minding one's own business, trusting only a chosen few, standing one's ground, and looking out for oneself. Upper-working-class mothers from Beach Channel, displaying a "soft defensive" individualism, frequently used sports metaphors or slogans to encourage perseverance in their children (e.g., "break through the front line," "just do it") as well as metaphors associated with upward movement and momentum (e.g., "try stepping out," "put your best foot forward"). Both groups of mothers frequently slid between an emphasis on individualism and an emphasis on sociocentrism in talking to and disciplining their children.

Mothers from the upper-middle-class community of Carter Hill, however, chose very different metaphors that conveyed what Kusserow termed a "soft offensive" individualism (this term seems close if not identical to Bellah and his colleagues' notion of "expressive individualism," as we discussed it in chapter 2) in messages about their children's uniqueness and self-esteem, relayed through metaphors of "blooming" and "blossoming." Unlike the two other groups of mothers, this group, although frequently speaking of the importance of acquiring sociocentric traits, expressed concern that the cultivation of these qualities might threaten the development of individualism in their children. It is this "soft offensive" or "expressive" type of individualism towards which the self-in-relation theorists tend. In tortured locutions, self-in-relation apologists honor expressive individualism while declaring themselves to be firmly anti-individualist.

Autonomy and the Relational Self

Janet Surrey asserts

> The self-in-relation model assumes that other aspects of the self (e.g., creativity, autonomy, assertion) develop within this primary context [of

relationship]. That is, other aspects of self-development emerge in the context of relationship, and there is no inherent need to disconnect or to sacrifice relationship for self-development.[86]

Surrey is faced here with the sticky task of trying to explain how autonomy *does* develop in women, just after she has argued strenuously against our society's mistaken emphasis on autonomy as a goal of development (I labor over the problem of figure and ground here).

The philosopher Jennifer Radden, in an article entitled "Relational Individualism and Feminist Therapy," has attempted to offer a way out of the conceptual labyrinth in which the Stone Center's discussion of women's autonomy is embedded:[87]

> the relational self which is an ideal of mental health must not lose all sense of agency or relinquish . . . its autonomy. Indeed, we might say, the relationality valued in therapy has been shown . . . to presuppose some sort or sorts of autonomy. . . . relationality will be a capability as much as a desire. [A woman] will have the power to choose the nature, number, and quality of her relationships with others.
>
> . . . through feminist therapy, she will be led to discover, notice, and name her relationality. But she will also be led to applaud and celebrate it. . . . By making the choice to value her relationality [*sic*] traits in this way, the client exhibits one reflection of her own agency. . . . Valuing relationality she may also deliberately choose and actively seek community over isolation, relational self-identity and definition (self-concept) over individualistic self-identity and definition.[88]

The fact that "self relationality" is "a goal as well as an endowment," Radden argues, enables feminist therapy to build a bridge between autonomy and relationality and "embrace both as therapeutic ideals."[89] The freedom to value what has been devalued in the broader culture (i.e., women's ability to connect with others, an ability that, as we have noted, is not an atypical accomplishment for those in subordinate positions) is conceived of here as an indication of autonomy, as is woman's power "to choose the nature, number, and quality of her relationships with others."

Apart from the questionable use of the term "autonomy" to define itself, a concern that arises relative to the Stone Center theorists' definition of autonomy is whether it is at all possible to assume that the "empowered" woman has free relationship choices in a society in which women still carry much of the burden for childrearing, as well as in a world within which race, class, age, geography, and sexual orientation, among other factors, constrain the exercise of free will. Furthermore, given the differences in the social construction of female and male identities, one must question whether women have complete choice as to the nature and quality of their relationships with each other, even if they "liberate" themselves through therapy or some other allegedly empowering activity. And is not the idea of a free, contextless choice itself the artifact of the legacy of individualism?[90] The notion of autonomy outlined by Radden seems in its own way as decontextualized as the age-old notion of "man's" free will. According to Judith Jordan of the Stone Center, "mutual empathic understanding" is the cornerstone of a woman's relational self, challenging "the inner conviction of the 'separate self.'"[91] What Jordan and her colleagues fail to take into account is how sturdy that inner conviction of the separate self is. As we have discussed in chapter 2, the modern self has been characterized by a "private life of subjective emotion,"[92] and the individual by her or his ability to take an instrumental position with reference to her or his own wishes, feelings, thoughts, and propensities such that these are available to be "worked on" until they reach the desired state.[93] In America what we need to find is still considered to be within ourselves and is still believed to be malleable.

As Rachel Hare-Mustin and Jeanne Marecek argue, autonomy and relatedness are not polar opposites; each includes characteristics of the other. Autonomy is essentially a transactional phenomenon that acquires meaning only in a relational context. However, because of their attachment to gender, autonomy and relatedness are frequently placed in opposition to each other, so that only their observed differences are noted. When it is employed in caretaking, the exercise of power by women is frequently hidden; similarly, the exercise of men's "autonomy" often conceals their dependency upon women.[94] Also, as Jane Flax contends, when autonomy and relationality are placed in opposition to each other, such opposition "does not account for adult forms of being-in-relations that can be claustrophobic *without* autonomy—an autonomy that, without being-in-relations can easily degenerate into mastery" [my italics].[95]

At times theorists display an unwarranted optimism with regard to how easy it might be to escape our individualist legacy, when, in fact, even antitraditionalism is part of that legacy.[96] For example, when Laura Brown and Mary Ballou state that "feminist psychologists must turn to feminists in other disciplines to learn new perspectives, then use them to construct new psychological theories, thereby avoiding the tyranny of in-dividualistic viewpoints," they imply not only that one *can* step outside that framework, but also that disciplines outside psychology are not steeped in the tradition of individualism.[97] Brown claims that women's shame—that is, the experience of their "selves" as deficient, as needing to be concealed, as undeserving—results from the fact that many women have "selves" that may not match the culturally dominant view of the separate self. Women, she maintains, "have been encouraged not to know ourselves, not to speak the truth, but rather to engage in the lies of si-lence."[98] Here she uses the argument about women's right to know them-selves as a counter to individualism (i.e., the notion of a "separate self"). But the notion of right to own this not-so-separate self is sister to the idea of domestic individualism as we discussed it in chapter 5—the sense that we have a "different" self born out of the world of relationships. The no-tion of "truth" to be uncovered in the self's interior is a concept deeply influenced by individualism and, as we have discussed in relation to Fou-cault's ideas, it is not free from the relations of power in which it is em-bedded.

As John Meyer insists, "the rights, powers, and value of the self are central institutions in the modern world." The relational self is still an in-tensely subjective self, and, like all "selves" in our society, it is the prod-uct of an institutionalized and even "compulsory" subjectivity that de-mands, within the context of institutionalized individualism, that we con-stantly bear the consciousness of our own needs, desires, and motives. We are expected to choose everything from our brand of soft drink, to our partners, to our gods. At the same time, the institutionalization of the self that requires us to choose is also "accompanied . . . by available lists of reasons, motives, and aspirations that are equally institutionalized."[99]

power in the lower case

As has been mentioned previously, in the self-in-relation model, power and empowerment are viewed as nonhierarchical and noncompetitive. In *Toward a New Psychology of Women,* Miller defined power as "the ca-pacity to implement," or "self-directed effectiveness," and she stressed the particular importance of putting into play "the abilities women have already." Miller saw the possibility of bringing "womanly qualities" to power: "women can bring more power to power by using it when needed and not using it as a poor substitute for other things—like cooperation. . . . The goal is . . . a new integration of the whole area of effective power and womanly strengths as we are seeking to define them." Women have power, Miller asserted; they only need to "implement" that power and the new abilities that they "are developing." Ideally, she maintained, power should not be "*for* oneself" or "*over* others." She made a distinction "between the ability to *influence* others and the power to control and restrict them [my italics]. . . . Women need the power to advance their own development, but they do not 'need' the power to limit the development of others."[100] Such was the allergy to the idea of putting one's own needs ahead of the needs of others—ahead of relationship—that Miller felt compelled to caution women against avoiding the use of power on their own behalf. Womanly "influence," as we have noted, has been long celebrated; indeed, it was the sole power afforded to women within the cult of true womanhood. If the republican liberal ideal of individual sovereignty for which Elizabeth Cady Stanton fought in 1892 is based on the masculine model of "power over,"[101] is the nineteenth-century power of "relationality" to be restored to take its place in the new millennium?

In the Stone Center model, women's desire should be solely relational; it is feared that if desire is individual, it may open a Pandora's box of ills the patriarchal society has known so well. As Judith Jordan warns, "violent relationships [are] based on competition of need and the necessity for establishing hierarchies of dominance, entitlement, and power."[102] Of course the emphasis upon caretaking—in some cases to the point of self-abnegation—in the socialization of many girls dramatically reduces the possibility that they will elect to act in their self-interest rather than in the interest of others. Possessive individualism is not so easily dispensed with. As we discussed in chapter 5, the ideas of self-ownership and the realization of one's potential have formed part of our cultural legacy for centuries. It is easier to see how, in Miller's parlance, women could use "power to advance their development" without wielding power *over* others than it is to see how they could "advance their own development" without being *for* themselves.

When Miller asks whether "tradition made it difficult to conceive of the possibility that freedom and maximum use of our resources—our initiative, our intellect, our *powers*—can occur within a context that requires simultaneous responsibility for the care and growth of others and of the natural world" [my italics],[103] she defines "powers" as personal abilities and conjoins "responsibility," "care," and the "natural world" in a manner strongly reminiscent of the discourse of women's sphere. To my mind, the use of the term "powers" and the frequent conflation of "power" and "powers" offer an inelegant compromise solution to the problem that power poses for self-in-relation theory (or, in fact, for feminist psychotherapy theory in general, a subject that will be pursued in the chapter to follow). The interchangeable use of the terms "power" and "powers" indicates a troublesome trend in much of the literature that posits a relational identity for women: it defines power principally in personal terms.

Miller clearly locates the roots of women's discomfort with "self-determined" action in a history of patriarchal oppression and decries the fact that society sanctions the use of power in gendered ways, such that "using one's powers for others . . . is prescribed for one sex only, along with the mandate that one must not act on one's own motivation and according to one's own determinations." She maintains that "without power or something like it . . . on both the personal and political level, women cannot effectively bring about anything"[104] Although Miller asserts that "it is important for women to recognize that we do need to use our powers," she believes that there is "enormous validity in women's *not* wanting to use power as it is presently conceived and used." Women, she suggests, may prefer being "powerful in ways that simultaneously enhance, rather than diminish, the power of others" because they have reason to fear using power in the traditional way.[105] At the same time, Miller contends, women are afraid to admit their desire or need for power because to "act out of one's own interest and motivation is experienced as the psychic equivalent of being a destructively aggressive person," a self-image intolerable to many women.[106] What women have absorbed, she maintains, is the cultural notion that "I exist only as I need," and in support of this argument she offers up the example of "Connie," a psychotherapy client who expresses the fear that if she continues to work productively "I would be too powerful and then . . . I would not need anyone else."[107] Miller makes the interpretation that, as is the case with many women, "being a person who needs" was so central to Connie's identity that "the prospect of not needing felt like . . . a loss of the known and familiar self." For Connie, then, change explodes the relational universe and her place in it. However, if Miller were to put Connie's relationship to power in a larger social context, perhaps she might conclude that it is not a relational *self* that Connie fears losing, but any chance she might have of receiving care for *herself,* an interpretation that draws its validity from the history of women's "natural" burden of physical and emotional responsibility for others.

Eschewing the term "nurturing" in favor of "mutual empowerment"[108] or "empowering the relationship" proves as problematic in self-in-relation theory as does the discussion of women's "powers." The connotation of empowerment as "power in connection" or "relational power" is explicated in Jean Baker Miller and Irene Stiver's book *The Healing Connection: How Women Form Relationships in Therapy and in Life*. In the book the example of an interaction between two friends, Ann and Beth, is used to illustrate the concept of mutual empowerment:

> As part of this basic emotional connection, Ann grows in several ways. First, she is able to state her feelings and thoughts directly. . . . This is movement toward greater authenticity. . . . Ann (and Beth too) feels empowered to act in the moment of the immediate exchange. In this interplay each acts and has an important impact on the other—each creates change. This extremely valuable form of action in the immediate relational interplay is often overlooked. . . . Next, as a result of the action within the immediate interplay—the conversation itself—Ann feels empowered to act in realms beyond, to be with Emily in a fuller way and to take action within her relationship with Emily.[109]

Here the attempt is to equate empathic attunement with action and relational interplay with power; relational action leads to mutual empowerment and individual growth.

Ann's husband, Tom, makes a short and unhappy entrance onto the scene. In a discussion with Ann about the grave illness of her friend Emily, Tom, the graven image of "disconnection," rather than "connecting" with Ann empathically, as Beth would do, proceeds to make suggestions about how Emily "should get a second opinion."[110] The authors point out that in the course of a lifetime each individual develops a "basic inner sense of his or her ability to act—of empowerment—as a result of the experience of seeing that he or she can have an impact on others." Miller and Stiver believe that in our culture only "action as the result of the forceful exertion of the lone individual" is valued, often leaving women, empathic supporters and empowerers of "men's actions," without the empathic support *they* need.[111] The differences between the types of behavior encouraged in women and men can be bridged, they state, but only "so long as one person can see a possibility of engaging with another in thoughts and feelings—the possibility of connecting."[112] However, if the conditions that have fostered these differences are not addressed (and they are barely addressed in Miller and Stiver's book), it will be difficult to build that bridge. Ellyn Kaschak in her review of *The Healing Connection* points out that in their emphasis on growth Miller and Stiver

> do not note the paradox implicit in prescribing expansion for women in a world that still values and defines the feminine as diminutive and contained by the masculine. . . . Would that their prescription were so easily fulfilled—but while this is certainly a fine feminist goal, much like increased assertiveness, the real-life outcome is not always possible or desirable, and the complex mixture of possible material consequences must always be combined with any strategy for individual change. Individual change alone does not do the job.[113]

The idea that changing the world means one individual having an impact on another through an essentially interpersonal exchange does not stand as a repudiation of the legacy of individualism. The idea of transformation through connection and of empowerment through mutuality might not exactly serve as a basis for the curriculum in Mama Gena's School of Womanly Arts, but it would certainly not close down the institution.

The notion of nurturing as power is but one of the incantatory illusions that we must examine, for the power the therapeutic culture purports to give women is not the power to control institutions, governments, or laws, but is an "inner" power that is there to be tapped through the reclamation of "an essential inner self," the psychological ability to "get in touch" with an "authentic, natural female self," a self that can guide its own actions and have freedom to make choices. Viewed in this way, power is a conscious appreciation of the fact that one already possesses power, albeit a type of womanly power unrecognized by our society.[114] For Miller and Stiver "the goal of therapy is . . . mutual empowerment."[115] Perhaps what therapeutic feminism seeks is an illusory "set of neutral rules" that offer the promise that, in following them, no one else's truth will be violated.[116]

As Mary Poovey has suggested, some concepts do "ideological work" by managing or containing important contradictions that exist within an ideological construction, work that may be essential to the widespread acceptance of that larger ideology as "common sense."[117] I believe that the notion of empowerment is currently performing the ideological work of managing feminism's contradictory notions about women's power. Theories that stress women's affiliative capacities aim to locate women's power in women's difference from men. These theories, while denying or concealing their inherent individualism, represent power and empowerment in individual, personal ways. Through this means, the idea of empowerment, as it is often currently employed in psychotherapy with women, has become a container for what Nancy Cott calls the "double aims" of feminism[118]—the contradictory notions of difference and equality. In the therapeutic culture the rights/equality principle that signifies political power is retained as a vestigial symbol named "empowerment," while the paradigm of women's difference that represents personal power reigns supreme. This "difference" paradigm not only governs the most popular theories of women's psychological development,[119] but it is becoming implicit in professional psychotherapy practice as well as in the popular and professional discourse about women and stress, as we shall see in the chapters that follow.

7

The Myth of Empowerment

Consider this bit of dialogue, reconstructed from a conversation I overheard recently as two workers talked together behind the counter at my local Starbucks:

> *Server #1*: You know that guy with the red car? He's definitely got issues.
> *Server #2*: Yeah, you're right, but everybody's got issues.

The word "issues," formerly used to refer to problems in the public and political world, is now frequently used to refer to personal problems. Much of what we do, even what we do morally or politically—not to mention how we conduct relationships—is discussed and evaluated in terms of how it causes us to *feel*.[1] One of the themes that Celia Kitzinger has prized from the psychological canon in order to illustrate to what extent psychology has achieved a personalization of the political is the "revolution from within" theme, aptly named after Gloria Steinem's book of the same name.[2] In therapy, a deeply personal activity, it is often thought to be a political act to "love ourselves, to heal the wounds of patriarchy, and to overcome self-oppression."[3] If these goals are met, the thinking goes, real social change will have been achieved. The disappointments of feminist therapy are in many ways the disappointments of an often unintended translation of the political into the purely personal.

For bell hooks the 1960s and 1970s feminist project of using the self as the "starting point for politicization" through consciousness-raising proved a dangerous business because for many women a sense of the connection between themselves and the larger political reality was difficult to grasp. For women uncertain of the political, the personal was easier to understand. Although the idea that politicization transforms consciousness formed the complex nucleus of the catchphrase "the personal is political," that slogan seemed to have more utility for women as an entry point to the favored cultural practice of exploring self and identity. With no apparent impetus for moving beyond the personal to make a connection with the political, feminist politics could be easily transformed into identity politics.[4] Critics have claimed that the women's movement took "the personal is political" too literally. However, to do just that—to take the slogan *very literally,* as Barbara Cruikshank points out, is truly to understand how "the political has been reconstituted at the level of the self." It is not, then, that we are avoiding dealing with "real" political problems, but that we are reconfiguring the way in which we are able to deal with those problems.[5] And the medium for addressing those problems has become the discourse of the therapeutic.

Therapeutic Feminism?

Are psychology and psychotherapy compatible with feminism? This question has been asked frequently, and perhaps more insistently these days. For many women, it would seem, the psychological is what remains of feminism.[6] Early on, psychology was clearly viewed as antithetical to feminist aims;[7] currently, feminist authors frequently and sometimes inadvertently explain the political in psychological terms. Psychology has always been political in the sense that it often reduces social and political problems to the personal and pathological. Whereas the women's movement explained women's problems as arising from their oppression, psychology transforms them into mental phenomena.[8]

Few would dispute that we are living in a conservative era, and the emphasis on biology within psychology reflects the conservatism of our time. The biological emphasis is nowhere more evident that in relation to sex differences, and media attention is riveted on whatever research purports to uncover a biological basis for those differences.[9] The relationship between hormones and a variety of mental illnesses is being vigorously pursued.[10] Even feminist researchers in psychology experience profound ambivalence about a discipline that in its anxiety to be "scientific," suffers acutely from what Evelyn Fox Keller terms "physics envy."[11] As Michelle Fine and Susan Gordon suggest, in order for women to be accepted in mainstream psychology they may need to join in the pretense that the discipline of psychology is apolitical "by representing [themselves] uncritically as objective researchers; by misrepresenting gender, within frames of sex roles, sex differences, or gender-neutral analyses without discussing power, social context, and meanings; and by constructing the rich and contradictory consciousness of girls and women into narrow factors and scales."[12] A focus on the individual is supported in professional journals, by academic tenure review committees, by agencies that control funding, and in the larger society in which feminist psychologists live.[13] Although feminist psychology could be a vital domain of political and intellectual thought, it is constrained by a discipline "designed to flatten, depoliticize, individualize."[14] Kitzinger sees feminist psychology as a "successor science" easily incorporated into the mainstream, just one more perspective in a field overrun with perspectives, creating barely a ripple on the smooth surface of the profession or a disturbance in the consciousness of most of its members.[15]

The action we take to remedy social problems—mental health problems included—depends largely on whether we find the causes of those problems within individuals or in the contexts in which individuals live. Many psychotherapists focus attention primarily upon the effects of intrapsychic phenomena that are believed to cause a variety of behaviors, often overlooking situational factors that influence those behaviors.[16] The bias in favor of personal as against environmental factors may pose particular obstacles for women, because personal factors are more often used to explain women's behavior that men's. Gender, itself a personal variable, is often used in such explanations, even though gender, status, and power are rarely completely separable from one another.[17] Bruna Seu found that the women she interviewed about their experiences as psychotherapy clients came out of therapy convinced that their problems were located mainly in their psyches—that both action and identity resided in a self that was "unitary, responsible, and capable of change." Seu concluded that these women viewed therapy as part of a medical discourse involving "cure" or confession and believed that a major aim of therapy was to uncover "hidden parts of the self" that their therapists were believed to be more capable of accessing than they were. The women's experience was largely an ahistorical and apolitical one.[18]

Feminist therapy is thought to provide a corrective for these ideas and to challenge the dichotomization of private and public, as Laura Brown has maintained. However, to insist that feminist therapy should "subvert patriarchy one life at a time, one therapy hour at a time" as Brown does, is paradoxically to employ individualism in the service of its own overthrow.[19] I can summon considerably more enthusiasm for Brown's more skeptical statement that whereas "feminism seems to have been good for therapy" in the sense that it has created more work for therapists, it remains uncertain whether "therapy is good for feminism." In an honest appraisal of her concerns, she states:

> While a feminist therapist may bravely describe herself . . . as engaged in acts of resistance and revolution, it is entirely possible that all we are witnessing is a feat of verbal legerdemain in which heroic-sounding justifications are advanced by a (usually) white and middle-class woman about the manner in which she makes her living.[20]

Many contemporary therapists, we must remember, belong to a generation that suffered an early and profound disillusionment with political life.[21]

Psychotherapists' attempts to "empower" their clients may well be assisting women to *experience* an increased sense of control while those women remain firmly situated within an oppressive social context. Without a corresponding increase in her actual ability to make changes in that context, a woman may gain from therapy only an illusory sense of agency in the world.[22] Judith Myers Avis, who defines power as "control over one's own life choices as well as . . . the ability to influence others and to influence the outcome of decisions that affect one's own life," is clear both with herself and with her clients that this context cannot be altered through therapy, a position quite infrequently articulated by therapists.[23]

Class, Race, Social Change

The question arises as to whether the kind of autonomy and personal authority that is often conceived of as attainable through a process of "empowerment" can be achieved in the absence of the kind of power—resources—endorsed by the culture at large. If therapists really seek to help women rebalance power in families, they may be stirring up trouble both inside and outside those families for the women whom they wish to empower. This effort requires us as therapists to take a very different view of ourselves; to learn how to tolerate "not being seen as helpful and healing" so that "we do not dampen the fire in order to soothe ourselves."[24]

Many African American women have long insisted that patriarchy was not their principal concern nor their overarching nemesis. In a racist society the emphasis in the phrase "black woman" is on "black." The white middle-class women who dominated the second wave of women's liberation were rightly taken to task for their failure to address important differences among women—differences in class and race, for starters. Elizabeth Spelman has argued that the origins of that failure lay in white middle-class women's general ignorance of the experience of women when it differs from their own. Ignorance, power, and authority make a potent cultural cocktail, she has maintained. Even now, when we routinely take account of race and class as well as gender, to persist in claiming that—black or white, poor or rich—we "are all the same as women" is to imply that "differences among women finally don't really matter" because they are located "in some non-woman part of [us]." And if the "woman part" of women is what we understand because of what we know about white middle-class women, then when we *seem* to be discussing women's differences we're really talking about white middle-class women. "This," Spelman argues, "is how white middle-class privilege is maintained even as we purport to recognize the importance of women's differences." In addition, when we talk about class and race, if we do not include ourselves as subjects to whom racial and class identities apply we end up discussing only what poor women and non-white women experience, not what we experience in our whiteness and privilege.[25]

In the wake of the struggle for civil rights and women's liberation in America, social change has hardly been the mantra for most women clients and their therapists, the focus of whose work together has increasingly been the self and its development, a private journey of self-discovery.[26] However, the transformation of self and the goal of self-fulfillment are poor substitutes for what has not been gained through political activity; these are narrow and even distracting objectives in the broader context of feminist politics. Lynne Segal refers to the mainstream culture of self-help and psychotherapy as part of a "growth industry designed to handle some of the more manageable [feminist] protests," accommodating to some variants of feminism while it discards or sneers at others.[27] The more toothless the "feminist" discourse—the more "feminizing" rather than "feminist," the more it valorizes the ethic of sensitive care— the more socially acceptable it is. This is a feminism without cultural or political challenge, a feminism "with a 'cozier' language of feelings."

> However, the particular structure of feeling . . . elaborate[d], although frequently attributed to the effect of pain and suffering, is one which is

always seen as adjustable. . . . The cozier therapeutic version of feminism can easily slide into, or at least be used in the service of, a wider culture of blandness and denial: one which collapses the political into the personal, the collective into the individual. Such a culture can accommodate governments which pretend that they cannot change what *is* only in their power to change, while demanding that individuals . . . *can* change what they have little hope of changing (given socially generated scarcity, deepening levels of inequality and ever-growing competitiveness).[28]

Unlike Kitzinger, who believes that psychology and therapy are completely opposed to the goals of feminism, Segal is loath to mock the aims of therapy, cautioning us not to expect "to find perfect harmony between our public and private selves, or any easy, even necessary integration of feminist theoretical work with effective, political practice."[29] Given its stated aims, however, if it is impossible even for *feminist* therapy to harmonize the personal and the political, then the enterprise is indeed built upon sand. In order to arrive at this or any other conclusion, however, it is necessary to move back in time and briefly review how the good faith attempts to marry the personal and political in psychotherapy took shape.

Consciousness Raising and Psychotherapy: From the Personal to the Political and Back

In her book *In Our Time: Memoir of a Revolution,* Susan Brownmiller discusses how Jane McManus, widow of the founder of the leftist magazine *National Guardian,* visited a meeting of the group New York Radical Women (NYRW) in 1968. "You girls have it all wrong, sitting around talking about your sex lives and your orgasms," she scolded. "Why don't you organize around the high cost of food in the supermarket? That's a real women's issue."[30] The women, barely suppressing their laughter, dismissed McManus as hopelessly out of tune with the times. This encounter represented the clash of old and new views of the "political." It was not long before consciousness-raising (CR) groups proliferated throughout the country. Brownmiller describes the phenomenon:

the New Yorkers were the fiercest champions of its political importance. Not everyone was temperamentally suited to the c.r. process, which required a high degree of honesty about intimate matters in front of relative strangers. Many of the "naturals" had been in group therapy or just adored talking about themselves. Others . . . had to overcome an inbred reluctance to speak confessionally, thinking it somewhat narcissistic. But we all believed in the political importance of our task. We expected that the pooled information would clear our heads and lead to analysis and theory, and it did.

Mimeographed sheets of suggested c.r. topics . . . found their way around the country, where they were used as guidelines for new groups that were forming. . . . by early 1972 a few NOW chapters had begun to offer "c.r. nights" in addition to their more structured programs; the first issue of *Ms.,* in July 1972, carried instructions on how to organize a consciousness-raising group, along with a list of sample topics. The free and simple technique of "going around the room and speaking from your own experience" on a given subject with no formal leader was the movement's most successful form of female bonding, and the source of most of its creative thinking. Some of the small groups stayed together for more than a decade.

As the new women's discourse reached into the mainstream during the next few tumultuous years, many original perceptions that the pioneer consciousness-raising groups had struggled to express would become received information, routine and unexceptional, to a new generation that would wonder what the fuss and excitement was all about. I can attest that in New York City during the later sixties and early seventies, nothing was more exciting, or more intellectually stimulating, than to sit in a room with a bunch of women who were working to uncover their collective truths.[31]

There are divergent opinions as to whether consciousness-raising contributed a great deal toward the organization of political action. At the time some women were already equating CR with feminist psychotherapy, which had its origins at roughly the same time.[32] NYRW, founded in 1967, debated the importance of consciousness-raising and discussed what form it should take. According to Kathie Sarachild, a group member and originator of the term "consciousness-raising," CR was intended to "awaken the latent consciousness that . . . all women have about our oppression." Its purpose was to help women begin to understand personal problems as "social problems that must become social issues and fought together."[33] As early as 1968, however, criticism arose from within the women's movement that women's groups were focused on consciousness-raising at the expense of action, and criticism of this kind continued to be leveled intermittently at consciousness-raising by women involved in the movement.[34] Some women negatively appraised CR as a form of therapy—self-indulgent "navel-gazing," as Betty Friedan put it.[35] It did not help that every time CR was discussed in *Ms.*, the feminist magazine, it was described as group therapy, with a heavy emphasis on self-improvement as power.[36] Although it was not uncommon for members of CR groups to have been in therapy previously,[37] its defenders strongly maintained that the aim of CR was to analyze male domination in order to lay waste to it, whereas the goal of therapy was to concoct personal answers to the subordination of women. Other participants viewed the CR group principally as a support group of unconditionally accepting peers. Some former CR participants now argue that, although it was not therapy, CR *was* therapeutic in that truth-telling made people feel better and reduced women's tendency toward self-blame.[38]

The popularity of CR groups, which peaked in the 1970s, was short-lived. After the period of the 1970s, gender inequality was more broadly recognized in American society, with the result that women could move into theory-building and political activity without engaging in the intervening stage of self-discovery. But for some women the supportive atmosphere and emphasis on self-actualization seemed worth hanging onto.[39] Some believed, as David and Joy Rice stated in 1973, that no matter how well groups of women could support individual members "to solve their own problems . . . this does not seem likely to relieve many of the emotional problems of women that require the skill of a trained psychotherapist."[40] Soon, with a call for leaders who could skillfully take on the task of helping women move beyond stereotypical ideas and behaviors, consciousness-raising groups gave way to feminist therapy collectives whose mission was not only to offer women personal help, but to create social change. As Ellen Herman points out, "the curious courtship of psychology and women's liberation" resulted in a paradox. Psychological understanding could either promote feminist awareness and social change or merely reproduce social norms: "At times the state of affairs was extremely perplexing. . . . Would it matter if women achieved institutional gains, only to have their subjective experience remain mired in dependence and powerlessness? Could a line even be reasonably drawn between psychological and social experience?"[41]

Early on, CR was considered a crucial component of feminist models of therapy. Literature on early feminist therapy groups highlighted the democratic nature of those groups, their focus on "pathological" forces in society that were injurious to women, and their emphasis on change beyond the intrapsychic. However, as groups continued to flourish they became more structured and increasingly focused on the agendas of individuals, with the roles of leaders and members becoming ever more distinct. Even though in group therapy the power of the group can offset the power of the therapist to some degree, a power differential between therapist and clients continues to exist. The dream of transporting the CR style into therapy may well have been punctured by the difficulty participants had in seeing each other as peers. Thus, early on, feminists had to develop ways of dealing with power inequities in the absence of societal models for a power-equal therapeutic encounter.[42] Only too aware of the subordinate position women had occupied for decades in their encounters with male physicians and psychiatrists, feminists struggled not to replicate traditional therapeutic situations. The new therapy, derided by one feminist as an "unproved and expensive tyranny," had its critics.[43] Nonetheless, early feminist therapy *was* identifiable as the offspring of its activist parent, consciousness-raising, and it offered a clear alternative to conventional psychotherapy. Its refusal to pathologize women, its disdain for therapeutic neutrality, its transformation of the traditional doctor/patient hierarchy, its turning away from androcentric personality theories— all these marked feminist therapy as a breed apart. Miriam Greenspan, a pioneer of feminist therapy, reflecting on the early days of her therapy practice in the mid-1970s, recalls that

> what was most precious to me in these years . . . was the sense of belonging to an ongoing cultural questioning and critique of received wisdom, the emotional/intellectual buzz of collective feminist enterprise . . . . the best and most important contributions of the grassroots feminist therapy movement . . . to me, . . . are: the unabashed and outright rejection of Freudianism and of the medical model as a basis for understanding and treating women; trusting ourselves to be experts in our own lives; developing theory from the ground of our own experience; understanding empowerment as a *social* and not simply individual psychological process; . . . trying things out in a "beginners' mind" sort of way; the rejection of professionalism as defined by the medical model and the psychiatric establishment; the efforts to work collectively rather than hi-

erarchically, developing models of work and study, theory and practice in which degrees and credentialization were less important than learning from one another and treating each other with equality and respect, regardless of our rung in the professional hierarchy.

In many ways, these contributions seem as important today as they were 20 years ago. The original principles of feminist therapy could still serve as guideposts by which to evaluate our work.[44]

In its early days feminist therapy embraced assertiveness training for women as a tool for empowerment in order to encourage women "to experience a feminist definition of power based on the ability to express oneself rather than on power over others."[45] In addition, a model of androgyny was widely endorsed by feminist theorists and practitioners.[46] It did not take long, however, for the enthusiasm over assertiveness training and androgyny to wane, vitiated by the burgeoning awareness that personal change does not always predict social change. Assertiveness training, for example, was criticized for potentially helping women adjust to a patriarchal, individualistic model of success and goal attainment.[47]

In the 1970s it was easier than it is today to see how feminism could make a positive impact on the process of psychotherapy. Women could (and did) attempt to dismantle Freudian ideas about "penis envy" and the belief in the essential passivity of women that ruled the day; they could unmask sex bias, sex-role stereotyping, and the pathologization of behaviors associated with learned role behavior; they could begin to challenge the predominance of male therapists in the field and encourage women to move beyond the constrictions of their prescribed roles.[48] Even so, in the early 1970s some therapists could not deceive themselves that "aiding a handful of individuals to paths of greater self-esteem and personal fulfillment," as personally satisfying as this may have been for the therapist, could replace the need for social action. Therapists like David and Joy Rice believed that they should be prepared to help a client seek such alternatives to psychotherapy as CR groups, social agencies, and/or other individuals who might be of assistance—that they should make use of any and all means to help a woman realize "that her 'personal' problem is in part a societal one."[49] However, many feminists working in mental health, far from focusing on social action, turned away from analyzing the problems within their own profession and focused on making therapy more "feminist" or taking feminist activist projects and repackaging them into therapeutic enterprises. As Laura Brown has pointed out, shelters for battered women and rape crisis hotlines were two such projects that were quickly transformed "into new employment settings for therapists," losing "their feminist identification and politics" in the bargain.[50]

Feminist group therapy in the mid-1980s differed substantially from the consciousness-raising groups of the early 1970s. Therapists surveyed at the time reported a lesser demand for feminist groups, and fewer and fewer therapists were running the type of collective therapy groups that had proliferated just a handful of years earlier.[51] No longer was it the commonality of their feminist perspectives, but a particular "issue" or problem that brought women together in groups. A study of CR groups in the mid-1970s had found that 70 percent of members had joined in order to "examine women's roles and experiences." In a later study, group members who were interviewed said that they had joined a group in order to garner peer support so that they could manage some parts of their lives better and gain an improved understanding of the experiences of women.[52]

The leaderless support groups that exist today are no more closely related to CR than is psychotherapy itself. These are groups in which women "become therapists for each other," and they are rarely formed with political intentions, all protestations to the contrary. A great deal of the time spent in support groups is taken up with members nurturing each other. As Barbara Kirsh points out, it is indeed ironic that CR groups, begun as vehicles for social change, should have devolved into support groups whose aim is to help women cope with some of the sequelae of the changes brought into being by second-wave feminism.[53]

By the early 1980s individual work with clients had become the preferred mode of feminist therapy practice and, despite criticism from some quarters that Freud's perspective on women was irredeemably flawed, there was a resurgence of interest in forms of therapy heavily influenced by psychoanalysis—feminist object relations theory, self psychology, and a feminist psychology of Jungian archetypes among these.[54] This predominance of the one-to-one encounter between client and therapist was a worrisome development. Although many therapists can and do bring a strengths perspective and an understanding of the effects of the social ecology upon individuals into their practice, by its very nature individual therapy encourages a focus on intrapsychic phenomena and individual pathologies, with the result that women clients may experience greater isolation and less motivation to make changes in the conditions of their lives.

CR, it can be argued, is not easily incorporated into work with individuals. As Carolyn Enns has pointed out, "in face-to-face sessions with individual clients it is extremely difficult to maintain awareness of the class and status issues involved. The unique incapacities of people are made so evident that it is next to impossible not to treat those incapacities as *the* problem.[55] In addition, attempts by the therapist to reduce the client-therapist power differential can be less successful in individual than in group therapy, increasing the possibility that the therapist's "ideology will become imposed rather than considered." A decade after its inception, although the core principles of the personal as political and the diminution of hierarchy in the therapeutic relationship continued to be espoused, feminist therapy was not as easily identifiable as it had been in the 1970s. Feminists cleaved not only to different philosophical positions within feminism, but also to different "schools" of therapy, from the psychoanalytic to the behavioral.[56]

Even in social work, where one might expect a consistent exploration of social forces upon individual development, the person/environment equation seemed to be shifting in favor of a focus on the individual. In 1980 social workers John Longres and Eileen McLeod in their article "Consciousness Raising and Social Work Practice" argued that CR "presupposes a simultaneous concern for [private] troubles and [public] issues but gives primary attention to the way in which public issues penetrate private troubles." This separation of "troubles" from "issues," when the two are in reality conjoined, is a false dichotomy. Longres and McLeod saw that the involvement of social workers in public issues was becoming increasingly restricted to the particular problems of particular institutions rather than to structural problems inherent in society at large; they cautioned social workers not to allow their strong commitment to honor individual differences to preclude consideration of how the class status of those individuals might be at the root of their problems.[57]

Feminist Therapy as Oxymoron?

Miriam Greenspan, whose fulsome description of the early days of feminist therapy was cited earlier, has warned of current dangers in the commodification of feminist therapy:

while there are numerous pockets of cultural resistance and rebellion, there is no social movement per se to speak of. Feminist therapy seems to coexist quite happily in the capitalist marketplace of therapeutic commodities. Feminist therapists can be purchased along with all the other brands of therapists in the ever-expanding multi-million dollar new age/recovery/therapy/healing industry. So it's easy to lose our sense of where we come from, or that we ever had a vision of changing the world.[58]

Hard-won gains in the acceptability of feminist therapy have been accompanied with new dangers.[59] Widespread acceptance, although it does confer legitimacy, may serve only to mute necessary criticism of feminist therapy.[60]

Two important studies limn the contrasts between feminist therapy today and the feminist therapy of the mid-1970s. When Susan Thomas published the results of the earlier of these studies of feminist therapy theory and practice in 1977, she explained feminist therapy as "more [a] part of a social movement than as a type of psychotherapy."[61] From her interviews with women who identified themselves as feminist therapists, Thomas culled a number of salient themes. One of these was the therapists' "desire to free women of the roles that prohibit them from realizing their individual potential." For most of the therapists, it was important to put forward their own feminist values; to place action above "awareness or introspection"; to engage in consciousness-raising. Over half the therapists in the study believed that it was essential to give the client "a sense of her unity and commonality with other women." Therapists in the study were quite concerned with helping the client find the means of achieving their goals outside therapy, within the women's movement. They made a point of giving their clients information concerning a variety of women's groups, with the stated aim of decreasing the clients' time in therapy and moving them into the wider community of feminists as quickly as they could, or, at the very least, attempting to decrease the women's dependence on therapy. One therapist stated that her goal was to "see the women she worked with become feminists themselves and work for societal change"—to help women "try to further the cause of women . . . not an individual solution, but a total change of the system."[62] Thomas concluded from her study that

the techniques ultimately chosen by the feminist therapist are less important to her than the shift in values that was engendered by her

feminist beliefs. . . . Unlike most forms of therapy, feminist therapy is
not merely a means to be used from time to time to alleviate stress
but a way of life for the therapist and, potentially, for the client as
well.[63]

Over twenty years later Jeanne Marecek and Diane Kravetz, relying on
lengthy interviews with twenty-five experienced feminist therapists, made
very different observations. The therapists in their study invariably talked
of therapeutic processes rather than therapeutic goals, and few made
mention of political transformation, consciousness-raising, or the like. In
the view of these therapists, what distinguished feminist therapy from
other therapies were the "respectful, kind, informal, and nurturing"
properties of the therapist-client relationship and interactions, features
that, the researchers pointed out, hardly diverge markedly from today's
professional status quo. Descriptions of interaction in feminist therapy
were couched in terms rooted in stereotypes of femininity and essentialist notions of femaleness, as in one therapist's description of the aim of
therapy: "trying to unearth the feminine character."[64]

Many of the therapists in this study used terms derived from popular
interpretations of Stone Center theories (see chapter 6), which they con-
strued as "invoking an inevitable and universal female nature, and celebrating the 'connectedness' and 'relationality' inherent in all women."[65]
Here, gender difference and gratification through feminine ways and
womanly activities were emphasized. These ideas, as Marecek and
Kravetz suggest, are probably quite familiar to many women clients and
are readily assimilable as a basis for a therapeutic alliance.

Therapists in the study felt in a bind vis-à-vis calling themselves feminist therapists in the wake of the current backlash against feminism. The
researchers were dismayed by how little connection existed for the therapists between practicing therapy and their commitment to producing social and political change, an aim central to the women's movement. The
identity that the therapists espoused most readily was not that of feminists but that of therapists "positioned . . . within the culture of psychotherapy," a culture that "set the terms of the discourse." The therapists introduced feminist elements into their work only when they believed it would not endanger therapeutic goals. In the main, however,
therapy reflected a conceptualization of the self as private and bounded,
and in their work with clients the therapists relied on specific constructs
related to that self (e.g., "womanly 'relationality,' self-empowerment,

self-discovery, self-fulfillment") that were consistent with what they viewed as a feminist model of therapy.[66]

For Laura Brown, therapy, if it is to be truly feminist, cannot merely be some variant on "women's therapy with women" that assists the client in adjusting to a patriarchal status quo, but must be "a conscious and intentional act of radical social change, directed at those social arrangements in which oppressive imbalances of power hold sway."[67] Brown defines feminist therapy as

> the practice of therapy informed by feminist political philosophy and analysis, grounded in multicultural feminist scholarship on the psychology of women and gender, which leads both therapist and client toward strategies and solutions advancing feminist resistance, transformation, and social change in daily personal life, and in relationships with the social, emotional, and political environment.[68]

In her view, feminist therapy "approaches the task of ending inequities by addressing patriarchal oppression as it is manifested as distress in people's lives."[69] It would seem that there are not many practitioners who would qualify as feminist therapists according to this description.

Marecek and Kravetz, who entered the "real" world of feminist therapy, a world at a far remove from academic theorizing, found important differences between feminist therapy as written about and feminist therapy as practiced.[70] They saw feminist practitioners who were relatively isolated from each other and, therefore, isolated from the sort of intellectual environment that might afford opportunities for sustaining a critical awareness. The therapists they interviewed were barely acquainted with the literature on feminist therapy or academic writing in feminist social work, psychology, or women's studies. Occasional exposure to training institutes such as those conducted at the Stone Center constituted, for some, their sole means of taking in new developments in the field. In this the therapists in the study differed not at all from therapists in the mainstream, the majority of whom do not keep up with the literature, obtaining information principally from trade books, organization newsletters, and workshops.

Becoming increasingly cut off from the critical practices of their graduate school training, therapists "tend to drift toward the kinds of clients and methods that enhance their feelings of professional competence," perhaps achieving success with their clients even though their methods may not be grounded in theory,[71] despite the fact that, as Lynne Segal reminds us, "therapeutic efficacy . . . does not establish theoretical adequacy, beyond the therapeutic relationship."[72] As we have seen, therapists' ideas about psychotherapy reflect deeply rooted beliefs about human development and behavior, and their orientation reflects convictions about treatment that are often stronger than the models or methods in which they are embedded. Training focuses on the theoretical and technical intricacies of a particular framework, but rarely on the selection of the framework itself, a selection generally "left to fate and unconscious motivations."[73]

Feminist theories and philosophies have become more and more widely varied—not to say complex—over the past two decades or more. Thus the beliefs and practices of feminist therapists have been shaped by theories propounding quite different notions about the root causes of sexism and about how to eliminate the oppression of women.[74] Although many psychologists are unfamiliar with a wide range of feminist theories, this does not keep them from making assumptions about the bases for sexism and how it should be eradicated that affect their psychological formulations or choices of interventions. Since the literature on feminist therapy has not inspired therapists to engage in any methodical examination of how their work with clients is influenced by particular feminist philosophical viewpoints, it is possible that therapists may wrongly assume that most feminist therapists share their own perspective on feminism.[75]

When Laura Brown states that ideally "a theory of feminist therapy should emerge from some version of political feminist theory," she is well aware that this is very often not the case in practice, where most feminist therapists are distinctly more conversant with the mainstream models of therapy with which feminism has been combined than with feminism itself.[76] The feminist therapy literature, in fact, contains more references to "mainstream theorists whose work it criticizes than to feminist scholars and theoreticians," an irony when we consider that it is feminism, not an understanding of cognitive theory or object relations, that defines the feminist therapist. Perhaps this situation represents feminist authors' ambivalence about the overall utility of such a personal, "inner-directed" activity as therapy in the achievement of political theory and action.[77]

It is to the liberal and cultural philosophical traditions that most contemporary feminist psychotherapy is moored.[78] The *liberal* tradition in feminist theory tends to minimize male-female differences, as we have previously noted, tracing a strong relationship between sexism and practices of socialization as well as delineating institutional constraints on women's access to various roles and to equal opportunities. Precepts of male-female difference embodied in *cultural* feminism—essentialism—are, as we have likewise discussed, given pride of place in the "self/being-in-relation" theories. Because the liberal and cultural traditions tend to emphasize individual agency and the interior life of the individual, they are particularly congenial to feminist psychotherapists, most of whose training in psychological theory and research emphasizes individual factors.[79]

Even when feminist therapists are as well versed in theory and as committed to social change as Brown and others believe they should be, a question that they must ask themselves is to what extent they defer, compromise, or otherwise distort their interventions in order to "meet clients where they are," as social workers put it, and to maintain a strong working alliance with them. A study performed to examine women's perceptions of two types of counseling interventions—"personal" and "sociocultural"—offers a glimpse into the difficulty inherent in any attempts to deliver a social change message—or indeed any social message—to clients.[80] The relatively demographically homogeneous group of single white university women who were studied had very different orientations to the two types of interventions. It was found, paradoxically, that those women who had *traditional* sex-role attitudes preferred a counseling approach that emphasized sociocultural factors because they felt that these approaches offered them a deeper insight into their problems, whereas, those with *nontraditional* attitudes were skeptical "that change in social attitudes and expectations [would] occur quickly enough to accommodate personal change." For those clients with nontraditional attitudes, the researchers reported, "the approach emphasizing personal sources of distress appeared more practical."[81] Essentially, then, the group to whom therapists might believe sociocultural interventions are most likely to appeal (i.e., those with nontraditional attitudes) was found to be the group least receptive to that emphasis in therapy. The authors of the study recommended that counselors

> assess clients' receptivity to a counseling attribution emphasizing the sociocultural basis of the problem. . . . An examination of sociocultural contributing factors must augment, not replace, exploration of internal, personal sources of client problems. . . . it is plausible that attributing

the cause of the problem to either personal or sociocultural factors, especially in the initial phase of counseling, will be most effective when the counselor's focus meshes with the client's attributions of the problem cause.[82]

Should feminist therapists conclude from this, then, that a "stealth" approach to social change should be taken, with discussions of the contribution of sociocultural factors to the client's problems only gradually inserted—if at all—into therapy sessions? Although there is no doubt that a brickbat approach is neither desirable or workable, it is worrisome to consider (all the more so, given what Marecek and Kravetz have contributed to our understanding of some versions of feminist therapy as it is currently being practiced) how many therapists and clients are ill prepared to venture outside the intrapsychic realm.

RuthAnn Parvin and Mary Kay Biaggio in their article "Paradoxes in the Practice of Feminist Therapy" assert that not all therapists who claim to be feminists necessarily subscribe to an activist political agenda for therapy, and that "there has been little, if any, articulation of these conflicting ideas and demands as they relate to feminist therapy." They ask: "What is the place of political advocacy in the therapy room? When does it primarily serve the therapist's agenda and when does it primarily serve the client? . . . When does our activist agenda impose an unsolicited value system on our clients?"[83] What Parvin and Biaggio fail to take into account, as they fret over how to combine the political and the therapeutic, is how *political* psychotherapy truly is. How can we separate "the private," "the political," and "the social" when power relations pervade all three realms, not just the political?[84] As we have discussed in chapter 2, a subject is both an individual who submits to the authority of another *and* an agent of her own actions. In a liberal democracy the "conduct of conduct," as Foucault puts it, ensures that people govern themselves. Psychological intervention is a form of recruitment into self-governance:

> "The professionalization of being human" . . . does not pit the interests of the experts against the interests and self-knowledge of the people. Rather, bio-power . . . seeks to unite the interests of the individual with the interests of society as a whole. . . . Instead of excluding participation or repressing subjectivity, bio-power operates to invest the citizen with a set of goals and self-understandings, and gives the citizen-subject

an investment in participating voluntarily in programs, projects, and institutions set up to "help" them.[85]

This "professionalization of being human" occurs increasingly at a time when the professional therapeutic realm is becoming more exclusively the domain of women. Of course woman has always been engaged in teaching others how to be human; she has, as we have seen, long represented man's "heart" and served as children's source of nurturance. Now, however, as a result of her "expert" position in the "psy" complex, she can become the agent of technologies of the self, through whose intervention society's teachings about psychological woman—the gendered self—are transmitted.

It seems clear that a social change mission is not easily—or often—accomplished in therapy, even in feminist therapy. It is not only therapists who enter psychotherapy imbued with therapeutic ideas; in the twenty-first century many clients have absorbed a sort of "street-corner" psychology (or, today, one might better term it "cablevision" psychology), and in some cases a real sophistication about psychology and psychotherapy. It is no longer self-help books or magazine articles alone that carry a psychological message, as was the case in earlier times. News media, entertainment programs, talk shows—all these send forth dendrites of the therapeutic culture that root themselves imperceptibly into our thinking. While self-help is, as a "market," rampantly middle class, white, and female, the medicalization and psychologization of human problems is infusing our culture more broadly. Naturally, for some individuals these messages are more reinforcing than others. Middle-class mothers, deluged with messages about relational responsibility, absorb these messages with special ease.

The Will to Empower

First, . . . empowerment is a relationship established by expertise, although expertise is constantly tested. . . . Second, it is a democratically unaccountable exercise of power in that the relationship is typically initiated by one party seeking to empower another. Third, it is dependent upon knowledge of those to be empowered, typically found in social scientific models of power or powerlessness and often gained through the self-description and self-disclosure of the subject to the empowered. The will to empower ourselves and others has spread across academic disciplines, social services, neighborhood agencies, social movements, and political groups, forging new relationships of power alongside new conceptualizations of power. Fourth, relationships of empowerment are simultaneously voluntary and coercive.[86]

—Barbara Cruikshank

The "will to empower"[87] has its origins in nineteenth-century reform movements designed to help the unfortunate who had problems that were defined as "social"—poverty, immorality, dependence, and the like—help themselves. As Cruikshank maintains, the aim was to "lift people out of themselves, to get them to objectify their own selves so that they would have no further need to be the objects of help."[88] Even in 1877, as social worker Octavia Hill made clear, the creation of a professional class of middle-class women devoted to that project was to be viewed with skepticism: "If we establish a system of professed workers, we shall quickly begin to hug our system, and perhaps to want to perpetuate it even to the extent of making work for it."

When women therapists experience the "will to empower" other women, they must carefully consider what this help will look like. In our society, power and dependency are frequently falsely dichotomized when, in fact, "all social relationships involve elements of social control, and yet there is no possibility for power except in social relationships."[89] For all the good intentions of those who seek to empower others—whether they are feminists, civil rights workers in the 1960s, or AIDS activists—the aim of empowerment "is to act upon another's interests and desires in order to conduct their actions toward an appropriate end." Empowerment itself, then, is a relationship of power.[90]

In social work, empowerment is generally considered to be a *process*,[91] a social rather than a political/power relationship. This conceptualization of empowerment, which dichotomizes power and powerlessness, characteristically does not assume that empowerment relations are power relations; the "process" definition does not identify empowerment relationships as "sites of resistance and participation in and of themselves."[92] In our previous discussion of power and subjectivity, it was made clear that the subjectivity of the "empowered" individual, the one allegedly without power, cannot be transformed without the use of power. The question of how this works—of how an "empowered" person is constructed from a powerless one, is a complicated one. Generally it is considered that to empower someone is to increase the amount of power she or he possesses. However, the existence of the powerless does not precede the *will* to empower.

Power and Empowerment in Psychotherapy

In 1976 Jean Baker Miller's exploration of how society had "assigned" women the necessary activity of participating in the empowerment of others made an important contribution to the field of psychology. In 1991 Miller, by her own admission, continued to struggle with her ideas about power. Whereas in the 1970s she had defined power as "the capacity to implement," or "self-directed effectiveness," her later attempts to grapple with the idea of power, as we have seen in chapter 6, have yielded the notion of mutual empowerment. Miller laudably suggests that the time is now ripe "to propose a form of development in which everyone would interact in ways that foster the psychological development of all the people involved." Although she critiques the major theories of psychological development for their failure to "reflect the societal situation," her recommendation with respect to altering those theories is to change their emphasis on "psychological separations from others." Apart from urging therapists to focus on interrelationships among family members rather than on promoting separation—in 1991 not at all a novel idea, particularly for family therapists—Miller did not clearly explain how we are to "build mutually empowering connections" without the kind of structural change from without that would promote different gendered arrangements at home, within families.[93] Many mothers, for example, are still taking on a "second shift"[94] of housework and childcare after a day in the outside working world, and if they are also performing a good deal of the emotion work within families, the prescription to build "mutually empowering connections" may not be the answer.

Power is not, at core, an "attitude problem." To feel powerful and to have power are not the same thing, and challenging societal definitions of power cannot imply that women cease to demand power in the public arena and within the family, which they must do if they are not once again to be left out in the cold.[95] Thelma Jean Goodrich, family therapist and editor of the volume in which Miller expressed her ideas about power, has formulated a definition of power quite different from Miller's: *"Power is the capacity to gain whatever resources are necessary to remove oneself from a condition of oppression, to guarantee one's ability to perform, and to affect not only one's circumstances, but also more general circumstances outside one's intimate surroundings"* [Goodrich's italics].[96] In this definition the capacity to obtain necessary resources may rest on the exercise of power in a variety of forms. Power can be seen as related to the degree of control one has over resources and the degree of access to key institutions.[97]

As we have seen with respect to the valorization of feminine influence in the nineteenth century, one can be accorded respect and honor and yet be denied any actual control over one's situation. Answers to the question of what kind of power women want are constrained both by the way power is employed and understood as well as by familiar institutions (e.g., motherhood, the economy, obligatory heterosexuality) that are supported in the culture at large—through religion, law, media, and "managed" popular opinion. The problem of getting power, for women, is paralleled by interior conflicts about what it *means* to get it, conflicts engendered by "the culture's stories of what women should want and by the culture's version of powermongering."[98]

The therapists in Marecek and Kravetz's study had very specific ideas about power, and those ideas, although not identical with Miller's, lean more in the direction of the "mutual empowerment" model than they do toward Goodrich's formulation of power. These therapists assumed, first, that women in general are powerless. They also distinguished, very much in line with the Stone Center theorists, that *power-over* (i.e., power that implies control and authority as well as the ability to "name and define things") was bad and that *power-to* (i.e., the capacity to do or make things) or *power-with* (i.e., relational power, also called "power for") was good.[99] For the therapists, power that involved others was viewed as potentially dangerous to oneself or to others, whereas safe power was power found *inside* the individual, usually defined by the therapists as psychological resources, expertise, and wisdom. In Marecek and Kravetz's estimate, the therapists managed their discomfort with power by "re-locating it away from the arena of social relations and into the private realm of the psyche,"[100] a problematic shift, given the way in which it ignores the transactional nature of power.[101] When, as has been the case in the psychology of women, power is dichotomized through the bad/competitive/male power-over and the good/relational/female power-for, not only are these categories unnecessarily linked to gender differences, but the complex uses of power are obscured, despite ample situational evidence that women exercise power differently in different situations. Parenting, for example, combines both kinds of power in ways that cannot be evaluated as either bad or good.[102] In addition the persistently negative connotations that cling to power-over may contribute to therapists' discomfort with their *own* power, a phenomenon we will take up shortly.[103]

The Uses of Empowerment

The purist's vision of feminist therapy is of an endeavor in which consciousness-raising leads to socially directed action, a vision that is seldom realized in practice, as we have noted. Empowerment is used to induce in women the sense of power, competence, self-esteem, and freedom to make choices in life in the absence of any significant structural change in social conditions.[104] For therapists the empowerment of clients connotes activism, a balm for any unease they may have with therapy's innate individualism. Therapists in Marecek and Kravetz's study often used phrases such as "feelings of empowerment," "moving the client into a state of empowerment," and "empowering the woman's voice." This is how one therapist defined power to the interviewer:

> *Interviewer*: How do you define power for yourself?
> [*Therapist*:] Well, I guess empower. I guess that's what I'd say. It enhances. Well, I guess it can be positive or negative. To me a positive way of experiencing power, viewing power, is one of empowering. It's viewing someone's strengths, sort of looking at their resources, what they have inside, their own expertise.[105]

The term "empowerment" as the therapists employed it seemed roughly equivalent to self-esteem, confidence, and self-knowledge; it did not refer to interpersonal relationships or the social structure. If some feminist therapists believe that power is an intrapsychic phenomenon then it should come as no surprise that those same therapists believe that women can be can be empowered through the therapeutic relationship alone.[106] This presumes that if her individual awareness is heightened in therapy, a client will be able to direct her new-found psychological energies in the direction of social change.[107] In this paradigm a fixed quantity of psychic "energy" is released through therapy along new channels, the "political" being one of these. However, in the real world of therapy, what actually occurs most frequently is that the personal and the political are emphatically separated, with the personal work taking place in the therapy room, divorced from any political action the client may take in the world. We return to the proposition put forward earlier in this chapter: that the notion of therapy as empowering proposes the political as outside, as the work of petitions, protests, and marches, but fails to take into account the notion that if the personal is *truly* political, then therapy itself is an eminently political process.[108]

It may be that many American women view empowerment much as the therapists in Marecek and Kravetz's study did. In a 1992 study Cynthia Miller and A. Gaye Cummins asked 125 women, ages 21 to 63, the majority of whom were white and heterosexual, to consider how they defined and used power in their lives.[109] Although the majority believed that having money and having control over other individuals was typical of society's definitions of power (i.e., the "power-over" model), over 90 percent stated that their *own* definition of power was autonomy and "personal authority," and almost as many maintained that power operated as autonomy and personal authority in their own lives. The women used the term "empowerment" far more frequently than they used the term "personal authority," however. Power signified personal control or "self-enhancement" to them, whether in the sphere of learning, health, or feeling positive about their bodies; powerlessness was defined as loss of personal control, exemplified by feeling dependent on others or asking someone for money.

In Marecek and Kravetz's study, a number of therapists discussed how they tried to give back power to the clients who came to them. As one therapists saw it, she had developed "from a more feminist perspective, that continual kind of awareness especially with women of how much they come into our offices and kind of hand over power. And we have to continually empower and empower and give that message very strongly."[110] Here the therapist's statement "from a *more feminist* perspective" is certainly revealing, given our discussion of the differences between the aims of feminism and the aims of feminist therapy. Empowerment is, in a sense, just that—a *more* feminist perspective than may exist in mainstream psychotherapy, but far from a feminist perspective.[111] To the therapists, empowering clients meant, among other things, being respectful, tendering acceptance, and "allowing" clients to set the therapeutic agenda. Typical of this perspective on donated power is the view that "in listening to our clients, we give them power."[112] Marecek and

Kravetz challenge this view of power as a transferable commodity in a closed system—the idea that if therapists handed over some of their power to their clients, clients will themselves have more power. They ask: Do all women who come to therapy perceive themselves as powerless inside and outside of therapy? Can the therapist, by force of will, "equalize" power within the therapeutic relationship? How does the fact of increased power in that relationship affect the client's life outside therapy?

Therapists in the study spoke of "going back"—uncovering—an "authentic" feminine self untainted by the influences of culture and society. This notion of the authentic feminine self can easily lead to a therapy unfettered by consideration of the sociocultural context of the "self"; a therapy devoted to helping clients to "become themselves," presumably through setting before them a smorgasbord of options and assisting them in selecting from among those options (this notion of freedom of choice resonates with the research study cited in chapter 2 that showed that the majority of Americans of all demographic groups believed that in America you could "be pretty much who you wanted to be").[113] Therapists' strongly stated belief in the necessity of free choice for women may be ultimately incommensurable with the notion of a fixed feminine self. A professed belief in the goal of client autonomy is at variance with therapeutic nudges in the direction of a previsioned representation of womanhood.[114]

A related theme in the feminist therapeutic discourse on power is that of "giving" a woman the power to define *herself*, as exemplified by Laura Brown's insistence that in feminist therapy "the client is explicitly, carefully, and persistently *given back* the power to define self and the meaning of self in the manner most attuned to the person's present identity and cultural context and heritage" [my italics].[115] Here, although the therapist "gives" power in line with her best judgment about how, when, and by what means this should occur, it is assumed that the self and its meanings are for the client to decide, that the therapist's ideas about what constitutes the self and its meanings can be easily put aside. Unlike the more naive practitioner, Brown understands that the self is a social construction; what she does not acknowledge is that therapists cannot leave their own construals of the self at the door of the therapy room.

To Brown empowerment of the client depends upon the therapist's ability to help the client articulate what she wants and how she will know what is working for her, among other things. If the client cannot "allow" herself to know what she wants, the therapist must persist in helping her to answer the question.[116] In my experience there are many clients for whom this type of "empowerment" strategy will not be helpful. What of clients whose culture, race, class, and/or ethnicity (contexts Brown believes must always be taken into account) emphasize reliance on the authority of the therapist and for whom the therapist's authority is a precondition for taking the therapeutic relationship seriously? What of those clients who may, given their own problems and histories, feel overwhelmed and overburdened by a therapy situation in which they are called upon to be the experts about themselves? If class status, education, or other factors have already rendered the therapist/client power differential very great, can we really speak blithely about "equalizing power" in the therapeutic relationship? I assume that, in such situations, Brown uses her judgment and does not dump the therapeutic chess pieces all over the table, leaving clients to figure out the game, but neither does she address the potential for problems in this domain. Experience working with poor African American single mothers as well as with middle-class Caucasian women has convinced me that many of the precepts of feminist therapy are a better "fit" for the latter than the former. Autonomy and self-determination, indeed, may be viewed as individualistic, middle- to upper-class values[117] that therapists who work mainly with middle- and upper-class clients may find it unnecessary to question. One must ask how much power resides in a "gift"—even a gift of illusory power—when it is made at the therapist's discretion and is received well by only a subset of psychotherapy clients. When practitioners work in agencies or institutions "where care is interwoven with social control," ideas about power and empowerment that situate power primarily within the therapist-client relationship cannot be sustained.[118]

In the previous chapter we discussed the idea, common among feminist therapists, that the therapist is there to help the client access the power she already has. A variation on this theme is the precept, here articulated by Laura Brown, that "a step toward construing the client as powerful is to acknowledge that entering into such a relationship of dependency in therapy is itself a statement of a certain type of power." Brown maintains that, given the opprobrium attached to dependency in a our society as well as our cultural adherence to the fiction that "to be powerful is to transcend dependency," for the client voluntarily to "risk a dependent stance in a relationship" is to resist "patriarchal norms."[119] This is the type of reasoning about power that therapists frequently employ when they don their therapeutic vestments—that in acknowledging a problem the client has taken powerful steps toward conquering it, that in the client's adverse circumstances lie challenges that the client has the power to take on. It is also the kind of logic that has led feminist theorists at times to view some "female" disorders—hysteria, for example, in the nineteenth century and anorexia in the twentieth and twenty-first—as protests against stereotyped notions of femininity and to romanticize madness as a form of commendable rebellion rather than understanding it as "the desperate communication of the powerless."[120]

Autonomy, Beneficence, and Choice

Two key psychotherapeutic principles, autonomy and beneficence, frequently collide.[121] Whereas beneficence (i.e., the obligation to maximize the welfare and happiness of others) necessarily sets limits on the client's autonomy and freedom of choice, helping clients make their own choices implies that we will not deter them from acting, at times, against their best interests. There are some therapists who fail to realize that, insofar as the therapist decides what is "healthiest," the client does not have autonomy. As Rachel Hare-Mustin and Jeanne Marecek conclude,

> no matter how hard a therapist might try to be egalitarian, she or he is still "in charge." Even to assert that the client shall ultimately determine the goals of therapy denies the reality that all therapists hold certain normative concepts of health and sickness, growth and stagnation, male and female. It is naïve to claim that the therapist merely evokes what is in the client.[122]

What often goes unremarked is how much the concepts that undergird our theories—autonomy, self-fulfillment, freedom of choice, equality—owe to the liberal-humanist tradition. This tradition disguises male domination by asserting that equality is the inheritance of every individual, that free choice is ours for the making, and that the individual's fate is in her or his own hands. What these ideas and the terms that characterize them—"choice," "power," and "freedom"—mean to us, how we define, use, or misuse them, is a question we must ask ourselves.[123]

In feminist psychological discourse, the notion of choice can be quite deceptive. The options available to women all exist within the prevailing social order. What is lost in psychological translation is the reality that within a culture some choices are more costly than others, and that none is "free." In second-wave feminism the "right to choose" did not imply a woman's getting "in touch with" her "inner needs; it was not a personal, private value."[124] For women, choices must be understood as socially constructed and, as a result, affected by power inequities.[125] Consider the freedom of choice women have relative to men: we can have power over those who are weaker than we are; we can sabotage, use "feminine" wiles, and employ the tactics of protest; we can refuse to consent to a male definitions of us. We *can* employ power, but it is often not of the same quantity and kind as men's power.[126]

The Empowerment Perspective in Social Work

One might assume that social work clinicians would be particularly sensitive to the uses of power. Many social workers devote themselves to helping those who have the least power in society—the homeless, the chronically mentally ill, the addicted. In social work the "empowerment perspective" and "empowerment-based practice" have been endorsed for many years. The social work dictionary defines empowerment in the practice of social work as "the process of helping individuals, families, groups and communities increase personal, interpersonal, socioeconomic and political strength and influence toward improving their circumstances."[127] Empowerment, in this rendering, is a multidimensional concept that encompasses both societally based (macro-level) and personal (micro-level) approaches to working with clients. Through conducting interviews with a small sample of social work practitioners about their conceptualizations of the meaning of "empowerment," Barry Ackerson and David Harrison found that the term, although widely employed, was quite indistinct in practitioners' minds. Practitioners strongly associated empowerment with "the social work value of self-determination," but when asked to make a distinction between empowerment and self-determination, they defined self-determination as "the ability to make choices, to set goals to accomplish desired change, and to recognize that one has the ability to make choices and set goals to improve one's life." The social workers "typically portrayed empowerment as the action side of the same process," albeit acknowledging barriers to the achievement of empowerment, given the limitations of client abilities, the limits imposed by agency policies, and the like.[128]

When the social workers discussed control they typically made references to their efforts to help clients take control of their own lives, make choices, or take personal responsibility. Although the social workers often decried the paternalism of family members and staff workers in the agencies in which they were employed, they rarely associated client powerlessness with larger social forces. Even when the researchers asked them questions designed to tease out this "macro" perspective, several clinicians were at a loss as to how to conceive of empowerment as distinct from a personal, therapeutic meaning.[129] Empowerment was viewed as relative, limited by the practice setting and/or the client's individual resources. The researchers were struck by how this discussion of limits and limitations was reminiscent of the idea of *protective beneficence,* a form of paternalistic intervention sometimes required on behalf of extremely vulnerable individuals such as the chronically mentally ill, rather than empowerment, although the clinicians did not appear to grasp the inherent differences between these two disparate practice models.[130]

Another study, by Amnon Boehm and Lee Staples, found clear differences between social workers' and clients' notions of empowerment. Although both groups spoke of the process and the outcomes of empowerment, clients placed much more emphasis on the relationship of the process to tangible *outcomes* (e.g., changes in living situation, improvements in health, better relationships with others), whereas social workers emphasized process itself (e.g., "the *ability* to control different situations" and "*awareness* of the different connections in the conditions of their lives" [my italics]).[131]

Ackerson and Harrison were disconcerted to find that none of the social workers they interviewed recalled having had specific discussions about empowerment in the course of their social work education. They expressed their fear that "if tomorrow's practitioners lose touch with the value dilemmas underlying the idea [of empowerment], they may learn to espouse and practice approaches that are in conflict with basic social work values." When the profession whose very mandate it is to tackle social problems supplants a focus on broader social and organizational change with a focus on the personal aspects of client problems that can be more easily addressed, the meaning of "empowerment" is vitiated.[132]

Agencies often control workers' decision making and influence the information to which workers have access, thereby limiting the range of options from which workers may choose in ways that interfere with the aim of client empowerment. Marcia Cohen has questioned whether feminist social work goals of "shared power, mutuality, and collaboration" can be met "when client/worker relationships are embedded in a hierarchical power structure that simultaneously transcends and impacts on power relationships within the dyad." She endorses the need to acknowledge "all sources of power over clients in a collective effort to struggle against them" as well as to analyze and resist power levied over social workers in the form of institutional barriers to client/social worker collaboration. This resistance might mean taking on "funding sources, accrediting bodies, agency hierarchies, and our own power as professionals."[133] One of the difficulties that has attended the professionalization of social work, as it has psychology, is the vested interest that members of the profession necessarily develop in the status quo, so that few are willing to engage in the most effective form of resistance—collective resistance.

Power of the Therapist

Although therapists are not always aware of it, their role is invested with power in the form of "authority, expertise, and wisdom."[134] Feminist therapists have had to confront the problem of how to reduce the power differential in therapy without at the same time abandoning boundaries that appear necessary to the professional conduct of therapy. Laura Brown astutely points out that discussions of therapists' power often make a spurious distinction between "real" power, that is, the power vested in the therapist role with its attendant functions, such as fee-setting and boundary-drawing, and "symbolic" power, or the meaning of the therapist's position to the client, a power that she may not herself experience and thus may fail to appreciate.[135] Brown has been struck by the difficulty that feminist therapists in this country and abroad seem to have in acknowledging that they have power. This is particularly disturbing, given how dangerous power can be when ignored or denied.[136] When I was training to become a therapist I can recall being taught (and well taught, too, if one goes by how long I continued this practice) that if clients tried to thank me for helping them, I should always insist that they credit themselves alone for change ("You did the work"). When I shrugged off any responsibility for my part in helping the client to effectuate change, I was always surprised at how insistent clients were in conveying their gratitude. I now am in agreement with Brown that the failure to accept credit from the client represents a sort of "false equality" that "tends to . . . frustrate clients, because it denies the meaning of their internal experience of the therapist as powerful in their lives." Such actions on the part of the therapist deny the therapist's symbolic power.[137]

Unfortunately discussions on the subject of power and therapy in much of the feminist therapy literature either focus completely upon or swiftly and inevitably devolve into discussions of ethics in therapy (e.g., boundary violations and the like). While it is critically important to attend to the therapist's ethical responsibilities toward the client, ethics should not furnish the sole forum for discussing power in therapy. The worry about boundaries is an obvious artifact of the professionalization of feminist therapy and, some contend, a symptom of feminist therapy's rigidity and artificiality. Miriam Greenspan, looking at today's preoccupations in light of what seemed important early on in feminist therapy, cites the "boundary" issue as an example of the development of the "historical myopia" that has accompanied hard-won gains in feminist therapy's mainstream acceptability. She has expressed concern that through fear of being labeled unprofessional, feminist therapists will yield to a "fear-driven, pseudo-objective distancing" in therapy with their clients.[138] Kitzinger and Perkins contend that the need for therapeutic boundaries, the creation of a distinction between "client" and "friend," has only been made because what we used to call friendship has been institutionalized as therapy. In our time, they claim, friends do not expect to have to deal with each others' suffering; therapy takes care of that. Although I would not go this far, it does appear that people worry more than they used to that they may be meddling where only experts should tread. To the extent that we view distress as something better handled in a private therapeutic relationship, we increasingly come to believe that we cannot manage our unhappiness and that we need therapy. As Celia Kitzinger and Rachel Perkins put it, "we are deskilled by the belief that coping with distress is a specialist job."[139]

The Therapist as Oprah's Best Friend?

According to Laura Brown, in order for the therapy relationship to be truly egalitarian, the client must "come to value her own needs and knowledge as central and authoritative." The therapist is not to substitute her own knowledge for the client's expertise about herself, "but rather to resonate with, mirror, and engage the client in this process and to assist the client in learning how such self-knowledge and self-value are obscured by patriarchal processes and institutions."[140] As a therapist I have found that the expectations many of my middle-class and upper-class women clients hold for therapy have been shaped by a media thrumming with psychological talk and insights. That this "information" is embedded in discourses—frequently medicalized—about women's psychology further complicates the notion that a good part of the therapist's job is to validate the client's "needs" and "knowledge." For psychological woman the world in which she will learn about herself is already set up for psychological business. The question is not how a therapist should hand over to a client a therapy of whatever form as the expected commodity, but how the self-knowledge of this more highly psychologized client, shaped by the cultural discourses we have named, individualism not the least of these, influences any therapeutic exchange. As I have mentioned (see chapter 1), a generation educated to advocate for themselves within the medical bureaucracy expects to shop for "answers" and "advice." Many middle-class women have only recently acquired this type of power. How far can—or should—the "professional" depart from the mainstream psychological canon without encountering not merely deeply held beliefs absorbed in transactions with the culture but psychological knowledge gleaned from psychological gurus like Dr. Phil, among others? The dilemma, I believe, is no longer how to achieve a more egalitarian therapist/client relationship, but what to do when the client, therapist, or both are unable to extricate themselves from the "expertise" provided so amply by the culture of the therapeutic? While popular knowledge has always affected how women view themselves, representations of women's experience masquerading as psychological theory have never been as pervasive as they are today.

It has interested me for some time how in the psychotherapy literature self-help has been considered as "other," as apart from what "real" therapists do and how we think. But in the contemporary therapeutic culture, self-help and "real" therapy are no longer quite so distinguishable from each other, despite the continuing rage in the "psy" industry for further scientization and professionalization. Not only do many clients bring well-formed ideas of their psychological selves into the therapy room, but therapists may be strongly influenced by popular ideas as well. My clinical students come to class talking about individuals' "issues" and their "emotional baggage." Of course they will learn theory, but like the rest of us they are not immune to the cultural assumptions that underlie these colloquialisms, and these assumptions may have a more pervasive influence than a dose or two of theoretical knowledge (likewise socially constructed) can provide.

What is brought to therapy by clients necessarily influences the therapeutic agenda and, frequently, the outcomes. For Goodrich, "the deeply held beliefs of our clients that structure their relationships unequally, the commitments that hold the unequal structure in place, the cultural ratification and rewards that accompany it, the material realities that limit alternatives—those will usually win over our one hour a week."[141] For Michelle Fine the changes therapists can help women achieve in their "microenvironments" are limited. Relative to redressing inequities in women's lives, the therapist's options are restricted to blaming women for the existence of those inequities, denying their occurrence, or helping women to see what is personally changeable as against what must be structurally altered.[142]

Psychotherapy, when it is conducted by women for women, is a strange undertaking, remarkable in many ways for what it is not. It is not a chat over the garden fence, nor an intimate telephone conversation with a friend; it is not lunch with a colleague or mentor. It is not the cosseting of an injured child by a mother, the gossip of schoolgirls in the playground, or whispered confidences shared by sisters from their beds. And yet when women sit together in a room, echoes of all these relationships and others I have omitted to name are present. The scrim of "professionalism" helps women therapists worry less that the conversations that occur in the therapy room have anything in common with those that I have mentioned; professionalism offers distance from this worry, and it is power.

How are feminist therapists to think about the value of what they do? Kitzinger and Perkins believe we should jettison the entire enterprise of psychotherapy. My own sentiments are best expressed in these wise words of Thelma Jean Goodrich:

> Knowledge of the limits [of therapy] grants us no solace; nor does it let us resign. Too many come to us and nowhere else. We cannot be victorious, yet we dare not be defeatist. We commit not to oversimplify, not to mystify, not to temporize, not to back away. We ready ourselves for the squeeze play.[143]

8

American Nervousness Redux
Women and the Discourse of Stress

In a recent two-page magazine ad for the antianxiety medication Paxil, we see a woman, probably forty-something, attractive, walking in a crowd, her hand tightly grasping the strap of a messenger bag. Her face has a worried expression. In bold highlighted text is written: "Millions suffer from chronic anxiety." Superimposed on the picture are the words "fatigue," "sleep problems," "worry," "restlessness," "muscle tension," "anxiety," and "irritability." On the next page we are treated to a head shot of the same women, broadly smiling. To one side is the caption, "Your Life is Waiting." The ad tells us that if she has experienced these symptoms for more than six months the woman has qualified for a diagnosis of Generalized Anxiety Disorder. The good news, we are told, is that "*Paxil . . .* works to correct the chemical imbalance believed to cause the disorder." This would be particularly good news for the woman if she happened to be suffering from the "Hurried Woman Syndrome," a condition freshly minted by Dr. Brent Bost and recently discussed on ABC's *Good Morning America*. Perhaps she doesn't even need to take Paxil; by following Dr. Bost's advice she can cure herself by just "simplifying" and "organizing" her life.[1]

The medicalization of human problems constitutes a type of social control that obscures the contribution larger social forces make to their development.[2] The artifact of stress has been an increasingly important vehicle for explaining human dilemmas, and, as we saw in chapter 4, one that has been wide open to cultural influences. By way of example, a recent brochure advertising a workshop for nurses, psychologists, and social workers entitled "The Mysteries of the Female Brain" offered education in differences between "female vs. male cognitive styles" as well as discussions of "reproductive hormones and the brain," "anxiety and stress-related disorders," and "post-traumatic headache." It likewise offered to answer the pressing societal question: "Are women more prone to dental anxiety?"

Post-traumatic headache? Dental anxiety? Were George Beard among us now he might feel right at home. The symptoms of stress are, as in the nineteenth century, many and varied, and, as might be imagined, the message that women experience stress differently than men do has been continuous. Panic over the stress of middle-class life is escalating, and middle-class Americans still believe that the amount and nature of the stress they experience is unique among nations. And, as we have also seen, Americans have had a staunch faith in scientific explanations that, in combination with the renewed ascendancy of a somatic psychiatry, has particularly reinforced medicalized explanations of stress. These days it is possible to talk of being "under stress" without ever having to reveal the causes of the stress, which may range from an excess of spam in one's inbox to an excess of crack dealers moving onto the block.[3] And when the language of stress is personal and individual, it should come as no surprise that the proposed solutions to stress are personal and individual as well.

In both 1957 and 1976 the *Americans View Their Mental Health* (ATVMH) surveys were designed to capture Americans' perceptions of their mental health and their willingness to seek help for their problems. In particular the surveys asked people to respond to the question of whether they have ever had the feeling that they were on the verge of a "nervous breakdown"; in 1996 a similar survey was conducted, and the results were compared.[4] Not surprisingly a significantly larger number of individuals answered this question in the affirmative in 1996 than previously. The researchers who conducted the study concluded that Americans had become "more willing to admit to having feelings of an impending nervous breakdown than they were 40 years ago."[5] What had not changed over the decades was the fact that being a woman increased the odds that a person would report an impending breakdown. The researchers did not conclude from this that women are more psychologically fragile than men or even that women are necessarily exposed to greater stress in their lives; indeed, the conclusion they reached was one that has most often been used to explain this consistent finding: that it is more permissible for women in our society to admit to and talk about personal problems than it is for men.[6]

There continues to be greater social support for women's help-seeking than for men's, but, as we have seen, not all of this support has been created equal. There has been plenty of support for the idea that women are hyperemotional (i.e., emotionally reactive), and this support has traditionally taken the form of medical intervention; there has been a great deal of support for the notion of women as more sensitive and caring than men, and this belief has helped maintain a social structure in which women do the lion's share of the nurturing and caretaking. Although these days we rarely call women hysterical and we do not insist on a middle-class separation of spheres, our *problematizations* (see chapter 3)— the kinds of problems that psychological expertise is deemed able to solve, and in turn, the kinds of human dilemmas that the therapeutic culture has viewed as particularly troublesome—reveal quite a bit about the ways in which that culture has helped maintain the status quo for women.[7] Recall how, in George Beard's day, women were thought to be more easily traumatized than men. Then, as today, the most frequent causes of nervous problems were thought to be biological, and ideas about the origins of nervous diseases and their symptoms were refracted through the lens of the dominant cultural view of women and their roles. Then, as today, scientism and radical medicalization came to the fore at times of particular stress associated with existing gender arrangements, and nervous (i.e., stress-related) illness became a social option for women faced with contradictory societal mandates. Now, at a time when few would question its existence in middle-class gender arrangements, stress has become a significant problematization for women.

The stress discourse has, in its ubiquity, taken both popular and professional forms, but the differences between them are sometimes less than distinct. Popular discussions, for example, rely heavily on professional research and expertise for their credibility, even as they frequently reproduce untrustworthy evidence or selectively cull from sound research those findings that support their conclusions. In the stress discourse, talk of gender generally confirms male-female differences in ways that support the status quo. Even as discussions of posttraumatic reactions following the terrorist attacks of 9/11 have amplified and merged the professional and popular discourses about stress, the familiar drumbeat of male-female difference can be heard. For example, a Pew Research Center survey showed that over 50 percent of women, as opposed to 30 percent of men, described themselves as "very" or "somewhat" worried after the attacks, noted the author of a piece in *Self* magazine, who went on to describe how the women she saw around her were coping—or, rather, not coping well—in the aftermath of the attacks by engaging in "nonstop gluttony," "overzealous shopping," redecorating, and obsessive exercising.[8] Although it is highly doubtful that poor women were responding in these ways, the stress discourse is remarkable for what it excludes—inequality, poverty, racism, and other forms of discrimination. And yet in a society in which poverty has a female form, these are the most acute stressors faced by women.[9]

Medicalization and the Posttraumatic Stress Disorder Diagnosis

Popular discussions about traumatic reactions to the events of 9/11 have enhanced public familiarity with the term "posttraumatic stress disorder," if not the psychiatric classification itself. In the more than twenty years that have passed since the diagnosis of posttraumatic stress disorder (PTSD) was first introduced in the *Diagnostic and Statistical Manual* (*DSM*) of 1980,[10] its description and application have changed dramatically.[11] In the 1980 and 1987 editions of the *DSM* it was made clear that the event that precipitated the disorder had to be something "outside the range of human experience."[12] This definition was consistent with the earliest descriptions of posttraumatic phenomena (e.g., the "shell shock" experienced by World War I soldiers and the responses of people exposed to natural disasters).[13] However, it excluded many traumatic experiences that were by no means uncommon in the lives of women: among these, child sexual abuse, rape, and wife-battering. In acknowledgment of the fact that these forms of male-to-female violence are common in our society, later editions of the *DSM*[14] abandoned the requirement that the precipitating cause of PTSD be outside the range of human experience. Rather, it was stated that the triggering events must have posed "actual or threatened death or serious injury, or other threat to the physical integrity of self or others" and to have "involved intense fear, helplessness, or horror."[15]

This alteration in the PTSD diagnosis has proven to be a mixed blessing. Initially many feminists applauded the inclusion of a diagnosis in the *DSM,* the psychiatric bible, that recognized the psychological effects of external events in the creation of women's problems as a refreshing change from the consistent emphasis on the intrapsychic origins of those difficulties. As time passed, however, some worried about the consequences of opening up the PTSD diagnosis to millions of women who otherwise would never have received it.[16] The transformation in the applicability of the diagnosis is a phenomenon that bears comparison with the epidemic of "cases" that appeared in the wake of nineteenth-century reconceptualizations of hysteria. Although the "fact" of PTSD has effectively been used to advocate for female trauma victims, there is growing concern about the use of a diagnosis of mental disorder to normalize women's reactions to sexual and physical abuse.[17] We can only question why, if PTSD symptoms are *not* abnormal responses to abuse, we are calling them, in the aggregate, a mental disorder.

Scientism in psychiatry has led to an insistence on validating diagnoses by identifying so-called biological markers of disorder, and countless studies attempt to trace the biological concomitants of PTSD.[18] However, an excessive reliance on biologization can de-emphasize the social context of abuse and encourage the separation of mind and body.[19] Even where the biology of PTSD is not reified, the separation of the psychological from the environmental persists, as this statement by Jessica Wolfe and Rachel Kimerling attests: "Whether a differential vulnerability for PTSD in women relates to underlying or intrinsic characteristics . . . *as opposed to external factors* remains unclear" [my italics].[20]

Elsewhere I have argued that broadening the criteria for PTSD has served to carry on a legacy of medicalizing women's problems and to de-emphasize the societal problem of male-to-female violence. In these ways widespread use of the PTSD diagnosis may fail our clients in the very task that alterations in its criteria were meant to achieve—that is, to ensure that women will *not* be regarded as the pathological sources of their own misery.[21]

The Discourse of Stress Meets the Discourse of Difference

It has been suggested that there may be hormonal differences in the ways women and men respond to traumata[22] as well as everyday stress, and some discussions in the popular literature hold that women actually *experience* more stress than men. Women experience greater stress, it is said, because they are the nurturers of others, inhabit multiple roles, and/or feel guilty about not being able to balance home and work life effectively. Views of caretaking in recent articles, books, and television programs dealing with women and stress generally take the essentialist view that caring for others is a naturally and inevitably gender-linked activity. This position is one that effectively joins together the relational and stress discourses.

The different ways in which men and women cope with stress have been given much play in the media, with particular attention paid recently to research performed by Shelley Taylor and her colleagues showing that stress may engender a "tend and befriend" rather than a "fight or flight" response in women. These researchers have hypothesized that the "tend and befriend" response, which they believe has evolutionary origins, biologically predisposes women to nurture their children and to lean on social supports when the survival or well-being of their children is threatened, because to respond by fighting and running from danger would leave the young unprotected.[23] In the preface to *The Tending Instinct*, the book that expanded on this much-ballyhooed research, Taylor insisted that she realizes that the pairing of instinct with caregiving can swiftly devolve into a biology-is-destiny argument that forms the "slippery slope to mothering instinct . . . and other terms . . . used to box women into roles they may not choose to play."[24] However, not only has Taylor's work been used to shore up the notion of a "natural" caretaking instinct in women; some of the very evidence that she herself marshals in support of the existence of the "tend and befriend" response flies in the face of her disclaimers. For example, Taylor cites research conducted by Rena Repetti that has shown differences in how men and women react at home following a stressful day at work. In Repetti's study a significant number of children reported that whereas their fathers responded either by wanting to be alone or by "picking" at everyone, their mothers were often even more affectionate than usual after a stressful work day.[25] Rather than attributing these perceived differences between men and women to differences in power and role demands,[26] Taylor and her colleagues found their answers in women's neurocircuitry, particularly in the effects of oxytocin, a hormone released when women are under stress that is said to induce calm feelings (Taylor calls this a "social hormone," as if there were nothing at all odd about calling a hormone "social").[27]

The following message from one anonymous woman reader was characteristic of the glut of e-mail sent to Taylor that she says relieved her fears about how the public would respond to her challenge to established theory. The woman wrote, "I've been reading popular accounts of science for years, and finally, here is something I recognize." I would argue here that proof of the validity of Taylor's ideas cannot lie in the intuitive appeal of her conclusions for women already primed to take notice of male-female differences and unquestioningly to accept ideas about the instinctual nature of women's nurturing role. But the appeal of those ideas and their societal function *is* reminiscent of the uses to which Gilligan's and Chodorow's work have been put (see chapter 5).

Research such as Taylor's that can be used to demonstrate the biological origins of girls' and women's relational tendencies is seized upon and its conclusions swiftly disseminated. A recent Associated Press article entitled "Girl Power Brings on Brand New Kinds of Pressures" begins with the theme that today's "girl power," although associated with "the feminist movement from the 1970s," does not consist in "trying to be like men"; rather, "girls today are being taught to embrace their own gifts." Taylor's (unattributed) research is then referred to by the author of the 2002 pop psychology book *Girls Will Be Girls,* who is quoted in the article as saying that "girls, and later women, are biologically wired to be compassionate, and when they are faced with challenges, they often produce hormones like oxytocin which make them want to create bonds and connect with people. To fight these reactions would be counter intuitive."[28] Next, the editor of *Elle Girl* magazine is quoted to the effect that "'feminism' is not a dirty word to this generation but they're not interested in burning bras either. Instead, it's about getting what they want, because they feel they should have it whether it's a sports team or a spot in a class." It is clear that girls' "getting what they want" is not associated with any need to transform the culture; the association of feminist activism with bra-burning ensures that any taint associated with rabid, "non-feminine" women will cling to girls who might think about "getting what they want" through antifeminine means such as social activism. The backlash against feminism is alive and well here.[29]

Hickory, Dickory, Dock: Middle-Class Women's Race against the Clock

Female voiceover—as alarm clock loudly ticks in background: "Listen to the voices of women under the influence of a very common, very destructive force—stress. They feel pressure to do it all—the job, the house, the kids."

Bearded, white, male authority: "We're talking about stress levels that approach those you see in combat."

Female voiceover: "Tonight, a life-changing hour for every woman and the men who care about them. What does stress do to a woman's body? Her mind? Her sex life?"

Female interviewer (to a group of seated women): "Does stress interfere with having a normal sex life?" *Women, as a group, laugh uproariously.*

Female voiceover: "You will hear the most intimate revelations from women." *Visual of blonde woman, looking puzzled as she says*: "We just couldn't make love, I mean, it just . . ." *(shrugs)*.

Female voiceover: "—and the latest research about the loss of sexual desire after children." *Visual of African American child, pacifier hanging out of mouth, screaming.* "Did you know that constant stress packs on the kind of fat that can kill?" *Visual of a store with a neon sign advertising sundaes and chicken wings.* "—and triggers explosive, damaging anger." *Cut to an African American woman in bathrobe, standing in a somewhat messy room, calling angrily over her shoulder to a child* (throughout the hour-long program, white women are never shown standing in messy rooms or screaming at their children).

Bearded, white, male authority: "It's [stress is] actually causing little nicks and tears in the inner lining of the arteries that feed our heart."

Female voiceover returns, ominously: "If you often feel overwhelmed, the next hour is for you." *Visual of several women looking distressed, wrinkling their brows as if they have headaches.*

These are the opening minutes of a show produced by *ABC News* entitled "STRESS HURTS: A Wake-Up Call for Women." In the show, scenes of women rushing between work and home, struggling to feed or pick up children, trying, as members of the "sandwich" generation, to care for elderly parents, and wincing from migraines, alternate with brief commentary by the women themselves and interviews with "experts" on the physiological and psychological effects of stress upon women.

Fear-inducing rhetoric saturates the discussion of the effects of stress. The cortisol that is pumping through the one's system under conditions of chronic stress "actually *ages* the brain" and is associated with heart disease, "the leading *killer* of women." The language employed is frequently the idiom of combat (e.g., stress "kills"; hormones may be "*sabotaging* our bodies"). Stress may cause us to overeat, but "stress fat" is different from other fat; "stress fat can *kill.*" Dr. Pamela Peeke, whose book *Fighting Fat over Forty* has received a good deal of play on television, in women's magazines, and on a variety of Web sites, argues that women are not "fighting and flighting" in response to stress; they are "stewing and chewing." Stress fat "is the only fat in the human body that is associated with disease, high blood pressure, stroke, diabetes, cancer." It is *lethal* fat" associated with "toxic stress"—stress that Dr. Peeke defines as "any stress that you see in your life—*it's all individual*—that is, associated with hopelessness, helplessness, and defeat [my italics]. If you don't *perceive* something as being completely out of control, hopeless and helpless, your cortisol doesn't rise. How you *think* ends up at your waistline" [my italics]. The discussion of "lethal fat" not only plays on the fear of fat that is endemic among women in our culture, but it also insists on women's clear responsibility for both the fat and its killer aspects. If only women would only think differently, they would not be dying from lethal fat. One can only recall with a grimace Elizabeth Towne's 1905 advice to a reader (see chapter 3): "I believe that a cheerful right-thinking attitude of mind along with fasting properly and persistently applied will cure any kind of disease except broken bones. You are on the right track. Keep cheerfully along."[30]

The goals of both self-care and self-abnegation are often rather paradoxically intertwined in the stress discourse. The message is that empowerment *is* self-care. We should take care of ourselves with the aim of achieving serenity and happiness; at the same time we absolutely need to take care of ourselves so that we can continue to nurture others without yelling at the kids, refusing our partners sex, or cursing at drivers on the road. Women's anger is often viewed as pathological when it is not unleashed in the service of others, even when situations present themselves that promote a great deal of it.[31] After all, as Jean Baker Miller has dryly observed, "any anger is too much anger in women."[32]

When, in the *ABC News* program, the host, Nancy Synderman, MD, says that "stress brings out the anger in all of us. But it's especially true for women. We try to keep it under control at work but that means we often carry it home," we can see how the term "stress" itself immediately masks any discussion of the causes of women's anger; after all, it is the *stress* that evokes the anger, not the husband, the employer, political or economic institutions. That the sources of woman's anger are seen to be local is useful in ascribing personal responsibility both for the experience and the expression of it. The idea that the woman "carries it home" implies that the anger originates at the workplace and is merely displaced onto the innocents awaiting her arrival. The notion that the anger may travel back and forth with her is anathema; to hold this view would be to imply that others—or other institutions—might be implicated in it. The subtext of women's hyperemotionality is close to the surface here in the message that women *should* keep their anger under control. To say that it is "especially true" that stress brings out anger in women is at once to imply that stress results in more anger in women than in men and at the same time to deny that manifestations of "stress-induced" rage in men can result in rape, wife-battering, and child abuse. Women themselves have adopted a language of minimization when it comes to their own anger. In the television special, "Maria," a single parent, describes her mornings:

> I would say I get angry from stress a lot. [The children's] misbehaving sets off my anger. It's the only way I get through my morning—is to yell. I sometimes feel a little trapped because of the fact I can't go places and do things like I would be able to if I had, you know, some help some-times with the kids, and things like that.

Work, Sex, and Anger Management

Early in the same television program a young white couple is interviewed, and in response to being asked what his wife does when she gets home after work, the husband states, "It's just amazing to watch her; she'll just flow into the kitchen and the kids are really hungry, so they want to eat really fast, so they're tuggin' on the pantlegs, and after we eat she runs up to give them a bath. That's really my down time." To the interviewer's question, "When does she get *her* down time?" the husband replies "She kind of doesn't make that time for herself, I guess. But you know, it just flows the way it does right now, and . . ." (*wife interjects*) "—he's O.K. with that." The wife smiles slightly and raises an eyebrow, and the husband, laughing, says "But, uh, it just seems to flow right now." Although the interviewer suggests through her question that there is inequity in these arrangements, the "flow" of the program is definitely in the direction of the husband's conclusion that his wife is responsible for her lack of "down time."

If we heard that as a result of fatigue, inequality of domestic responsibility, anger towards her spouse over this injustice, and his seeming obliviousness to that disparity in domestic arrangements, the wife's sexual appetites have been somewhat blunted by the end of the day (and later in the program this particular woman confesses that this is so), we would register no astonishment. But the program never mentions any of these potential causes of her lack of libido. Instead it insistently focuses on how stress interferes with women's sex lives. The drumbeat of sexual failure throughout the program, I believe, represents obeisance to what Rachel Hare-Mustin calls the "male sexual drive discourse" that privileges men's "natural" and dominant need for sex.[33] For women to be "overstressed" and uninterested in having sex might imperil the marital relationship.

Interestingly, on the television program it was not the women themselves who brought up the subject of sex. Indeed, the laughter with which they greeted the question "Does stress interfere with having a normal sex life?" might well have been a response to their perception of the inanity of the question in the context of the many other more pressing problems on their minds. The solutions offered to the sex dilemma involved hormonal tinkering in order to restore women's sexual desire when what seemed to be required was a discussion of workplace policies that discourage shared parenting; the lack of affordable childcare; and the impact of an imbalance in domestic responsibilities on couples' relationships in general, not merely on their *sexual* relationships—all of which factors— and more—contribute to working mothers' "stress" and diminished desire for sex.

Working Mother magazine (we need hardly ask ourselves why there is no equivalent *Working Father* magazine) is, unsurprisingly, awash in the stress discourse. In the piece "Shifting Gears: How to Go from Stressed-Out Professional to Way-Calm Mom during Your Drive Home," the phenomenon of working mothers' road rage is explored: "It's the 'second shift' awaiting at home that brings out the worst in women drivers, says Barbara Curbow, Ph.D. . . . A study she conducted showed that working women who assume most of the household responsibilities and get little emotional payback are more likely to exhibit road rage."[34] The assumption that the duties of the second shift will be more tolerantly borne if greater "emotional payback" is forthcoming, presumably from spouses and other family members, is reminiscent of our discussion of domestic individualism in chapter 5—the notion that women supply men with an "interiority" grounded in domestic life and are rewarded through generous praise for their moral qualities. In this piece, as in others we have discussed, research that might, in different hands, contain larger social ramifications is used to buttress an essentially individualistic psychology.

The *Working Woman* "road rage" piece limns the paradox posed by Arlie Hochschild, originator of the term it borrowed, the "second shift": that the increase in woman's power through her participation in the economy, when it is paired with "the growing instability of marriage creates an anonymous, individualistic 'modern' form of oppression."[35] Hochschild believes that this oppression is related to the fact that the specter of divorce and its attendant economic instability may breed caution in many women still inside marriages.[36] One might think that the twin pressures of the need for women to contribute to the family economy and for men to participate in domestic labor might lead us toward "an egalitarian gender ideology" that would have us radically restrategizing and reconfiguring "the division of labor at home." Instead, as attractive as this notion may be, Hochschild's study of working couples with children shows us how two quite different forces combine to work against it. The effects on women of the difference between men's and women's pay and the increased divorce rate, taken together, lead away from visions of domestic equity and back toward very conventional notions of gender and their related "solutions" that run, on the woman's side, to supermomism and, on the man's, to a resistance to taking an equal share in domestic life.[37]

Since the ill effects of maternal employment on child development have not been demonstrated over the past several decades (and hardly for want of researchers' attempts to demonstrate them), media attention seems to have shifted to the guilt-inducing arguments between working and stay-at-home mothers about the value of their respective positions. There is a burgeoning literature on and media interest in women's competition with other women that, I believe, has served as a well-timed distraction from the issues raised by Hochschild and others.[38] And a focus on the decision some women have made to "opt out" of high-level professional and corporate positions in order to stay at home with their children is yet another unwarranted digression, in my view.[39] The "opting-out" discussion posits the working mother's choice as solely between working outside the home and staying at home with the children. Presumably there is not an option, for example, to advocate for workplace conditions that are congenial to co-parenting.

The popularity of Allison's Pearson's novel *I Don't Know How She Does It* speaks to the broad identification middle-class women have made with the prototype of the guilty working mother, her role conflicts, and her task overload. Perhaps many would also identify with the comments of one reviewer who characterized the predicaments of Pearson's protagonist, the overwhelmed working mom, Kate Reddy, as "some of feminism's unintended fruits."[40] If we can't blame Kate's problems on social conditions, and we like Kate too much to blame them on *her,* we can always blame them on feminism. Beyond the stark reality that millions of women do not have the "choice" to opt out of the labor market, stories of professional women leaving their jobs for the homefront deflect attention from the larger question of whether women in fact can choose to fashion a subjectivity that does not include the heterosexual mandate to nurture. Even women like Kate, who may be able to leave their paid employment eventually, still cannot "opt out" of that societal expectation, a requirement that second-wave feminism, for all its flaws, *did* attempt to alter.

Stress, Self-Blame, and Self-Change

Stressed Out? Keep a Stiff Upper Lip and Relax

The "opting-out" discussion is persuasive precisely because the discourse of stress renders it the individual working mother's responsibility to choose to quit her job in order reduce the stress of multitasking and the guilt feelings that frequently assail her. But if she does not make this decision, she had certainly better take care of herself via one of the many means available to her—yoga, naps, breathing exercises, visualization, aromatherapy.[41] The proposed solutions to the problems created by chronic stress seem all the more mild in comparison to the widely touted lethality of the effects of stress. Of course the milder the solutions, the more amenable they are to consumerist intervention—scented candles, pastel yoga mats, spa treatments, and the like.

The stress discourse not only insists that men and women experience stress differently, but also that women are responsible both biologically and psychologically for the fact that they are more "stressed" than men, as exemplified in the following excerpt from an article in *Harper's Bazaar* entitled "How to Reduce Your Stress":

About a decade ago, state-of-the-art scans confirmed what many of us have always suspected: Women's brains have more connections between the two cerebral hemispheres than men's, which may explain why women can multitask from dawn to dusk while men, even presidential alpha males, cannot chew pretzels and watch television simultaneously. . . . In this new no-leisure age, we take a perverse pride in being the busiest woman on the block. . . . our sense of self-worth has somehow become wrapped up in our impossibly exacting schedules. . . . Can't we live without the heart-thumping rush of stress hormones coursing through our veins?[42]

Although the author goes on to suggest that we are "culturally pro-grammed" to overcommit, she never discusses what societal expectations have contributed to that sense of commitment. She asks the question "Could a change of attitude, rather than a change of life, be the solution to stress?" and concludes with a rhetorical shriek: "Can we let go of our pathological perfectionism?"[43]

In the world of self-help, the overfocus on internal, individual solu-tions to what are viewed as personal problems leads to the blaming of women on the one hand, and to a continuing and unjustifiably optimistic view of self-change on the other. Wendy Simonds in her study of women and the self-help culture found that the authors of self-help books, rely-ing on the notion that we must "learn to know and love" ourselves, con-sistently "bombard women readers with the message . . . that we can gain complete control over what happens to us; we simply have to elect to begin the process of change that will . . . mean a better life."[44] Of course the rhetoric of male-female difference obtrudes into discussions of the change process as it does everywhere else. Women can change; but men may not be able to do so, although they *should*. If we could only care less about relationships with men, so the wisdom goes, then "we would be better off in every way." What makes for problems in this rendering, however, is "that women's approach to forging connections is assumed to be more detrimental than men's distance." Women are shown to be over-involved, whereas men's distance from women is steady, invariant, and unproblematic.[45]

As Elayne Rapping concluded when she studied the relationship be-tween women and the recovery movement, that movement addresses only "the effects of [women's] confusion and pain, not the causes," setting forth cut-and-dried guidelines for the management of distress. Although this gives the movement an apolitical feel, the acontextual description of women's suffering and its anodynes is as political as any message broad-cast by women during the height of second-wave women's liberation; it is just that, in this case, the message is "reactionary and repressive" rather than progressive and liberating.[46]

Practitioners and Stress

The stress discourse has not left behind those who are in the expert position. At professional organizations, workshops offer therapists opportunities to "de-stress" and to consider how they are coping with stress. Therapist training frequently involves helping clinicians learn how to "'set limits' on how much responsibility they take for and develop 'distance' from client problems."[47] For those practitioners who work with clients vulnerable to the onslaughts of poverty, racism, discrimination, and other social ills, a paradox lies in the societal message that they need to take personal responsibility for dealing with their own "stress" while, at every level, "this society's structured response to social problems creates stress for the worker, whether it be conflicting, punitive national policy or bureaucratic work design which makes rational response impossible."[48] At the level of policy, neither yoga nor antidepressants will effect a cure.

The Stress Discourse and the Medicalization of Women's Poverty

Our current stress discourse, although it may originate in the middle classes, does not concern itself with the middle class alone. It appears to be infecting the way we conceptualize poverty, and, given the fact of the feminization of poverty, it affects the way we view poor women.[49] Poverty has long been characterized as a stressor, but although poverty and its attendant stresses will never make the pages of *Harper's Bazaar,* the middle-class "take" on stress is evident in a recent focus on the individualization of the stress *response* in poor people. Recently the following statement was emblazoned on the cover of the *New York Times Magazine*: "There's a killer haunting America's inner cities. Not drugs. Not handguns. But . . . stress?"[50] The article followed several poor African American[51] inner-city dwellers suffering the effects of chronic illnesses such as diabetes, asthma, arthritis, cancers, and kidney disease. These individuals are not elderly; some are young, others middle-aged. It was made clear in the piece that there are no absolute answers or explanations for differences in the severity of health problems between the poor and the non-poor. Although eating habits, smoking, and/or the lack of health insurance can explain the exacerbation of disease, it was maintained, these cannot explain why, for example, a rich person who has the same cigarette habit as a poor person is less likely to develop lung cancer. Explanations, the author asserted, "fall into two main schools of thought. One school holds that the problem has mainly to do with stress (e.g., pressures of 'family responsibilities,' racism, discrimination); the other holds actual deprivation responsible. These two factors are often intertwined, but the emphasis is important." The author of the piece makes certain to remind us that "stress is subjective, a feeling, and it means different things to different people."[52] To the reader who wonders why it is so important to determine where the "emphasis" belongs—on stress *or* on deprivation—the answer is soon given:

> If stress is a major cause of ill health, interventions to alleviate it—counseling, antidepressants, even yoga—might be beneficial. A recent article in *The British Medical Journal* suggested that building self-esteem actually helped a group of Native Americans manage their obesity and diabetes. . . . On the other hand, if material disadvantage is a major cause of ill health among the poor, then extensive changes in the environment in which the poor live . . . are needed.[53]

It is clear from these statements that far from being "intertwined," as the author suggested is frequently the case, the "stress" hypothesis and the "environmental" hypothesis are placed in opposition to each other.

Although the *New York Times* article's only subjects—"cases"—are women, neither gender nor the feminization of poverty is ever mentioned, nor is single motherhood discussed, although the stories of single mothers abound. When the health problems of Juanita Moody, a married fifty-two-year-old woman, are discussed, those of her husband, William, are never brought up; however, our old friends cortisol and "lethal fat" make an appearance as Mrs. Moody's switch from fried foods to a healthy diet is discussed:

> It is well known that junk food can make anxious people feel better. Researchers from the University of California recently discovered . . . [that] in response to constant stress, the brain makes a hormone called corticotripin-releasing factor, which instructs the adrenal gland to manufacture stress hormones, including adrenaline and cortisol. These hormones cause a range of physiological changes that over long periods can be

harmful. When people with high levels of cortisol eat sugary, fatty foods, fat is deposited in the abdomen. The researchers theorize that these abdominal fat cells can temporarily inhibit the brain from making corticotripin-releasing factor, reducing feelings of stress and anxiety. If this theory is correct, it could explain how the stress of poverty creates a biological urge to overeat, thus putting poor people at greater risk of obesity and its consequences—diabetes, heart disease, stroke, and certain types of cancer.[54]

The fact that there are fewer supermarkets selling fresh produce in close proximity to poor neighborhoods than in the suburbs is not mentioned. It is clear, too, from her words that Mrs. Moody herself has absorbed the language of stress to describe her problems. Here, she talks about the low-income housing development where she used to live: "it was stressful just to walk out of that place. You were always scared for the kids. . . . You wake up stressed, go to sleep stressed, you see all the garbage and the dealers. That is depressing. In a bad environment like that you say, 'What's the use of doing anything?'"[55]

In this discussion, depression replaces anger; "stress" replaces rats, racism, uncaring landlords, and preoccupied politicians as the cause of depression. The reader may recall the optimistic hypothesis of the 1980s California Task Force to Promote Self-Esteem and Personal and Social Responsibility (see chapter 2), when it announced that "self-esteem [is] the likeliest candidate for a *social vaccine,* something that empowers us to live responsibly and that inoculates us against the lures of crime, violence, substance abuse, teen pregnancy, child abuse, chronic welfare dependency, and educational failure." When poor women are enjoined to take charge of their health (not an unworthy goal, surely; but not a goal that will not go far toward eradicating poverty and crime in the inner city), the medicalization of poverty, through the stress discourse, finds a home in the discourse of empowerment.

Afterword

If history has told us anything, it is that middle-class woman's informal, domestic involvement in the psychological has been constant, necessitated by her social role, consistent with the creation of her subjectivity, and fed by consumerism. As women have gained more authority in the world at large, their ideas, needs, and desires have had to be taken into account in the therapeutic professions and in the therapeutic marketplace. And as the distance between women's and men's spheres has lessened, the distance between a popular culture that embraces therapeutic ideas and the culture of professional psychotherapy practice has diminished and the medicalization of women's problems has become commonplace. When a headline on AOL's "Welcome" page reads "In Need of Retail Therapy? Shop at malls and shopping districts," we know we are in the maw of a wide-ranging therapeutic beast.[1] Recall Foucault's idea of how technologies of the self offer us selective options for judging and adjusting our "selves," options that give the appearance of having been chosen freely.[2] We might well say then, to subvert Pogo's catchphrase, that "we have met the professional and she or he is us."

Decrying the fact that psychology is joining a list of "female" occupations that includes nursing and social work, Irene Philipson insists that the feminization of psychology is robbing "society of an institution in which men traditionally have involved themselves in emotion work, in tolerating and immersing themselves in the intimate and messy problems real people experience on a day-to-day basis." To Philipson, men's leaving the field "confirms the idea, nurtured in families, that if one is hurting inside, if one is depressed or anxious, it is women's job to fix it."[3] I would argue that mere fact of the existence of male psychologists and psychiatrists has never leant substance to the notion that men were involved in day-to-day emotion work. The history of medical professionalization has told us that the "messiness" of human existence has not been

186

at the core of the psychological professions' attractiveness; if anything, the authority vested in the therapeutic professions has given more weight to the need to clean up human disorder than to the need to achieve caring immersion in it. It has been through science and the pretensions of science that professionals have sought to contain the mess.

Caring has always been viewed as women's preserve, and men's long monopoly over the therapeutic professions never altered that fact. When dealing with human problems could be considered science, men were not averse to pronouncing on those problems and their cures; now that the middle classes have more than a passing acquaintance with psychological ideas, the mystery—and the money—are gone. Women, ever associated with the world of the interpersonal, are left to consider the human untidiness, and many men are moving on to more "scientific" psychological pursuits to which women, too, may need to commit themselves if they are to be taken seriously as professionals. However, if the only way women can achieve authoritative positions in the field is to embrace science as the central means of addressing human dilemmas, we will have unwittingly joined in a tradition of medicalizing women's problems that has not served women well.

Just as the backlash against the popular Emmanuel Movement gained steam when its originators claimed that any layperson could adopt its practices, so the popularization of psychotherapy in our time has once again required a professional answer. The first response, I believe, has been the co-option of feminist psychotherapeutic ideas into mainstream practice (see chapter 7). The second has been characterized by efforts to "re-scientize" the field, and many of the men who remain in the "psy" professions have been leading the charge. It was not so very long ago that psychiatry, then a male-dominated field in danger of professional extinction, greatly expanded its diagnostic system, the *Diagnostic and Statistical Manual of Mental Disorders* (*DSM*), to include many more problems of daily living. With this move, psychiatry separated itself from psychoanalysis, thereby re-medicalizing the profession, and psychiatrists entered a high-stakes bid, as psychopharmacologists, for market share in a reborn somatic psychiatry. Psychology, too, has had its turf to defend. After 1970 psychologists found themselves in the odd position of vigorously asserting "that mental illnesses were not really diseases" while simultaneously pushing to obtain health insurance reimbursement for their services. In Larry Beutler's view, this was indeed a Pyrrhic victory, because in ensuring that psychologists are included as providers of mental and more recently, of health services . . . [we] . . . became subjugated to the vagaries, inconsistencies, and demands of a healthcare environment that seems to care little for the people it serves. . . . When the tent of medical dominance of the healthcare industry came down, . . . we were successfully ensconced within its folds.[4]

In 2002 Kurt Salzinger, head of the American Psychological Association's Science Directorate, put out a call for APA members to transform "people's perception of what psychologists do" through writing op-ed pieces about "how psychology as a science reveals fundamental aspects of behavior." He reminded members that from time to time it might be "useful . . . to write about a current topic, such as the psychological variables acting on a populace anxious about an anthrax attack."[5] Exhortations such as these come at a time when psychologists have both lobbied for the right to prescribe psychotropic medication[6] and focused a great deal of attention on their new growth industry, neuropsychology—the "hot" scientific pursuit of those looking to make their mark in the field.

It may be that with the feminization of the psychological professions we will inevitably walk down the path already taken by social work in the first quarter of the twentieth century. As we have seen, social work followed where psychiatry led, away from immersion in the untidiness of the human condition and toward the scientific analysis of it. As Ann Withorn has pointed out, beginning in the late 1920s, apart from short bursts of activism, social workers increasingly viewed their task as that of helping people "cope with and transcend their social situations." By and large they chose not to interpret "their activity in ideological terms or [to become] involved in direct political activity that would jeopardize their objectivity."[7] The low status of the profession led to a hunger for scientific methods and specialization. John Ehrenreich suggests that when, in 1915, Abraham Flexner asked his now famous question, "Is social work a profession?" (he answered his own question resoundingly in the negative), perhaps instead of endlessly struggling to prove him wrong, social work should have been trying to answer another question: "Do we really want to be a profession?" Ehrenreich's concerns about the professionalization of social work apply equally to all the psychological professions: if professionalism implies "a frantic search for status, abjuring social action, . . . evaluating theory for its occupational benefits, defending turf against other professionals, maintaining agency or 'professional' concerns as prior to those of clients, then 'professionalism' hardly seems a desirable or respectable goal."[8]

In this book I have suggested historical precedents for some of the dilemmas the therapeutic culture poses for women. There are some in our profession who do not view psychotherapy as an essentially political activity, and for them it is difficult to imagine what Andrew Polsky has called the "darker possibilities" of power.[9] If psychotherapy with women means invading "personal autonomy . . . in order to create a more desirable kind of autonomy," then we have, indeed, employed our individualist heritage to women's disadvantage. Finding ourselves awash in a therapeutic culture that helps maintain the social status quo for women, must we abandon all professionalism, as Withorn proposes, or can we still hope along with Steven Brint that "some of the earlier community-minded forms of professional idealism [will] remain relevant?"[10]

Ehrenreich's nightmare scenario does not need to come to pass; there are therapists at work at this moment who are committed to helping women engage with the larger sociopolitical context within which their individual problems are situated. I propose that an understanding of the politics of therapeutic empowerment will encourage, if not professional idealism, then at least care and caution on the part of those who practice psychotherapy. The pervasiveness of our tendency to view women's problems as personal rather than political demands that we work to make ourselves suspicious of the uses of empowerment.

Notes

NOTE TO THE PROLOGUE

1. Ann Douglas, *The Feminization of American Culture* (New York: Noonday Press, 1977/1987), xv.

NOTES TO CHAPTER 1

1. See Ellen Herman's discussion of the burgeoning industry of psychotherapy for the normal that followed in the wake of World War II in chapter 9 of *The Romance of American Psychology: Political Culture in the Age of Experts* (Berkeley: University of California Press, 1995).

2. Philip Rieff, *The Triumph of the Therapeutic: Uses of Faith after Freud* (New York: Harper & Row, 1966).

3. I use "psychological woman" here and elsewhere as the unacknowledged counterpart of Rieff's "psychological man."

4. See Celia Kitzinger and Rachel Perkins, *Changing Our Minds: Lesbian Feminism and Psychology* (New York: NYU Press, 1993) for strong opposition to the idea of psychotherapy as an empowering enterprise.

5. Richard A. Cloward and Frances Fox Piven, "Hidden Protest: The Channeling of Female Innovation and Protest," *Signs* 4 (1979): 651 – 669, esp. 666.

6. I have borrowed this term from Ann Douglas, who uses it liberally *in The Feminization of American Culture* (New York: Noonday Press, 1977/1998).

7. This is Arlie Hochschild's term. See *The Managed Heart: Commercialization of Human Feeling* (Berkeley: University of California Press, 1983).

8. Elizabeth Fox-Genovese, *Feminism without Illusions: A Critique of Individualism* (Chapel Hill: University of North Carolina Press, 1991), esp. 25.

9. Ibid., 32.

10. Gillian Brown coined this term in her book *Domestic Individualism: Imagining Self in Nineteenth-Century America* (Berkeley: University of California Press, 1990).

11. See John P. Hewitt, *Dilemmas of the American Self* (Philadelphia: Temple University Press, 1989), esp. 9 – 11, for a discussion of a definition of discourse influenced by Emile Durkheim and George Herbert Mead. See also Hewitt's discussion of optimistic versus pessimistic views of the self in his chapter 1, "The Ubiquity of the Self," 3 – 18.

12. I am indebted here to Jeanne Marecek and Diane Kravetz's discussion of what they term the "connectedness discourse" that conflates such divergent conditions and actions as "care, respect, empathy, kindness, unity, collaboration, and community," in "Putting Politics in Practice: Feminist Therapy as Feminist Praxis," *Women & Therapy* 21 (1998): 17 – 36, esp. 32.

13. See Arlie Russell Hochschild, *The Second Shift: Working Parents and the Revolution at Home* (New York: Viking, 1989).

14. Douglas, *The Feminization of American Culture*, 64.

15. Irene Philipson, in *On the Shoulders of Women: The Feminization of Psychotherapy* (New York: Guilford, 1993), esp. 67, describes deskilling as "the process by which work requiring the exercise of conceptual and judgmental abilities is separated off from that requiring only routine execution" (67). It permits employers to hire less-skilled, lower-paid workers to perform more routinized functions. Philipson has concluded that the increase in the number of women psychotherapists is a Pyrrhic victory, since it is occurring against this backdrop of deskilling and the reduction in the occupational status of psychotherapy.

16. I would consider the relationship between social workers and psychiatrists to have had this semiprofessional character for many decades. See Elizabeth Lunbeck's discussion of the relationship between social work and psychiatry in the early twentieth century in *The Psychiatric Persuasion: Knowledge, Gender and Power in Modern America* (Princeton, NJ: Princeton University Press, 1994).

17. Rieff, *The Triumph of the Therapeutic*, 32 – 33.

18. Christopher Lasch, *The Culture of Narcissism: American Life in an Age of Diminishing Expectations* (New York: Norton, 1979).

19. Virginia Woolf, *A Room of One's Own* (New York: Harcourt, Brace, Jovanovich, 1929), 35.

20. See Rupert Wilkinson, *The Pursuit of American Character* (New York: Harper & Row, 1988), esp. 48 and chapter 5, for his description of the themes — the "four fears," as he calls them — that he believes dominate descriptions of the American character.

21. Richard Sennett, in *The Fall of the Public Man* (New York: Knopf, 1977), argued that, as the public and private worlds have become increasingly conjoined, what is public is now evaluated only in terms of manifestations of the inner self: intimacy, warmth, and openness.

22. David M. Potter, "American Women and the American Character," in *History and American Society: Essays of David M. Potter,* Don E. Fehrenbacher, ed. (New York: Oxford University Press, 1973), 278 – 303.

23. Ibid., 300.

24. Ibid., 302.

25. Robert D. Putnam, *Bowling Alone: The Collapse and Revival of American Community* (New York: Simon & Schuster, 2000).

26. The sometimes-uneasy relationship between feminism and psychoanalysis has been admirably chronicled and analyzed by Mari Jo Buhle in *Feminism and Its Discontents* (Cambridge, MA: Harvard University Press, 1998).

27. Susan Bordo, "Feminism, Postmodernism, and Gender Skepticism," in *Theorizing Feminism: Parallel Trends in the Humanities and Social Sciences,* Anne C. Herrmann and Abigail J. Stewart, eds. (Boulder, CO: Westview Press, 1994), 458 – 481, esp. 465.

NOTES TO CHAPTER 2

1. Warren I. Susman, *Culture as History: The Transformation of the American Society in the Twentieth Century* (New York: Pantheon, 1984), esp. 273, 274.

2. I was led to the essay through a reference to it by Edward E. Sampson in his "Reinterpreting Individualism and Collectivism: Their Religious Roots and Monologic versus Dialogic Person-Other Relationship," *American Psychologist* 55 (2000): 1425 – 1432. See

also Richard Powers, "American Dreaming: The Limitless Absurdity of Our Belief in an Infinitely Transformative Future," *New York Times Magazine* (May 7, 2000), 66 – 67.

3. See John W. Meyer, "Myths of Socialization and of Personality," in *Reconstructing Individualism: Autonomy, Individuality, and the Self in Western Thought*, Thomas C. Heller, Morton Sosna, and David E. Wellbery. eds. (Stanford, CA: Stanford University Press, 1986), 208 – 221.

4. Initially, the term was used pejoratively as a result of conservatives' overwhelmingly negative reaction to the Enlightenment appeal to individual rights and interests that had sparked the French Revolution. For the French, in particular, *individualisme* connoted a focus on the individual that was harmful to the political order and the important concerns of society at large. Some feared that the teachings of eighteenth-century philosophers such as Locke, Kant, Voltaire, and Rousseau would lead to anarchy. See Karl W. Swart, "Individualism in the Mid-Nineteenth Century (1826 – 1860)," *Journal of the History of Ideas* 23 (1962): 77 – 90; Steven Lukes, *Individualism* (New York: Harper & Row, 1973). Also see the discussion of the historical context of American individualism in chapter 6 of Robert N. Bellah, Richard Madsen, William M. Sullivan, Ann Swidler, and Steven M. Tipton, *Habits of the Heart: Individualism and Commitment in American Life* (Berkeley: University of California Press, 1985/1996).

5. Alexis de Tocqueville, *Democracy in America, Volume II* (New York: Knopf, 1840/1945), 98, 99.

6. See Lukes, *Individualism*, 14. For all his admonitions about the perils of individualism, however, Tocqueville found Americans to be more public-spirited than they would admit: "They are more anxious to do honor to their philosophy than to themselves; . . . each American knows when to sacrifice some of his private interests to save the rest." See Tocqueville, *Democracy in America, Volume II*, 122 – 123.

7. Lukes, *Individualism*, 19.

8. See J. W. Burrow, *The Crisis of Reason: European Thought, 1848 – 1914* (New Haven, CT: Yale University Press, 2000), esp. 154 – 155, for a discussion of Burkhardt's understanding of Renaissance individualism.

9. Swart, "Individualism," 86.

10. Lukes, *Individualism*, 26.

11. As the medieval Christian concept of fulfillment through salvation waned, so did the idea that moral behavior — virtue — was the key to that fulfillment. See Alisdair MacIntyre, *After Virtue: A Study in Moral Theory* (Notre Dame, IN: University of Notre Dame Press, 1984).

12. Roy F. Baumeister, "How the Self Became a Problem: A Psychological Review of Historical Research," *Journal of Personality and Social Psychology* 52 (1987): 163 – 176.

13. Gillian Brown, *Domestic Individualism: Imagining Self in Nineteenth-Century America* (Berkeley: University of California Press, 1990), esp. 169.

14. Philip Rieff, *The Triumph of the Therapeutic: Uses of Faith after Freud* (New York: Harper & Row, 1966), esp. 68. See Susman, *Culture as History*, for further discussion of the self and the system of meanings that attend it.

15. Nikolas Rose, *Governing the Soul: The Shaping of the Private Self* (London: Routledge, 1990), esp. 218.

16. Philip Cushman, *Constructing the Self, Constructing America: A Cultural History of Psychotherapy* (Reading, MA: Addison-Wesley, 1995), esp. 259.

17. See Baumeister, "How the Self Became a Problem"; also see Charles Taylor, "The Moral Topography of the Self," in *Hermeneutics And Psychological Theory: Interpretive Perspectives on Personality, Psychotherapy, and Psychopathology*, Stanley B. Messer, Louis

A. Sass, & Robert L. Woolfolk, eds. (New Brunswick, NJ: Rutgers University Press, 1988), 298 – 320; see also Charles Taylor, *Sources of the Self: The Making of the Modern Identity* (Cambridge, MA: Harvard University Press, 1989).

18. Susman, *Culture as History,* 271.

19. I use the male pronoun here to reflect the historical conceptualization of the self as masculine.

20. Taylor, in *Sources of the Self,* lays out with the greatest care the progression of historical thought that led up to modern notions of the self.

21. Heller et al., *Reconstructing Individualism,* 5.

22. See Taylor, "How the Self Became a Problem," 308.

23. Ibid., 314. Citation from Augustine's *De Vera Religione,* 313.

24. Robert L. Woolfolk, *The Cure of Souls: Science, Values, and Psychotherapy* (San Francisco: Jossey-Bass, 1998), esp. 95.

25. See Judith Butler, *Gender Trouble: Feminism and the Subversion of Identity* (New York: Routledge, 1990), 134.

26. Cushman, *Constructing the Self,* 332.

27. See Taylor, *Sources of the Self.*

28. See Lukes, *Individualism,* chapter 4.

29. Taylor, *Sources of the Self,* 18.

30. Bellah et al., *Habits of the Heart,* 143.

31. Ibid., 84.

32. Rieff, *The Triumph of the Therapeutic,* 68.

33. For an extended discussion about the relative influence of the Puritan, democratic, and the social-class visions relative to individualism, see chapter 1 of Richard M. Merelman's *Making Something of Ourselves: On Culture and Politics in the United States* (Berkeley: University of California Press, 1984). The term "loosely bounded culture" is Merelman's. Also see Bellah et al., *Habits of the Heart,* chapter 6, "Individualism"; and Heller et al., *Reconstructing Individualism.*

34. Bellah et al., *Habits of the Heart.* Richard Sennett, in *The Fall of the Public Man* (New York: Knopf, 1977), made perhaps the most vehement case for this dichotomization of public and private. See Christopher Lasch's equally vehement critique of Sennett's ideas in *The Culture of Narcissism: American Life in an Age of Diminishing Expectations* (New York: Norton, 1979), esp. 27 – 30. Lasch's critique nowhere mentions gender, however.

35. Herbert J. Gans, *Middle American Individualism: The Future of Liberal Democracy* (New York: Free Press, 1988), esp. 111 – 113. Among his other criticisms, Gans maintains that Bellah et al.'s notions of community are utopian. See also Woolfolk, *The Cure of Souls,* 28; he cites Nisbet's (1967) characterization of such communitarian critiques as a "nostalgia for Gemeinshaft."

36. Rupert Wilkinson, *The Pursuit of American Character* (New York: Harper & Row, 1988), esp. 37.

37. Elizabeth Fox-Genovese, *Feminism without Illusions: A Critique of Individualism* (Chapel Hill: University of North Carolina Press, 1991), esp. 119.

38. For the consideration of "social theory as cultural text," I am indebted to John P. Hewitt's discussion in his chapter of the same name (chapter 2) in his *Dilemmas of the American Self* (Philadelphia: Temple University Press, 1989). Hewitt makes the point that the fact that some ideas are oversimplified by the reading public and become part of a public discourse stems from a previously untapped cultural need to interpret our experience in a certain way. The cultural significance of certain works resides in the meanings ascribed to them, whether or not those meanings are accurate.

39. Of course, as Hewitt points out, the notion of an American turn toward con-

formism was what the general reader took from David Riesman's considerably more complex discussion in *The Lonely Crowd: A Study of the Changing American Character* (New Haven, CT: Yale University Press, 1953).

40. Wilkinson, *The Pursuit*, 53.

41. Christopher Lasch, *Haven in a Heartless World: The Family Besieged* (New York: Basic, 1977); see also Lasch's *The Culture of Narcissism*.

42. Merelman, *Making Something of Ourselves.*

43. Cushman, *Constructing the Self.*

44. Wilkinson, *The Pursuit*, 48. Although Wilkinson makes much of women's fear of being owned, I would suggest that although women may have been "owned" for many centuries, they could not fear being owned until they could begin to see a way out of that condition.

45. Lasch, *The Culture of Narcissism*, 10.

46. See Harriet G. Lerner, "Female Dependency in Context: Some Theoretical and Technical Considerations," *American Journal of Orthopsychiatry* 53 (1983): 697 – 705.

47. See Wilkinson's analysis of the communitarian critique in *The Pursuit*, 37 – 48.

48. Bellah et al., *Habits of the Heart*, ix.

49. Ibid., xi.

50. Jean Baker Miller, *Toward a New Psychology of Women* (Boston: Beacon Press, 1976); Carol Gilligan, *In a Different Voice: Psychological Theory and Women's Development* (Cambridge, MA: Harvard University Press, 1982).

51. Bellah et al., *Habits of the Heart*, 14 – 15.

52. Ibid., 23 – 24.

53. Ibid., 24.

54. Susman, *Culture as History*, 277.

55. Lasch, "Changing Modes of Making It: From Horatio Alger to the Happy Hooker," 52 – 70, chapter 3 in *The Culture of Narcissism.*

56. Wilkinson, *The Pursuit*, 69.

57. This term was coined by Marianne Walters, Betty Carter, Peggy Papp, and Olga Silverstein in *The Invisible Web: Gender Patterns in Family Relationships* (New York: Guilford, 1988).

58. Bellah et al., *Habits of the Heart*, 142.

59. Adrie Kusserow, "De-homogenizing American Individualism: Socializing Hard and Soft Individualism in Manhattan and Queens," *Ethos* 27 (1999): 210 – 234, esp. 211.

60. David Potter views the notion of self-reliance as an outgrowth of American frontier individualism; the "individualism of intellectual independence and personal self-expression" could only grow in a less physically punishing environment. See David M. Potter, "American Individualism in the Twentieth Century," in *History and American Society: Essays of David M. Potter*, Don E. Fehrenbacher, ed. (New York: Oxford University Press, 1973), 257 – 276, esp. 264. Adrie Kusserow discusses Potter's ideas in "Crossing the Great Divide: Anthropological Theories of the Western Self," *Journal of Anthropological Research* 55 (1999): 541 – 562, esp. 551 – 552.

61. Wilkinson, *The Pursuit*, 40.

62. Potter, "American Individualism," 276.

63. Frank Richardson and Timothy J. Zeddies, "Individualism and Modern Psychotherapy," in *Critical Issues in Psychotherapy: Translating New Ideas into Practice*, Brent D. Slife, Richard N. Williams, and Sally H. Barlow, eds. (Thousand Oaks, CA: Sage, 2001), 147 – 164, esp. 152.

64. Edward E. Sampson, "Psychology and the American Ideal," *Journal of Personality and Social Psychology* 11 (1977): 767 – 782, esp. 778.

65. Richardson and Zeddies, "Individualism and Modern Psychotherapy," 153. For the following discussion of the forms of liberal individualism and their impact on the therapeutic, see 153 – 156.

66. Bellah et al. in *Habits of the Heart* (particularly chapter 2) define and describe utilitarian and expressive individualism. For a thorough discussion of the origins of utilitarian individualism, see C. B. Macpherson, *The Political Theory of Possessive Individualism: Hobbes to Locke* (Oxford: Oxford University Press, 1962).

67. Bellah et al., *Habits of the Heart*, 124.

68. See also Alisdair MacIntyre's discussion of the therapist and manager in *After Virtue*, 30.

69. See Sheila McNamee and Kenneth J. Gergen, *Therapy as Social Construction* (London: Sage, 1992); Michael White and David Epston, *Narrative Means to Therapeutic Ends* (New York: Norton).

70. Jane Flax, *Thinking Fragments* (Berkeley: University of California Press, 1990), esp. 216 – 217.

71. Tocqueville, cited in Barbara Cruikshank's *The Will to Empower* (Ithaca, NY: Cornell University Press, 1999), esp. 99 – 101. In what follows, I rely heavily on Cruikshank's discussion of "liberation therapy," 88 – 104.

72. Ibid., 89. See also Nikolas Rose, *Inventing Ourselves: Psychology, Power, and Personhood* (Cambridge: Cambridge University Press, 1998).

73. Michel Foucault, *Discipline and Punish: The Birth of the Prison,* Alan Sheridan, trans. (New York: Vintage/Random House, 1979), esp. 201.

74. See Luther H. Martin, Huck Gutman, and Patrick H. Hutton, *Technologies of the Self: A Seminar with Michel Foucault* (Amherst: University of Massachusetts Press, 1988), esp. 18. Foucault maintains that technologies of the self enable "individuals to effect by their own means or with the help of others a certain number of operations on their own bodies and souls, thoughts, conduct and way of being, so as to transform themselves in order to attain a certain state of happiness, purity, wisdom, perfection, or immortality."

75. California Task Force to Promote Self-Esteem and Personal and Social Responsibility, appendixes to *Toward a State of Esteem: The Final Report* (Sacramento: California Department of Education, 1990), cited in Cruikshank, *The Will to Empower,* 102.

76. California Task Force to Promote Self-Esteem and Personal and Social Responsibility, *Toward a State of Esteem: The Final Report,* cited in ibid., 92 – 93.

77. Rose, *Inventing Ourselves,* 96

78. California Task Force, appendixes to *Toward a State of Esteem,* cited in Cruikshank, 91, 95.

79. Nikolas Rose, *Governing the Soul: The Shaping of the Private Self* (London: Routledge, 1990), esp. 23, 256.

80. Cruikshank, *The Will to Empower,* 102.

81. Celia Kitzinger and Rachel Perkins, *Changing Our Minds: Lesbian Feminism and Psychology* (New York: NYU Press, 1993), 33.

82. Gloria Steinem, *Revolution from Within: A Book of Self-Esteem* (Boston: Little, Brown, 1992).

83. Cruikshank, *The Will to Empower,* 102 – 103.

84. Sandra Lee Bartky, "Foucault, Femininity, and the Modernization of Patriarchal Power," in *Reflections on Resistance: Feminism & Foucault,* Irene Diamond and Lee Quinby, eds. (Boston: Northeastern University Press, 1988), 61 – 85, esp. 74, 75.

85. Ibid., 77.

86. Ibid., 82 – 83.

87. Biddy Martin, "Feminism, Criticism, and Foucault," in *Reflections on Resistance:*

Feminism & Foucault, Irene Diamond and Lee Quinby, eds. (Boston: Northeastern University Press, 1988), 3 – 19, esp. 9.

88. Ibid, 11, 14.

NOTES TO CHAPTER 3

1. Robert L. Woolfolk, *The Cure of Souls: Science, Values, and Psychotherapy* (San Francisco: Jossey-Bass, 1998), 2, 10. See particularly chapter 2, "Psychotherapy as a Social Institution of the Modern Era."

2. Nikolas Rose, *Inventing Ourselves: Psychology, Power, and Personhood* (Cambridge: Cambridge University Press, 1998), 46.

3. William James, *The Varieties of Religious Experience: A Study in Human Nature* (New York: Longmans, Green, & Co., 1902), esp. 91 – 92.

4. See Nikolas Rose, *Governing the Soul: The Shaping of the Private Self* (London: Routledge, 1990), 213 – 215.

5. Rose, *Inventing Ourselves,* 46.

6. Notably, Philip Rieff in *The Triumph of the Therapeutic: Uses of Faith after Freud* (New York: Harper & Row, 1966), esp. 24 – 25, and Christopher Lasch in *The Culture of Narcissism* (New York: Norton, 1979), esp. 13.

7. See Elizabeth Lunbeck, *The Psychiatric Persuasion: Knowledge, Gender and Power in Modern America* (Princeton, NJ: Princeton University Press, 1994), 76.

8. As Ann Douglas states in *The Feminization of American Culture* (New York: Noonday Press, 1977/1998), 7, the Protestant of 1800 was markedly different from the Protestant of 1875. Whereas in 1800 the churchgoer was on a primarily theological mission and adhered to a dogmatic ideology, for the congregants of 1875 attendance in church was more apt to fulfill social purposes and to be defined in terms of familial morality and responsibility to the community.

9. These included the Emmanuel Movement, spiritualism, Swedenborgianism, mesmerism, and Transcendentalism

10. In chapter 5 more will be said about women's central role in the revival movements.

11. See Roy M. Anker, *Self-Help and Popular Religion in Early American Culture: An Interpretive Guide, Vol. 1* (Westport, CT: Greenwood Press, 1999), esp. 148.

12. Ibid., 151, 168.

13. Ibid., 170.

14. This theme was particularly associated with Swedenborgian Transcendentalism. The historian Sydney Ahlstrom in *A Religious History of the American People* (New Haven, CT: Yale University Press, 1972) refers to this metaphysical perspective as "harmonialism."

15. Anker, *Self-Help and Popular Religion, Vol. 1,* 173 – 174.

16. Burton J. Bledstein, *The Culture of Professionalism: The Middle Class and the Development of Higher Education in America* (New York, Norton, 1976), esp. 116.

17. Barbara Sicherman, "The Paradox of Prudence: Mental Health in the Gilded Age," in *Madhouses, Mad-Doctors, and Madmen: The Social History of Psychiatry in the Victorian Era,* Andrew Scull, ed. (Philadelphia: University of Pennsylvania Press, 1981), pp. 218 – 240, esp. 220.

18. Cited in ibid., p. 220. From Women's Medical Association of New York City, ed., *Mary Putnam Jacobi: A Pathfinder in Medicine* (New York: Putnam, 1925), xxiii.

19. See Robert C. Fuller, *Mesmerism and the American Cure of Souls* (Philadelphia: University of Pennsylvania Press, 1982); see also Nathan G. Hale Jr., *Freud and the Americans:*

The Beginnings of Psychoanalysis in the United States, 1876 – 1917 (New York: Oxford, 1971).

20. Eric Caplan, in *Mind Games: American Culture and the Birth of Psychotherapy* (Berkeley: University of California Press, 1998), esp. 61, argues that, for these reasons, neurologists cannot be considered the true progenitors of psychotherapy.

21. See Fuller, *Mesmerism*.

22. Caplan, *Mind Games*, 62.

23. The inventor of mesmerism, Franz Anton Mesmer (1734 – 1815), a Viennese physician, asserted in the late eighteenth century that he had discovered an element called animal magnetism, an invisible fluid whose distribution throughout the body was responsible for all illness. Mesmer passed magnets over the body or the head to improve the balance of fluid and restore patients to health. Later, one of Mesmer's most illustrious disciples, Marquis de Puysegur, added the technique that Americans most frequently associated with mesmerism — hypnosis — to Mesmer's method.

24. Fuller, *Mesmerism*, 10. The following discussion of mesmerism in America owes much to Fuller's thorough narrative.

25. Fuller cites an estimate made at the time that put about twenty to thirty traveling mesmerists in New England and over two hundred non-traveling mesmerists in Boston by 1843.

26. See Fuller's argument, 132 – 133, that Quimby should be given credit for his part in the early development of psychotherapy.

27. Anker, *Self-Help and Popular Religion*, 184.

28. Eva Moskowitz, *In Therapy We Trust: America's Obsession with Self-Fulfillment* (Baltimore: Johns Hopkins Press, 2001), esp. 14.

29. Ibid., 15.

30. Quotations are from Quimby's book, *Science of Health and Happiness*, cited in Moskowitz, *In Therapy We Trust*, 15 – 16.

31. Anker, *Self-Help and Popular Religion*, 187.

32. Cited by Fuller in *Mesmerism*, 126, from Charles Braden's *Spirits in Rebellion* (Dallas: Southern Methodist University Press, 1963).

33. Annetta Gertrude Dresser, *The Philosophy of P. P. Quimby: With Selections from his Manuscripts and Sketch of His Life* (Boston: Geo. H. Ellis, 1895), 23. Cited in Caplan, *Mind Games*, 68.

34. During the period of the 1880s, the many metaphysical groups in existence used different names — Mental Science, Divine Science, Spiritual Science, Unity, Mind Cure, Science of Being, Home of Truth, and even Christian Science (until Mary Baker Eddy had the name copyrighted in the 1890s). See Beryl Satter's *Each Mind a Kingdom: American Women, Sexual Purity, and the New Thought Movement, 1875 – 1920* (Berkeley: University of California Press, 1999), esp. 3.

35. Eddy worked hard to distinguish her ideas from those of her contemporaries, making a number of important enemies in the process, many of whom viewed Christian Science as quite radical. Although both Christian Science and New Thought were essentially based on the same assumptions, the New Thoughters were less doctrinaire than Eddy, more tolerant both of traditional religious institutions and medical practices. Eddy insisted that only the Bible and her writings held the truth. Because of its more "mainstream" characteristics, New Thought is the subject of our discussion here. In addition to Caplan's discussion *in Mind Games*, see Satter, *Each Mind a Kingdom*, for an extensive discussion of both the New Thought and Christian Science movements and the distinctions between them.

36. Quotations are taken from James, *The Varieties*, 119, 100.

37. The neurologist Frederick Peterson, "The Nerve Specialist to His Patients," *Colliers* 42 (January, 1909), 11. Cited in Hale, *Freud and the Americans*, 231.

38. James, *The Varieties*, 102 – 103.

39. Elizabeth Barnett, *Practical Metaphysics or the True Method of Healing* (Boston: H. H. Carter & Karnck, 1889), 47. Cited in Moskowitz, *In Therapy We Trust*, 23.

40. Ibid., 26. Mental suggestion and mental "photography," methods we might today class as crude cognitive techniques, whereby one conjured up or repeated verbally certain thoughts in an effort to banish bad feelings, were recommended.

41. *Good Housekeeping, Ladies Home Journal,* and other popular magazines at the turn of the century discussed New Thought and psychology as though they were one. See Satter, *Each Mind a Kingdom,* 240.

42. See ibid., 234 – 238, for a detailed discussion of Towne and her writings.

43. Elizabeth Towne, "Family Counsel," *Nautilus* 8 (December 1905), p. 29. Cited in ibid., 27.

44. Satter, *Each Mind a Kingdom.* Satter argues that the long-held view of New Thought ideology as merely a well-fitting cloak for consumerist capitalism fails to take into account the movement's first thirty years. By no means were pampered consumers the parties most interested in late-nineteenth-century New Thought.

45. Interest in mind cure became even more widespread after 1905, when publicity about an onslaught of "American nervousness" grew to a fever pitch. See Hale, *Freud and the Americans*, esp. 232 – 233.

46. Fuller, *Mesmerism,* 142 – 143.

47. Hale, *Freud and the Americans,* 246.

48. Fuller, *Mesmerism,* 154. See also Anker, *Self-Help and Popular Religion,* 206 – 211, for a thorough discussion of Trine and his influence.

49. Satter, *Each Mind a Kingdom,* 7.

50. Anker, *Self-Help and Popular Religion,* 209.

51. Fuller, *Mesmerism,* 160.

52. See Anker's argument for the importance of Trine's little-noted contribution to American culture, *Self-Help and Popular Religion,* 206 – 210.

53. See Caplan, *Mind Games,* 118 – 148, for a comprehensive discussion of the nexus among psychotherapy, the Emmanuel Movement, and the medical profession. My discussion of the Emmanuel Movement owes a great deal to Caplan's meticulous research, as well as to Hale's discussion of the movement in *Freud and the Americans,* esp. 233 – 240.

54. Hale, *Freud and the Americans,* 228.

55. Quoted by Homer Gage in "The Emmanuel Movement from a Medical View Point," *Popular Science Monthly* 75 (October 1909): 363. Cited in Caplan, *Mind Games,* 123.

56. Richard C. Cabot, "The Literature of Psychotherapy," in *Psychotherapy: A Course Reading in Sound Psychology, Sound Medicine, and Sound Religion,* 3, 24. Cited in Caplan, *Mind Games,* 201.

57. Ray Stannard Baker, "The Spiritual Unrest, I. Healing the Sick in Churches," *American Magazine* 67 (December 1908), 199. Cited in Hale, *Freud and the Americans,* 247.

58. George Santayana, cited in Hale, *Freud and the Americans,* 245.

59. See ibid., 239.

60. Caplan, *Mind Games,* 126.

61. See ibid., 131 – 150, for a discussion of the galvanizing effects of the Emmanuel Movement upon the medical community's interest in and eventual domination of psychotherapeutics.

62. Hale, *Freud and the Americans*, 248.

63. Ibid., 248.

64. See Caplan, *Mind Games*, 130 – 150, for a discussion of attacks on the Emmanuel Movement.

65. Andrew Scull relates how, during the 1870s and 1880s, the neurologists mounted ongoing attacks on the asylum superintendents, who held a monopoly on the treatment of the insane. The quotation is from a letter from Frank R. Fry to Smith Ely Jelliffe, March 17, 1924, cited by Andrew Scull, "The Social History of Psychiatry in the Victorian Era," in *Madhouses, Mad-Doctors, and Madmen: The Social History of Psychiatry in the Victorian Era*, Andrew Scull, ed. (Philadelphia: University of Pennsylvania Press, 1981), 5 – 26, 18.

66. James Jackson Putnam, "Remarks on the Psychical Treatment of Neurasthenia," *Boston Journal* 132 (May 28, 1895), 505. Cited in Hale, *Freud and the Americans*, 121.

67. See Lunbeck, *The Psychiatric Persuasion*, for an engrossing history of this period in the transformation of psychiatry through her examination of psychiatry and social work at the Boston Psychopathic Hospital. Southard's statement is quoted on p. 72.

68. Sicherman, "The Paradox of Prudence," 233.

69. John Burnham, "The New Psychology," in *1915, The Cultural Moment: The New Politics, the New Woman, the New Psychology, the New Art and the New Theatre in America,* Adele Heller and Lois Rudnick, eds. (New Brunswick, NJ: Rutgers University Press, 1991), 117 – 127, esp. 118 – 119.

70. Caplan makes these very strong arguments in *Mind Games,* 8 – 9, 150 – 152.

71. The paper that excited such ridicule was entitled "The Influence of the Mind in the Causation and Cure of Disease — the Potency of Definite Expectation." Cited in ibid., 94.

72. Ibid., 94, 97.

73. From Charles L. Dana's (1908) discussion of "Rest Treatment in Relation to Psychotherapy," by S. Weir Mitchell, in *Transactions of the American Neurological Association* 34 (1908), 217. Cited in Scull, "The Social History of Psychiatry," 21.

74. Caplan, *Mind Games,* 95.

75. Ibid., 104. Prince and Putnam played influential roles in laying the groundwork for the new psychotherapy between 1885 and 1900. Nonetheless, bitter divisions continued to exist past the turn of the century between tradition-bound somaticists and advocates of a model of systematic mental therapeutics. See Hale, *Freud and the Americans,* 93 – 94. As Hale points out (pp. 138, 146), after the turn of the century medical interest in the burgeoning field of psychotherapy was spurred by a number of developments. In 1906, Prince founded the *Journal of Abnormal Psychology.* In 1909 alone, the first medical congress on psychotherapy in America was held in New Haven; psychotherapy was listed as a separate topic in *Index Medicus* and ninety or so articles about psychotherapy were referenced in it; and the Sixth International Congress of Psychology was held in Geneva.

76. See Hale, "American Psychotherapy 1885 – 1909," chapter 7 in *Freud and the Americans,* 116 – 150. Freud was studying with Jean Martin Charcot in 1886. The work of the French psychopathologists that pointed to the existence of a subconscious and to the effective uses of hypnotic suggestion in symptom induction and cure was widely influential, and by 1890 their discoveries had crossed the Atlantic. However, Janet's continuing insistence on the importance of heredity in mental disorder was not sufficiently optimistic for importation into America. In 1893 Freud and Joseph Breuer published their first article on hysteria, "On the Psychical Mechanism of Hysterical Phenomena: Preliminary Communication." For thorough discussions of the influence of the ideas of Jean Martin Charcot, Pierre Janet, and other European psychopathologists on Freud, see also Henri F. Ellen-

berger, *The Discovery of the Unconscious* (New York: Basic, 1970), esp. 89 – 101 on Charcot, and chapter 6, "Pierre Janet and Psychological Analysis," 331 – 417.

77. See Caplan, *Mind Games,* 103. Prince believed that because hysteria and other neuroses were caused by learned associations, therapists, employing "re-education," could help patients unlearn these associations and learn the "true" nature of their symptoms, as the products "of fixed ideas, apprehensions, false beliefs, and bad habits."

78. A number of Putnam's conceptualizations — the struggle between self and society, "the internalization of social forces in a sharply critical aspect of the self," the need to face up to distressing emotions and restore unity to the mind — bear a resemblance to Freud's. See Hale, *Freud and the Americans,* 133.

79. James Jackson Putnam, "The Bearings of Philosophy on Psychiatry," *British Medical Journal* (October 20, 1906): 1023. Cited in ibid., 133.

80. Ibid., 133.

81. James Jackson Putnam, *American Journal of the Medical Sciences* 135 (January 1908): 87 – 88. Cited in ibid., 136.

82. Ibid., 247.

83. Quotation cited by Sicherman, "The Paradox of Prudence," 233, from William James, *The Energies of Men* (New York: Dodd, 1914).

84. Hale, in *Freud and the Americans,* 136, 242, 243, discusses how, just as the Emmanuel Movement had fed the nation's hunger for a spirituality somehow based upon scientific principles, there was a groundswell of popular excitement about the ideas of Henri Bergson, a well-regarded French philosopher-scientist first brought to public attention in America by William James in 1909. Bergson's scientific justification for the existence of the soul had particular appeal for a young, questing, "unchurched" generation of Americans. Eschewing determinism, Bergson believed that humans were autonomous agents of the Life Force or energy — *élan vital* — that pushed human evolution. Perhaps more that what he actually said, however, it was what Americans made of Bergson's ideas that proved significant. For Americans, "it was easy to identify instinct and intuition in everybody with the beneficent subconscious and the Life Force." American interpretations of Bergson seem importantly to reflect a cultural synthesis: the coming together, among other things, of a high valuation on intuition and instinct with the influence of abnormal psychology and Freud's ideas.

85. Ibid., 248.

86. See Rose, *Inventing Ourselves,* 187; Burnham, "The New Psychology," 122.

87. Virginia Woolf, "Mr. Bennett and Mrs. Brown," in *The Captain's Death Bed and Other Essays* (London: Hogarth Press, 1950), 91.

88. See Joel Kovel, "The American Mental Health Industry," in *Critical Psychiatry: The Politics of Mental Health,* David Ingleby, ed. (New York: Pantheon, 1980), 72 – 101, esp. 80 – 82.

89. Lunbeck, *The Psychiatric Persuasion,* 76, 306 – 307.

90. Michel Foucault, *Discipline and Punish: The Birth of the Prison* (New York, Pantheon: 1977), 191, 192.

91. Ibid., 192.

92. John H. Ehrenreich, *The Altruistic Imagination: A History of Social Work and Social Policy in the United States* (Ithaca, NY: Cornell University Press, 1985), esp. 68.

93. See Rose, *Inventing Ourselves,* 72; see also John W. Meyer, "Myths of Socialization and of Personality," in *Reconstructing Individualism: Autonomy, Individuality, and the Self in Western Thought,* Thomas C. Heller, Morton Sosna, and David E. Wellbery. eds. (Stanford, CA: Stanford University Press, 1986), 208 – 221.

94. Roy Lubove, *The Professional Altruist: The Emergence of Social Work as a Career* (Cambridge, MA: Harvard University Press, 1965), esp. 84.

95. Lunbeck, *The Psychiatric Persuasion,* 306, 307.

96. See Ellen Herman, "The Growth Industry," chapter 9 in *The Romance of American Psychology: Political Culture in the Age of Experts* (Berkeley: University of California Press, 1995), 238 – 275, esp. 263.

97. Karen Horney, *The Neurotic Personality of Our Time* (New York: Norton, 1937).

98. Herman, *The Romance of American Psychology,* 262.

99. Woolfolk, *The Cure of Souls,* 30

100. See Alessandra Stanley, "Portfolios Depressed, Traders Seek Therapy," *New York Times* (July 7, 2002), 1; Bridget Murray, "Psychologists Help Companies Traverse the Minefields of Layoffs," *APA Monitor* 33 (April 2002), 50 – 51.

101. John C. Burnham, "The Influence of Psychoanalysis upon American Culture," in *Paths into American Culture: Psychology, Medicine, and Morals* (Philadelphia: Temple University Press, 1988), 96 – 110, esp. 99. Burnham distinguishes between the first and second phases of Freud's influence in America: "In that first phase, psychoanalysis was carried primarily within two successive, more general movements, psychotherapy and mental hygiene, and popularization was confounded with both general intellectual rebellion and a myriad of books and articles for the 'nervous.' " Although these phenomena — intellectual radicalism, mental hygiene, literature for the nervous — persisted for several decades, Burnham asserts that knowledge of psychoanalysis from the first phase "did not necessarily contribute to or even facilitate second-phase psychoanalysis," which began roughly in the 1930s and crested after World War II.

102. Hale, in *Freud and the Americans,* has suggested that this tone may be attributable to the fact that many of the new practitioners of psychoanalysis were Europeans who emigrated to America as adults and who may have put a premium on adaptation or social conformism.

103. Philip Rieff, *The Triumph of the Therapeutic,* 30.

104. Cited in Sanford Gifford, "The American Reception of Psychoanalysis, 1908 – 1922," in *1915, The Cultural Moment: The New Politics, the New Woman, the New Psychology, the New Art and the New Theatre in America,* Adele Heller and Lois Rudnick, eds. (New Brunswick, NJ: Rutgers University Press, 1991), 128 – 145, esp. 129, 131.

105. Ibid., 142.

106. See Burnham, "The New Psychology."

107. Nathan G. Hale Jr., *The Rise and Crisis of Psychoanalysis in the United States: Freud and the Americans,* Vol. 2 (New York: Oxford University Press, 1995), 346.

108. For the following discussion, I rely on Burnham's "The Influence of Psychoanalysis," 108 – 109.

109. Ibid., 108. Although we tend to ascribe the widespread recognition and acceptance of human sexuality to Freud, Burnham points out that, in fact, we might more accurately trace it to the social hygiene movement that had, albeit sometimes unwittingly, served as a vehicle for the popularization of Freud's ideas.

110. Ibid., 109.

111. Ibid.

112. Rieff, *The Triumph of the Therapeutic,* 100. As Daphne Merkin states in "The Literary Freud," *New York Times Magazine* (July 13, 2003), 43, "there has been criticism of James Strachey's translation of the standard edition for its "well-meaning but essentially falsifying effort to present Freud as an empirical and systematic . . . thinker rather than a subtle and allusive poet of the unconscious life." Strachey, "in the hope of making him more acceptable to a skeptical medical community, . . . set about 'scientizing' Freud,

adding concrete qualifiers like 'degree' and 'level' to Freud's metaphorical imagery, and introducing clanking Greek words like cathexis and parapraxis into the text in place of Freud's more colloquial and plainspoken German." Nonetheless, as Burnham points out in "The Influence of Psychoanalysis," 103 – 104, the medicalization of psychoanalysis may well have played a large part in its dominance in the post – World War II United States at a time when medicine and its "miracle cures" were king. Even the theoretical bent of psychoanalysis, long a sticking point with Americans enamored of the empirical, was now embraced, as theoretical science became increasingly accepted. See also Woolfolk, *The Cure of Souls,* 16, for a discussion of how Freud came to the conclusion over time that a medical education actually posed obstacles to the development of psychoanalytic expertise. Freud's use of the term *"Seelsorger"* (translated as "one who cares for souls" or "pastor" or "minister") to describe the analyst's function indicates how much closer Freud saw psychoanalysis to pastoral work than to the practice of medicine.

113. This is Bledstein's term for the social context created by professionalism. See *The Culture of Professionalism.*

114. Jill G. Morawski and Gail A. Hornstein, in "Quandary of the Quacks: The Struggle for Expert Knowledge in American Psychology, 1890 – 1940," in *The Estate of Social Knowledge,* JoAnne Brown and David K. van Keuren (Baltimore: Johns Hopkins University Press, 1991), 106 – 133, discuss how this co-optation began in the 1930s as one of the last-ditch attempts to deal with the competition that psychoanalysis posed to the psychologists' establishment of scientific psychology.

115. Bledstein, *The Culture of Professionalism,* 90.

116. See ibid., and Ehrenreich, *The Altruistic Imagination.*

117. Ibid., esp. 107.

118. Rose, *Inventing Ourselves,* 65, 82.

119. Barbara Sicherman, "The Uses of a Diagnosis: Doctors, Patients, and Neurasthenia," *Journal of the History of Medicine* (January 1977): 33 – 54, 40. Barbara Ehrenreich and Deirdre English, in *For Her Own Good: 150 Years of the Experts' Advice to Women* (Garden City, NY: Anchor Press/Doubleday, 1978), esp. 124, discuss how the hysteria broke the gynecologists' long-standing "monopoly of the female psyche."

120. Rose, *Inventing Ourselves,* 87.

121. See Nathan G. Hale Jr., *The Rise and Crisis of Psychoanalysis,* esp. chapter 9, "The Psychoanalytic Impact on American Psychiatry, 1917 – 1940."

NOTES TO CHAPTER 4

1. Roy Porter, "The Body and the Mind, the Doctor and the Patient: Negotiating Hysteria," in *Hysteria beyond Freud,* Sander L. Gilman, Helen King, Roy Porter, G. S. Rousseau, and Elaine Showalter, eds. (Berkeley: University of California Press, 1993), 225 – 285, esp. 240 – 241.

2. Elizabeth Fox-Genovese, *Feminism without Illusions: A Critique of Individualism* (Chapel Hill: University of North Carolina Press, 1991), esp. 181.

3. Arthur Kleinman, *Rethinking Psychiatry: From Cultural Category to Personal Experience* (New York: Free Press, 1988), 71 – 72. See also F. G. Gosling, *Before Freud: Neurasthenia and the American Medical Community, 1870 – 1910* (Urbana: University of Illinois Press, 1987), xiii, for speculations about diagnosis.

4. Carroll Smith-Rosenberg and Charles Rosenberg elucidate the nature of this relationship vis-à-vis Victorian women in "The Female Animal: Medical and Biological Views of Woman and Her Role in Nineteenth-Century America," *The Journal of American History* 60 (1973): 332 – 356.

5. See Porter, "The Body and the Mind," 240.

6. Charles E. Rosenberg, *No Other Gods: On Science and American Social Thought* (Baltimore: Johns Hopkins University Press, 1976/1997), esp. 10.

7. Ibid., 13. Rosenberg reminds us that the authority of science in the nineteenth century was largely restricted to the "elite and articulate."

8. Porter, "The Body and the Mind," 236.

9. Rosenberg, *No Other Gods,* 1.

10. See Cynthia E. Russett, *Sexual Science: The Victorian Construction of Womanhood* (Cambridge, MA: Harvard University Press, 1989), esp. 187 – 188, for a discussion of Clifford Geertz's and Roger Cooter's constructions of science and ideology.

11. Rosenberg, *No Other Gods,* 10.

12. Ibid., 19.

13. Philip Rieff uses the terms "language of faith" and "language of science" in *The Triumph of the Therapeutic: Uses of Faith after Freud* (New York: Harper & Row, 1966). As Louis Menand has pointed out in *The Metaphysical Club: A Story of Ideas in America* (Farrar, Straus and Giroux, 2001), 353 – 354, William James devised the concept of pragmatism in order to "defend religious belief in what he regarded as an excessively scientist and materialistic age."

14. Rosenberg, *No Other Gods,* 2, 3, 12.

15. Barbara Ehrenreich and Deirdre English, *For Her Own Good: 150 Years of the Experts' Advice to Women* (New York: Anchor Press/Doubleday, 1978), esp. 67 – 69.

16. Ann Douglas Wood, " 'The Fashionable Diseases': Women's Complaints and Their Treatment in Nineteenth-Century America," *Journal of Interdisciplinary History* IV(1) (1973): 25 – 52, esp. 32.

17. Ehrenreich and English, *For Her Own Good,* 61, 70; quotation on p. 70. For their discussion concerning how the displacement of women from their traditional roles as healers was accomplished through the commodification of medicine, see chapter 2, "Witches, Healers, Doctors."

18. Ibid, 70 – 74; Porter, "The Body and the Mind," 248 – 249. Over time, those physicians who were in the scientific vanguard used their energies to render medical education more scientific. Teaching and research became more institutionalized and medical discourse was aimed increasingly at a professional audience.

19. Gosling, *Before Freud,* 84 – 87. See also Russett, *Sexual Science,* 201 – 204.

20. William James, *A Pluralistic Universe: Hibbert Lectures at Manchester College on the Present Situation in Philosophy* (London: Longmans, Green, 1909), 211. Cited by John Burnham in "The New Psychology," in *1915, The Cultural Moment: The New Politics, the New Woman, the New Psychology, the New Art and the New Theatre in America,* Adele Heller and Lois Rudnick, eds. (New Brunswick, NJ: Rutgers University Press, 1991), esp. 118.

21. Russett, *Sexual Science,* 195.

22. George M. Beard, *American Nervousness: Its Causes and Consequences: A Supplement to Nervous Exhaustion* (New York: Arno Press, 1972), esp. 99.

23. In fact, rest cure was often prescribed for those who were overworked or overwrought.

24. Barbara Sicherman, "The Paradox of Prudence: Mental Health in the Gilded Age," in *Madhouses, Mad-Doctors, and Madmen: The Social History of Psychiatry in the Victorian Era,* Andrew Scull, ed. (Philadelphia: University of Pennsylvania Press, 1981), 218 – 240. Sicherman suggests that the preoccupation of physicians with the dangers within and without may have stemmed in part from the growing realization that no distinct boundaries could be drawn between normality and insanity.

25. Porter, "The Body and the Mind," 242.

26. Richard A. Cloward and Frances Fox Piven, "Hidden Protest: The Channeling of Female Innovation and Protest," *Signs* 4 (1979): 651 – 669.

27. Of all the definitions of gender that I have seen, I prefer Elaine Showalter's, in "Hysteria, Feminism, and Gender," in *Hysteria beyond Freud,* Sander L. Gilman, Helen King, Roy Porter, G. S. Rousseau, and Elaine Showalter, eds. (Berkeley: University of California Press, 1993), 286 – 344, esp. 288: "The term 'gender' refers to the social relations between the sexes, and the social construction of sexual roles. It stresses the relational aspects of masculinity and femininity as concepts defined in terms of each other, and it engages with other analytical categories of difference and power, such as race and class."

28. G. S. Rousseau, " 'A Strange Pathology': Hysteria in the Early Modern World, 1500 – 1800," in *Hysteria beyond Freud,* Sander L. Gilman, Helen King, Roy Porter, G. S. Rousseau, and Elaine Showalter, eds. (Berkeley: University of California Press, 1993), 91 – 221, esp. 129.

29. Smith-Rosenberg and Rosenberg, "The Female Animal," 332, 354. See also Carroll Smith-Rosenberg, "Hearing Women's Words: A Feminist Reconstruction of History," in *Disorderly Conduct: Visions of Gender in Victorian America* (New York: Knopf, 1985), 11 – 52, esp. 44. Smith-Rosenberg maintains that during periods when social turmoil is at its height, regulation of one group's values, behavior, or language by another is very difficult. However, when social order has been reestablished and economic and political power reasserted, constraints upon both disorder and freedom are reapplied. It is then that people who have social power will move to regulate others they believe are deviant, and the "deviant" will tailor their words and actions in synchrony not only with the new power arrangements but also with their own interests and perceptions.

30. Porter, "The Body and the Mind," 249 – 250; see also Ehrenreich and English, *For Her Own Good,* 26.

31. Carroll Smith-Rosenberg, "The Cross and the Pedestal: Women, Anti-Ritualism, and the Emergence of the American Bourgeoisie," in *Disorderly Conduct,* 129 – 163, esp. 143.

32. See Ehrenreich and English, *For Her Own Good,* 13, 19 – 26, on the Woman Question and the distinction between the "rational" and "romantic" answers to it.

33. As Barbara J. Harris concludes in *Beyond Her Sphere: Women and the Professions in American History* (Westport, CT: Greenwood Press, 1978), esp. 45, in the Romantic tradition, the "insistence on the unity of flesh and spirit, the glorification of the physical and emotional, the acceptance of man and all his drives as good, and the rejection of fixed social rules — all emphasize the physical side of human nature, male and female, and legitimize sexuality without any reference to marriage." The reification of the emotional and the physical/sexual that is part of the Romantic tradition was certainly not part of the conventional Christian view of woman as presented in the cult of domesticity. See also Douglas, *The Feminization of American Culture,* esp. 13; see also Chapter 1, this book, for discussion of the Romantic tradition.

34. *Ladies Magazine* 3 (1830), 83, 84. Cited in Ann Douglas, *The Feminization of American Culture* (New York: Noonday Press, 1977/1998), 45.

35. Ibid., 46, 48.

36. Russett, *Sexual Science,* 206.

37. Carroll Smith-Rosenberg, "Puberty to Menopause: The Cycle of Femininity in Nineteenth-Century America," in *Disorderly Conduct,* 182 – 196, esp. 195.

38. Ehrenreich and English, *For Her Own Good,* 105 – 107; see also Harris, *Beyond Her Sphere,* 57 – 58, on the influence of Darwinism and the rise of science; and Beryl Satter, *Each Mind a Kingdom: American Women, Sexual Purity, and the New Thought Movement,*

1875 – 1920 (Berkeley: University of California Press, 1999), 34 – 42, for a discussion of the use of evolutionary theory to support arguments in favor of women's domesticity.

39. William B. Carpenter, *Principles of Human Physiology: With Their Chief Applications to Pathology, Hygiene, and Forensic Medicine*, 4th ed. (Philadelphia, 1850), 727. Cited in Smith-Rosenberg and Rosenberg, "The Female Animal," 334. For the following discussion of science and women's sexuality see Smith-Rosenberg and Rosenberg, "The Female Animal," 335 – 338; Smith-Rosenberg, "Puberty to Menopause," in *Disorderly Conduct*, 182 – 196; Russett, *Sexual Science*, esp. 122 – 124; Ehrenreich and English, "The Sexual Politics of Sickness," chapter 4 in *For Her Own Good*; Porter, *The Body and the Mind*, 250 – 255.

40. Wood, " 'The Fashionable Diseases.' "

41. Showalter, "Hysteria, Feminism, and Gender," 335. Of course, as Showalter warns in *The Female Malady: Women, Madness, and English Culture* (New York: Pantheon, 1985), it is a mistake to consider hysteria and other such illnesses as feminist protests, as some scholars have.

42. See Showalter, "Hysteria, Feminism, and Gender," 288 – 293, 309 – 314 for a lengthy discussion of the perceived differences between male and female hysteria. See also Rousseau, " 'A Strange Pathology,' " 174.

43. Showalter, "Hysteria, Feminism, and Gender," 292. Showalter categorizes the pairings as: hysteria/melancholy (Renaissance); hysteria/hypochondria (seventeenth and eighteenth centuries); hysteria/neurasthenia (late nineteenth century); and hysteria/shell shock (World War I).

44. See Carroll Smith-Rosenberg and Charles Rosenberg, "The Hysterical Woman: Sex Roles in Nineteenth Century America," *Social Research* 39 (1973): 652 – 678; Showalter, *The Female Malady*, 133.

45. Porter, "The Body and the Mind," 229.

46. Nathan G. Hale Jr., *Freud and the Americans: The Beginnings of Psychoanalysis in the United States, 1876 – 1917* (New York: Oxford University Press, 1971), esp. 59.

47. Jane M. Ussher, *Women's Madness: Misogyny or Mental Illness?* (Amherst: University of Massachusetts Press, 1992), esp. 132.

48. Rousseau, " 'A Strange Pathology,' " 172.

49. Cited by Jean Strouse in *Alice James: A Biography* (New York: Bantam, 1980), esp. 112.

50. See Smith-Rosenberg and Rosenberg, "The Hysterical Woman," 201 – 204, for a thorough exploration of the evolutionary history of hysterical symptoms.

51. Beard, *American Nervousness*, 176.

52. Barbara Sicherman, "The Uses of a Diagnosis: Doctors, Patients, and Neurasthenia," *Journal of the History of Medicine* (1977): 33 – 45, esp. 45; Rosenberg, *No Other Gods*, 7.

53. Tom Lutz, *American Nervousness, 1903: An Anecdotal History* (Cornell, NY: Cornell University Press, 1991), esp. 18.

54. Beard first described the symptoms of neurasthenia in 1869.

55. Beard, *American Nervousness*, 7 – 8.

56. Sicherman, "The Uses of a Diagnosis," 38. See also Gosling, *Before Freud*, 9, and Rosenberg, "The Place of George M. Beard in Nineteenth-Century Psychiatry," *Bulletin of the History of Medicine* 36 (1962): 245 – 259, esp. 247.

57. Sicherman, "The Uses of a Diagnosis," 39. See also Eric Caplan, *Mind Games: American Culture and the Birth of Psychotherapy* (Berkeley: University of California Press, 1998), esp. 42 – 45, for further discussion of the resuscitation of "patient-centered therapeutics."

58. Sicherman, "The Uses of a Diagnosis," 53.

59. Lutz, *American Nervousness, 1903*, 28 – 29.

60. Gosling, *Before Freud*, 83.

61. Rosenberg, "The Place of George M. Beard," 256.

62. Cited in Russett, *Sexual Science*, 116, from Beard's *Sexual Neurasthenia: Its Hygiene, Causes, Symptoms*.

63. Showalter, "Hysteria, Feminism, and Gender," 293.

64. Sicherman, "The Uses of a Diagnosis," 42.

65. Lutz, *American Nervousness, 1903*, 35.

66. Others had noted an increase in insanity over the course of the nineteenth century. Andrew Scull has argued that the increase in the incidence of insanity is attributable in part to what he calls the "professional imperialism" — self-interest — that impelled asylum physicians to seek out more and more cases and to the ever-changing boundaries of what constituted insanity. In the nineteenth century, class considerations played a considerable role in physicians' labeling individuals as lunatics and placing them in asylums. The poor tended to be so labeled and so assigned more frequently than the middle or upper classes. See Andrew Scull, "Was Insanity Increasing?" in *Social Order/Mental Disorder: Anglo-American Psychiatry in Historical Perspective* (Berkeley: University of California Press, 1989), 239 – 249. Hale, in *Freud and the Americans*, 75 – 76, discusses the precipitously declining rates of recovery reported during the period between the 1870s and 1910 by alienists working in public hospitals. See also Rousseau, " 'A Strange Pathology,' " esp. 175 – 176, for a discussion of the blurring of the demarcation between hysteria and insanity.

67. Gosling, *Before Freud*, 15. See also Andrew Scull, "The Social History of Psychiatry in the Victorian Era," in *Madhouses, Mad-Doctors, and Madmen: The Social History of Psychiatry in the Victorian Era*, Andrew Scull, ed. (Philadelphia: University of Pennsylvania Press, 1981), pp. 5 – 26, esp. 17.

68. As Gosling discusses in *Before Freud*, 17, neurologists of the nineteenth century were much closer to the psychiatrists of today "because of their emphasis on the emotions and the social origins of stress." See pp. 17 – 22 for a discussion of the conflict between the neurologists and the alienists. For further discussion of that rivalry, see also Sicherman, "The Uses of a Diagnosis," 40, and Bonnie Ellen Blustein, " 'Hollow Square of Psychological Science': American Neurologists and Psychiatrists in Conflict," in *Madhouses, Mad-Doctors, and Madmen: The Social History of Psychiatry in the Victorian Era*, Andrew Scull, ed. (Philadelphia: University of Pennsylvania Press, 1981), 241 – 270.

69. Hale, *Freud and the Americans*, 45, 79 – 82; Sicherman, "The Uses of a Diagnosis," 49. Neurasthenia comprised disorders that in today's terms might include phobias, emotional stress, mild psychotic states, actual physical conditions not diagnosable in the nineteenth century, and psychosomatic illnesses.

70. W. A. McClain, "The Psychology of Neurasthenia," *Medical Record* 48 (1895): 81, cited in Caplan, *Mind Games*, 43.

71. Wood, "The Fashionable Diseases," 28; Lutz, *American Nervousness, 1903*, 31 – 34.

72. Gosling, *Before Freud*, 55 – 58, 98 – 99.

73. An extended discussion of rest cure is to be found in Showalter, "Hysteria, Feminism, and Gender," 297 – 300. See also Wood's discussion of early treatments and of rest cure in "The Fashionable Diseases," 30 – 31. See Lutz, *American Nervousness, 1903*, 34 – 36, for a discussion of men and neurasthenia.

74. Margaret A. Cleaves, "Neurasthenia and Its Relation to Diseases of Women," *Transactions of the Iowa State Medical Association* 7 (1886): 166 – 167, cited in Gosling,

Before Freud, 56. Gosling, on p. 59, suggests that a greater tolerance for female nervousness as a "natural" phenomenon may have led doctors to conclude more quickly that a woman's condition had improved or that she had been cured altogether of her symptoms.

75. See Gosling, *Before Freud,* 39. There were even hysterical types of neurasthenia, symptoms of which were believed to be more common in women than in men. The main symptoms of these "hysterical" forms of neurasthenia were obsessions or "fixed ideas."

76. Strouse, *Alice James.*

77. Cited in Sicherman, "The Uses of a Diagnosis," 41. As Sicherman demonstrates (see pp. 42 – 43), case records from the Massachusetts General Hospital over a twenty-year period show that those patients referred to as stupid, deceitful, or morally weak were frequently given the diagnosis of hysteria rather than that of neurasthenia. Physicians chose, in some cases, to call individuals neurasthenic rather than insane if they were well-to-do and had families willing to take responsibility for them.

78. Sicherman, "The Uses of a Diagnosis," 35 – 36; Gosling, *Before Freud,* 164.

79. Gosling, *Before Freud,* 173 – 174.

80. Ibid., 162. See also 143, 161 – 162; Sicherman, "The Uses of a Diagnosis," 44.

81. Cited in Gosling, *Before Freud,* 86.

NOTES TO CHAPTER 5

1. The phrase "collective illusions" is found in Pierre Bourdieu, *Le Sens Pratique* (Paris: Les Editions de Minuit, 1980), esp. 366, cited by Joan Wallach Scott in "Gender: A Useful Category of Historical Analysis," in *Feminism and History,* Joan Wallach Scott, ed. (Oxford: Oxford University Press, 1996), 152 – 180, esp. 169.

2. Elizabeth Fox-Genovese, *Feminism without Illusions: A Critique of Individualism* (Chapel Hill: University of North Carolina Press, 1991), esp. 114, 115.

3. Catherine Clinton and Christine Lunardini, *The Columbia Guide to American Women in the Nineteenth Century* (New York: Columbia University Press, 2000), esp. 26.

4. For this discussion about women's place in the Second Great Awakening, I am indebted to Carroll Smith-Rosenberg's "The Cross and the Pedestal: Women, Anti-Ritualism, and the Emergence of the American Bourgeoisie," in *Disorderly Conduct: Visions of Gender in Victorian America* (New York: Knopf, 1985), 129 – 164.

5. See Mary Douglas, *Natural Symbols: Explorations in Cosmology* (London: Routledge, 1970/1996), esp. 20 – 21. I credit Smith-Rosenberg's analysis of Douglas's argument, "The Cross and the Pedestal," 140, for drawing my attention to her work.

6. Smith-Rosenberg, "The Cross and the Pedestal," 152. I rely on Smith-Rosenberg's extension of Douglas's arguments in the following paragraphs.

7. Ibid., 163, 164.

8. Even though the revivals of the Second Great Awakening did not outlast the 1850s, and most of its female adherents turned to embrace the new bourgeois status quo, as has been the case with respect to women's movements since that time, those who had participated in the movement did not return to society completely stripped of power. Women retained the skills they had acquired, using them to create and run women's organizations at the regional and national levels. Despite the fact that these organizations were hardly revolutionary (indeed, they ultimately upheld the new capitalist order), they did enable middle-class women to gain important worldly knowledge of economics and politics. See Smith-Rosenberg, "The Cross and the Pedestal," 155.

9. Fox-Genovese, *Feminism without Illusions,* 125 – 128.

10. Lynne Segal, *Is the Future Female? Troubled Thoughts on Contemporary Feminism* (New York: Peter Bedrick, 1987), esp. 6.

11. Patrice DiQuinzio, *The Impossibility of Motherhood: Feminism, Individualism, and the Problem of Mothering* (Routledge: New York, 1999), esp. 9 – 10.

12. Ibid., 9.

13. Fox-Genovese, *Feminism without Illusions*, 140 – 141.

14. Nancy Cott, *The Grounding of Modern Feminism* (New Haven, CT: Yale University Press, 1987), esp. 16. See also chapter 1, "The Birth of Feminism."

15. Elizabeth Cady Stanton, "Address to the Legislature of New York on Women's Rights," February 14, 1854. Cited in Cott, *The Grounding of Modern Feminism*, 19.

16. Elizabeth Cady Stanton, "Solitude of the Self," address before the United States Senate Committee on Woman Suffrage, February 20, 1892, in *The Concise History of Woman Suffrage: Selections from the Classic Work of Stanton, Anthony, Gage, and Harper*, Mari Jo Buhle and Paul Buhle, eds. (Urbana: University of Illinois Press, 1978), 325 – 326.

17. The idea of self-ownership is closely associated with the seventeenth century idea of *possessive* individualism, the notion that the individual (naturally, in the seventeenth century, a free white male) was essentially the proprietor of his own person or capacities who, as a result of his being a free man, owed nothing to society in exchange for that proprietorship. See C. B. MacPherson, *The Political Theory of Possessive Individualism: Hobbes to Locke* (Oxford: Oxford University Press, 1962). Gillian Brown discusses MacPherson's ideas in her book *Domestic Individualism: Imagining Self in Nineteenth-Century America* (Berkeley: University of California Press, 1990). The idea of possessive individualism posits a human essence free from dependence on the will of others; freedom is a function of "self" possession. Society, in these terms, is a collection of equal individuals who are related to each other as proprietors of their own capacities and of what they have acquired through the exercise of those capacities. In McPherson's view, it was not only Bentham's idea of man as purely a "calculator of his own interests" that proved problematic for liberal individualism, but the fact that attempts to restore to liberal individualism "a sense of the moral value of community" inherent in its Puritan and Lockean incarnations have not succeeded in repairing an essentially flawed ideology.

18. Even though men were considered superior in the gender hierarchy, women were not uniformly relegated to positions of inferiority. Women might, for instance, act as temporary substitutes if fathers or husbands were absent. Although women were viewed as inferior to their male kin, they were not seen, as they would be later, as lesser than men of a lower class. See Smith-Rosenberg, "The Cross and the Pedestal," 158 – 159.

19. The works upon which my discussion of "separate spheres" draws include: Barbara Harris, *Beyond Her Sphere: Women and the Professions in American History* (Westport, CT: Greenwood Press, 1978); Ann Douglas, *The Feminization of American Culture* (New York: Noonday Press, 1977/1998); Barbara Ehrenreich and Deirdre English, *For Her Own Good: 150 Years of the Experts' Advice to Women* (New York: Anchor Press/Doubleday, 1978); and Fox-Genovese, *Feminism without Illusions*.

20. One must take care, however, not to overstate the difference between women's positions before and after the industrial revolution, as Barbara Harris warns, in *Beyond Her Sphere*, 19 – 22, 35 – 40. Women in colonial times contributed to the economy under conditions of subordination, and the women who escaped the sexual division of labor were generally women in atypical circumstances — such as widows — forced into new roles out of economic necessity.

21. Carroll Smith-Rosenberg summarizes the debate among women historians as to women's relative power before and after industrialization in "Hearing Women's Words: A Feminist Reconstruction of History" in Smith-Rosenberg, *Disorderly Conduct*, 11 – 52. Some historians strongly believe that women were more powerful in the agrarian society,

before they were stripped of their important role in the family economy; others insist that women's lot improved once pressures were exerted in the first half of the nineteenth century to enable women to take on responsibilities outside the home. Another debate has followed, related to the question of whether the roles middle-class women carved out for themselves were merely extensions of bourgeois attempts at social control (e.g., attempts to manage the sexuality of working class women; removing children from Catholic homes and apprenticing them to Protestant farmers) or, as Smith-Rosenberg believes, whether they represented important assertions of women's solidarity as well as platforms for gaining expertise in organization and urban and economic change.

22. Douglas, *The Feminization of American Culture*, 55.

23. See Barbara Welter, "The Cult of True Womanhood: 1820 – 1860," *American Quarterly* 18 (Summer, 1966): 151 – 174, for her seminal discussion of the characterization of women and women's roles during this period. It is important to note, as the historian Joan Scott reminds us, that the domestic ideology of Victorian times was vigorously contested even in its heyday. See Scott, "Gender: A Useful Category," 167.

24. Harris, *Beyond Her Sphere*, 22.

25. Robert N. Bellah, Richard Madsen, William M. Sullivan, Ann Swidler, and Steven M. Tipton, *Habits of the Heart: Individualism and Commitment in American Life* (Berkeley: University of California Press, 1985/1996). See also Alexis de Tocqueville, *Democracy in America, Volume II* (New York: Knopf, 1840/1945).

26. See Ehrenreich and English, *For Her Own Good*, p. 9 and following, for a discussion of the opposition of these spheres.

27. The Puritans were not responsible for institutionalizing the principles of capitalism as we know them today. Although their legacy has been debated at length by historians, it seems clear that, contrary to the popular portrayal of the Puritans as "money-grubbing misers responsible for the worst abuses of . . . American capitalism," the Puritans based their culture on mutuality and social harmony. In that society, it was thought that wealth and status should be proportionate to their employment on behalf of the social good. See Roy M. Anker, *Self-Help and Popular Religion in Early American Culture: An Interpretive Guide* (Westport, CT: Greenwood Press, 1999), esp. 49. See also Anker's discussion of the arguments of Perry Miller, Stephen Foster, and other historians in chapter 3, "The Protestant Ethic and Puritan New England."

28. Christopher Lasch, *Haven in a Heartless World: The Family Besieged* (New York: Basic, 1977).

29. Gillian Brown, *Domestic Individualism*, 23.

30. Ibid., 3 – 5.

31. Ibid., 68. As Brown suggests, one can speak of a female ("anti-market") as well as a male ("market") individualism in the nineteenth century.

32. Beryl Satter, *Each Mind a Kingdom: American Women, Sexual Purity, and the New Thought Movement, 1875 – 1920* (Berkeley: University of California Press, 1999), 31.

33. Brown, *Domestic Individualism*, 4 – 6.

34. Ibid., 4, 6.

35. Harriet Beecher Stowe, "Appeal to the Women of the Free States of America on the Present Crisis in Our Country," *The Liberator*, March 3, 1854. Cited in Brown, *Domestic Individualism*, 26.

36. Mrs. L. H. Sigourney, *Letters to Mothers* (Hartford, 1838), 10. Cited in Douglas, *The Feminization of American Culture*, 74.

37. See Satter, *Each Mind a Kingdom*, 49. Arguments in favor of women's rights based on the maternal nature of women (e.g., their inherent morality and domesticity)

had been met by critics with the argument that this maternal nature was basically animal and that women's spirituality was little more than irrationality. In an effort to thwart their opponents, women's rights activists had to fashion a definition of a scientific morality divorced from desire, sexuality, and the body. This led to a difficulty: only if women's selfless purity were innate, as the crusaders argued, rather than an artifact of their separation from the marketplace, could they go out into the world with their purity intact. But if what women were alleged to offer the world were disembodied, it is difficult to see how this unworldly influence could have genuine power outside the domestic sphere.

38. Harris, *Beyond Her Sphere*, 132 – 136, makes use of Andrew Sinclair's term "New Victorianism" to refer to the ideology that kept alive the notion of woman's difference well into the first decades of the twentieth century. See Sinclair's *The Emancipation of the American Woman* (New York: Harper, 1965).

39. Harris, *Beyond Her Sphere*, 86.

40. Nancy Cott, *The Bonds of Womanhood: "Woman's Sphere" in New England, 1780 – 1835* (New Haven, CT: Yale University Press, 1977), esp. 201.

41. Harris, *Beyond Her Sphere*, 85 – 86.

42. Clinton and Lunardini, *The Columbia Guide*, 95

43. Smith-Rosenberg, "Hearing Women's Words," 24.

44. See Douglas, *The Feminization of American Culture*, 7 – 10. As Douglas points out, sentimental novels flooded the market from the 1840s through the 1880s (see p. 62). The moral and psychological persuasion that these middle-class women aimed to achieve through the mass medium of literature, Douglas maintains, had less to do with religious tradition than it did with commerce.

45. Ibid., 64.

46. T. J. Jackson Lears, "From Salvation to Self-Realization: Advertising and the Therapeutic Roots of Consumer Culture, 1880 – 1930," in *The Culture of Consumption: Critical Essays in American History, 1880 – 1980*, Richard W. Wrightman Fox and T. J. Jackson Lears, eds. (New York: Pantheon, 1983), 1 – 38, esp. 27.

47. Mary P. Ryan, *Womanhood in America: From Colonial Times to the Present*, 2nd ed. (New York: New Viewpoints, 1979), esp. 180.

48. See Christopher P. Wilson, "The Rhetoric of Consumption: Mass-Market Magazines and the Demise of the Gentle Reader, 1880 – 1920," in *The Culture of Consumption: Critical Essays in American History, 1880 – 1980*, Richard W. Wrightman Fox and T. J. Jackson Lears, eds. (New York: Pantheon, 1983), 41 – 64.

49. Lears, "From Salvation to Self-Realization," 3 – 38.

50. Ibid., 25.

51. Ryan, *Womanhood in America*, 181.

52. Lears, "From Salvation to Self-Realization," 27.

53. "The Melancholy of Woman's Pages," *Atlantic* 97 (April 1906): 574 – 575. Cited in Wilson, "The Rhetoric of Consumption," 64.

54. Segal, *Is the Future Female?* 9.

55. The full quotation by Sherwood Anderson, writing in the 1920s about psychoanalysis, is as follows: "Dark hidden things came out and found expression for themselves, and the miracle was that, expressed, they became often very beautiful." Cited in John Burnham, "The New Psychology: From Narcissism to Social Control," in *Paths into American Culture: Psychology, Medicine, and Morals* (Philadelphia: Temple University Press, 1988), 69 – 93, esp. 79.

56. Ibid., 78.

57. Ibid., 78 – 79.

58. Cited by John Burnham in "The New Psychology," in *1915, The Cultural Moment: The New Politics, the New Woman, the New Psychology, the New Art and the New Theatre in America*, Adele Heller and Lois Rudnick, eds. (New Brunswick, NJ: Rutgers University Press, 1991), 117 – 127, esp. 124. The quotation was taken from Lippman's *Drift and Mastery: An Attempt to Diagnose the Current Unrest* (New York: Mitchell Kennerly, 1914), 269.

59. Joel Pfister, *Staging Depth: Eugene O'Neill and the Politics of Psychological Discourse* (Chapel Hill: University of North Carolina Press, 1995), 48, 49, 93. Critical response to *Long Day's Journey into Night* at the time it was produced suggests that O'Neill's representation of the Tyrone family as a self-contained psychological entity was at least in part responsible for the play's hold on the public imagination.

60. Not surprisingly, her husband James disparages her pianistic ambitions: "[Those were] put in her head by the nuns flattering her" (IV:140).

61. Pfister, *Staging Depth*, 205. See also Ryan, *Womanhood in America*, 169 – 170, on the subject of the ingredients proposed for adolescent girls' "heterosexual adjustment" in the early twentieth century.

62. Scott, "Gender: A Useful Category," 167.

63. Here and elsewhere I have placed O'Neill's stage directions in italics.

64. See Pfister, *Staging Depth*, 207, 211 – 212, for the implication that, in injecting the morphine into her veins, Mary gains power through undermining the cultural constructions of mother, wife, and woman.

65. See Elaine Showalter, *The Female Malady: Women, Madness, and English Culture* (New York: Pantheon, 1985).

66. See Susan Bordo, *Unbearable Weight: Feminism, Western Culture, and the Body* (Berkeley: University of California Press, 1993).

67. In John Berger, *Ways of Seeing* (Harmondsworth: Penguin, 1972), esp. 46 – 47.

68. Pfister, *Staging Depth*, 202.

69. See Elizabeth Lunbeck, *The Psychiatric Persuasion: Knowledge, Gender and Power in Modern America* (Princeton, NJ: Princeton University Press, 1994), esp. 208.

70. Helene Deutsch, *The Psychology of Women: A Psychoanalytic Interpretation, Vol. II* (New York: Grune and Stratton, 1945), esp. 17. Cited in Ryan, *Womanhood in America*, 166.

71. Ryan, *Womanhood in America*, 166.

72. Lunbeck, *The Psychiatric Persuasion*, 219 – 220.

73. Pfister, *Staging Depth*, 25.

74. Ryan, *Womanhood in America*, 170, 174.

75. Cott, *The Grounding of Modern Feminism*, 168; see also Ehrenreich and English, *For Her Own Good.*

76. See Ehrenreich and English, *For Her Own Good*, esp. 211 – 217, 219, 253 – 258, for discussions of "momism." See also Deborah A. Luepnitz, *The Family Interpreted: Feminist Theory and Clinical Practice* (New York: Basic, 1988).

77. Scott, "Gender: A Useful Category," 173 – 174.

78. See Paula J. Caplan and Ian Hall-McCorquodale, "Mother-Blaming in Major Clinical Journals," *American Journal of Orthopsychiatry* 55 (1985): 345 – 353, and Paula J. Caplan, *The New Don't Blame Mother: Mending the Mother-Daughter Relationship* (New York: Routledge, 2000).

79. Wendy Simonds, *Women and Self-Help Culture: Reading between the Lines* (New Brunswick, NJ: Rutgers University Press), esp. 179.

80. Pfister, *Staging Depth*, 28 – 29, 47.

81. Harold Bloom, "Foreword," in *Eugene O'Neill, Long Day's Journey into Night*, 2nd ed. (New Haven, CT: Yale University Press, 1987), v – xii, esp. vi, vii.

82. John H. Ehrenreich, *The Altruistic Imagination: A History of Social Work and Social Policy in the United States* (Ithaca, NY: Cornell University Press, 1985), esp. 57.

83. Roy Lubove, *The Professional Altruist: The Emergence of Social Work as a Career* (Cambridge, MA: Harvard University Press, 1965), esp. 60.

84. See Lunbeck, *The Psychiatric Persuasion*, 36 – 37. The quotation, cited in Lubove, *The Professional Altruist*, p. 77, is from Ada E. Sheffield, *The Social Case History, Its Construction and Content* (New York, 1920), 218.

85. Lunbeck, *The Psychiatric Persuasion*, quotations cited on 39, 41, 44.

86. Ibid., 26.

87. Ibid., 37 – 38.

88. Ibid., 38.

89. See Lubove, *The Professional Altruist*, esp. chapter 3, "Mind and Matter: Psychiatry in Social Work"; Ehrenreich, *The Altruistic Imagination*, 52, 60; Lunbeck, *The Psychiatric Persuasion*, 43.

90. See Ehrenreich, *The Altruistic Imagination*, 57.

91. I have borrowed this phrase from Lunbeck, *The Psychiatric Persuasion*, 76.

92. Ibid., 281 – 285.

93. For a discussion of the significance of the clinic to the mental hygiene movement and the place of social workers in it, see Lubove, *The Professional Altruist*, 90 – 100, esp. 97 – 98.

94. See Luepnitz, *The Family Interpreted*; also see Rachel Hare-Mustin's seminal article, "The Problem of Gender in Family Therapy Theory," *Family Process* 26 (1987): 15 – 33.

95. Virginia Goldner, "Feminism and Family Therapy," *Family Process* 24 (1985): 31 – 48.

NOTES TO THE INTERLUDE

1. Mari Jo Buhle, *Feminism and Its Discontents* (Cambridge, MA: Harvard University Press 1998), esp. 14.

2. Nancy Cott, *The Grounding of Modern Feminism* (New Haven, CT: Yale University Press, 1985), esp. 5, 6. See chapter 1, "The Birth of Feminism," in particular, for a nuanced discussion of the ideological duality of nineteenth- and early-twentieth-century feminism. As Cott points out, in the 1910s the debate over women's human rights as against women's difference was unusually vocal. Both Cott and Buhle (in *Feminism and Its Discontents*, 39 – 49) chronicle the bitter ongoing public argument between the Swedish feminist Ellen Key, who, despite radical views on women's sexuality that challenged the prevailing moral norms, championed women's difference, particularly with respect to motherhood, and Charlotte Perkins Gilman (1860 – 1935), who strongly challenged the notion of women's special talents for mothering and viewed men and women as equally suited for all kinds of work. For many Americans, the debate between Gilman and Key, well publicized at the time, furnished an introduction to feminist beliefs.

3. Joan W. Scott, "Deconstructing Equality-versus-Difference: Or, The Uses of Poststructuralist Theory for Feminism" in *Theorizing Feminism: Parallel Trends in the Humanities and Social Sciences,* Anne C. Herrman and Abigail J. Stewart, eds. (Boulder, CO: Westview Press, 1994), 358 – 371, esp. 366, 367, reprinted from *Feminist Studies* 14 (1988): 33 – 50.

4. Cott, *The Grounding of Modern Feminism,* esp. 39 – 40.

5. For the New Woman, the search for self-realization was not performed in isolation, as it often is today; rather, it took place within the context of a new *community* that itself promoted that self-expression and personal development. See Ellen Kay Trimberger, "Conflict and Contradiction in the Writings and Lives of Mabel Dodge and Neith Boyce," in *1915, The Cultural Moment: The New Politics, the New Woman, the New Psychology, the New Art and the New Theatre in America,* Adele Heller and Lois Rudnick, eds. (New Brunswick, NJ: Rutgers University Press, 1991), 98 – 115, esp. 113.

6. Elizabeth Fox-Genovese, *Feminism without Illusions: A Critique of Individualism* (Chapel Hill: University of North Carolina Press, 1991), 138.

7. Cott, *The Grounding of Modern Feminism,* 6. Marcia Westkott uses the term "imperative to nurture" in *The Feminist Legacy of Karen Horney* (New Haven, CT: Yale University Press, 1986).

8. Cott, *The Grounding of Modern Feminism,* 278, 279.

9. Lynne Segal, *Why Feminism? Gender, Psychology, Politics* (New York: Columbia University Press, 1999), 5. For a thorough explication of feminism's embrace of psychoanalysis, both Freudian and Lacanian, including a critique of the ideas of the French feminists Julie Kristeva and Luce Irigaray, see Lynne Segal, *Is the Future Female? Troubled Thoughts on Contemporary Feminism* (New York: Peter Bedrick, 1987), esp. 121 – 134. The intellectual preoccupation of a number of feminist theorists with the work of the psychoanalytic structuralist Jacques Lacan, according to Segal, created a schism between academic and activist feminists. This was due, at least in part, to the fact that the exploration of women's own experience, either individual or collective, did not have compelling interest for those of the Lacanian "persuasion." Segal believes that psychoanalytic ideas in the Freudian tradition, particularly those pertaining to the nature of the unconscious and of fantasy, can contribute greatly to an understanding of "the difficulty of developing a female identity in the context of male power," p. 128. For further discussion of feminism's relationship to psychoanalysis, see Buhle, *Feminism and Its Discontents.*

10. Michelle Fine and Pat MacPherson, "Over Dinner: Feminism and Adolescent Female Bodies," in *The Gender and Psychology Reader,* Blanche M. Clinchy & Julie K. Norem, eds. (New York: NYU Press, 1998), 285 – 307, esp. 291.

11. Patrice DiQuinzio, *The Impossibility of Motherhood: Feminism, Individualism, and the Problem of Mothering* (Routledge: New York, 1999), esp. xiv, xv.

12. Biddy Martin, "Feminism, Criticism, and Foucault," in *Reflections on Resistance: Feminism & Foucault,* Irene Diamond and Lee Quinby, eds. (Boston: Northeastern University Press, 1988), esp. 14.

13. Segal, *Is the Future Female?* 131.

NOTES TO CHAPTER 6

1. Jane Eisner, "Career Women Feeling Pinch of Fertility Issues: Business Policies Should Support Parents More," *Philadelphia Inquirer* (April 21, 2002), C-2.

2. See "Making Time for a Baby," *Time* (April 15, 2002), 48 – 54.

3. Lisa Belkin, "For Women, the Price of Success," *New York Times* (March 17, 2002), section 10, 1.

4. Gina Bellafonte, "Sic Transit Ally: A 90s Feminist Is Bowing Out," *New York Times* (April 21, 2002), section 9, 1.

5. Elizabeth Hayt, "Admitting to Mixed Feelings about Motherhood," *New York Times* (May 12, 2002), section 9, 1 – 2, esp. 1.

6. "Imperative to nurture" is Marcia Westkott's term. See Westkott's *The Feminist Legacy of Karen Horney* (New Haven, CT: Yale University Press, 1986).

7. Janis Bohan, "Regarding Gender: Essentialism, Constructionism, and Feminist Psychology," in *Toward a New Psychology of Gender,* Mary M. Gergen and Sara N. Davis, eds. (New York: Routledge, 1997), 31 – 47, esp. 37.

8. Celia Kitzinger and Rachel Perkins, *Changing Our Minds: Lesbian Feminism and Psychology* (New York: NYU Press, 1993), esp. 6.

9. Lynne Segal, *Is the Future Female? Troubled Thoughts on Contemporary Feminism* (New York: Peter Bedrick, 1987), esp. 13 – 14, 17, 37. Segal uses the term "maternal revivalism," which I have borrowed for the title of this section, on p. 144.

10. Michelle Fine and Susan M. Gordon, "Feminist Transformations of/despite Psychology," in *Disruptive Voices: The Possibilities of Feminist Research,* Michelle Fine, ed. (Ann Arbor: University of Michigan Press, 1992), 1 – 25, esp. 19.

11. Ibid., 37.

12. Jean Baker Miller, *Toward a New Psychology of Women,* 2nd ed. (Boston: Beacon Press, 1986), esp. 264.

13. See Bohan, "Regarding Gender," 35.

14. Ibid., 35 – 36.

15. Segal, *Is the Future Female?* 33.

16. Bohan, "Regarding Gender," 41. On the notion of "doing" gender, see Candace West and Don H. Zimmerman, "Doing Gender," in *Seldom Seen, Rarely Heard: Women's Place in Psychology,* Janis S. Bohan, ed. (Boulder, CO: Westview Press, 1992), 379 – 403. According to West and Zimmerman, doing gender "involves a complex of socially guided perceptual, interactional, and micropolitical activities that cast particular pursuits as expressions of masculine and feminine 'natures,' " p. 380.

17. Segal, *Is the Future Female?* 145.

18. Ibid., 146.

19. Lynne Segal, *Why Feminism? Gender, Psychology, Politics* (New York: Columbia University Press, 1999), esp. 6.

20. See Mari Jo Buhle, "Feminine Self-in-Relation," chapter 7 in *Feminism and Its Discontents* (Cambridge, MA: Harvard University Press 1998), 240 – 279, for an impressively clear and detailed discussion of the theoretical basis in object relations theory for the genesis of Chodorow's ideas as well as the ways in which Chodorow's formulation was subverted. In the discussion that follows I draw upon Buhle's careful analysis of the theories of Chodorow, Dinnerstein, Gilligan, and Miller and the uses to which the readings and misreadings of their work were put.

21. Given the persistence of Chodorow's ideas and their many contemporary uses, about which more shall be said shortly, I have chosen here to emphasize her work.

22. For this and the following discussion, see Nancy Chodorow, "Family Structure and the Feminine Personality," in *Woman, Culture, and Society,* Michele Zimbalist Rosaldo and Louise Lamphere, eds. (Stanford, CA: Stanford University Press, 1974), 43 – 66, and Nancy Chodorow, *The Reproduction of Mothering* (Berkeley: University of California Press, 1978).

23. See Westkott, *The Feminist Legacy,* 124, 131. Westkott believes that the need for affiliation is not related to "permeable" ego boundaries between mother and daughter, but that it results from "parent-child relations based on the cultural belief that all females should be nurturant" (p. 131), an imperative to nurture that derived from the historical entitlement of men to receive care from women.

24. Janice Doane and Devon Hodges, *From Klein to Kristeva: Psychoanalytic Feminism and the Search for the "Good Enough" Mother* (Ann Arbor: University of Michigan Press, 1992), esp. 6.

25. Segal, *Is the Future Female?* 142. As Arnold S. Kahn and Janice C. Yoder point

out, discussions by psychologists of Chodorow's early work misconstrued it as a theory of socialization. See their article, "The Psychology of Women and Conservatism: Rediscovering Social Change," *Psychology of Women Quarterly* 13 (1989): 417 – 432, esp. 424

26. Nancy Chodorow, "Feminism and Difference: Gender, Relation, and Difference in Psychoanalytic Perspective," in *The Gender and Psychology Reader,* Blythe McVicker Clinchy and Julie K. Norem, eds. (New York: NYU Press, 1998), 383 – 395, esp. 393, reprinted from *Socialist Review* 46 (July/August 1979): 42 – 64.

27. See Segal, *Is the Future Female?* 141 – 143, for a careful articulation of Chodorow's ideas and their implications.

28. Judith Butler, *Gender Trouble: Feminism and the Subversion of Identity* (Routledge: New York, 1990), esp. 36.

29. Elizabeth Spelman, *Inessential Woman: Problems of Exclusion in Feminist Thought* (Boston: Beacon Press, 1988), esp. 171; see also chapter 4, "Gender in the Context of Race and Class: Notes on Chodorow's 'Reproduction of Mothering,' " 80 – 113, for a lengthy critique. Concerns linger with respect to the construal of while, middle-class women's experience as *all* women's experience. The Stone Center's latest attempt to address the issue of diversity is represented in Judith V. Jordan, ed., *Women's Growth in Diversity: More Writings from the Stone Center* (New York: Guilford, 1997).

30. Carol Gilligan, *In a Different Voice: Psychological Theory and Women's Development* (Cambridge, MA: Harvard University Press, 1982); Jean Baker Miller, "The Development of Women's Sense of Self," in *Women's Growth in Connection,* Judith V. Jordan, Alexandra G. Kaplan, Jean B. Miller, Irene P. Stiver, and Janet L. Surrey, eds. (New York: Guilford), 11 – 26.

31. For example, Buhle, in *Feminism and Its Discontents,* 262, argues that "Gilligan had no trouble judging [the ethic of responsibility] superior." However, Anne Phillips, in *Democracy and Difference* (University Park: Pennsylvania State University Press, 1993), esp. 50, 52, maintains that this view constitutes a misreading of Gilligan.

32. Jean Baker Miller, *Toward a New Psychology of Women* (Boston: Beacon Press, 1976), esp. 68.

33. See Linda K. Kerber's critique "Some Cautionary Words for Historians. On *In a Different Voice*: An Interdisciplinary Forum," *Signs* 11 (1986): 304 – 310, esp. 307. Kerber also points to the small sample size in the studies upon which Gilligan's conclusions are based. The largest of the studies was based on a sample of women considering whether or not to have an abortion. If men facing an equivalent crisis (e.g., draft resistance) had been studied, Kerber suggests, Gilligan might have been able to draw similar conclusions about men's orientation to care and responsibility. Kerber likewise maintains that because Gilligan never addresses the "limitations of the female 'voice' that she identifies, . . . the effect of her argument is to encourage the conclusion that women really are more nurturant than, men, less likely to dominate, more likely to negotiate" (p. 307).

34. Joan C. Tronto, "Beyond Gender Difference to a Theory of Care," *Signs* 12 (1987): 644 – 663, esp. 652; Rachel T. Hare-Mustin, "Sex, Lies, and Headaches: The Problem is Power," in *Women and Power: Perspectives for Family Therapy,* Thelma Jean Goodrich, ed. (New York: Norton, 1991), 63 – 85, esp. 70. See also Lynne Segal's critique of Gilligan's theory of moral development in *Is the Future Female?* 146 – 148. Laura Brown is another scholar who believes that in focusing on "women's ways," feminist therapists have failed to do justice to the dilemma of how power can serve to delineate gender boundaries. See Laura Brown, *Subversive Dialogues: Theory in Feminist Therapy* (New York: Basic, 1994), esp. 51.

35. Westkott, *The Feminist Legacy,* 141.

36. Buhle, *Feminism and Its Discontents,* 263.

37. Rachel T. Hare-Mustin and Jeanne Marecek, "Autonomy and Gender: Some Questions for Therapists," *Psychotherapy: Theory, Practice, and Research* 23 (1986): 205 – 212, esp. 208.

38. Susan Bordo, in "Feminism, Postmodernism, and Gender Skepticism," in *Theorizing Feminism: Parallel Trends in the Humanities and Social Sciences,* Anne C. Herrmann and Abigail J. Stewart, eds. (Boulder, CO: Westview Press, 1994), 458 – 481, esp. 469, argues that the context for reading these works has changed significantly, even among feminist theorists. She is dismayed by the attacks on Gilligan, Chodorow, and others, arguing that this defensive position may have been adopted by feminists in the academy in an attempt to protect themselves from being accused of romanticism or sentimentality: "Of course, to romanticize anything is the last thing any rigorous scholar would do. . . . disdain for female "sentimentality" intersects with both the modern fashion for the cool and the cult of professionalism in our culture" (p. 471). Although I agree with many of Bordo's criticisms of feminist postmodernism and am certainly in favor of taking a critical look at why certain interpretations prevail at particular historical moments, I am not in agreement with her overall position here. In my view, the way in which these theories are currently interpreted has disturbing implications for the future of feminist theory and practice.

39. Buhle, *Feminism and Its Discontents,* 264.

40. Miller, *Toward a New Psychology of Women,* 88.

41. Buhle, *Feminism and Its Discontents,* 269.

42. Miller, *Toward a New Psychology of Women,* 61.

43. Ibid., 46.

44. Ibid., "Foreword," x.

45. Segal, *Why Feminism?* 156 – 157. See also Segal, *Is the Future Female?* 2 – 3.

46. Rachel T. Hare-Mustin and Jeanne Marecek, "Gender and the Meaning of Difference: Postmodernism and Psychology," in *Making a Difference: Psychology and the Construction of Gender,* Rachel Hare-Mustin and Jeanne Marecek, eds. (New Haven, CT: Yale University Press, 1990), 22 – 64. For the most part, analyses of the numerous studies that profess to show sex differences point up their weaknesses. See Bohan, "Regarding Gender," esp. 38. See also Catharine G. Greeno and Eleanor E. Maccoby, "How Different is the 'Different Voice,' " *Signs* 11 (1986): 310 – 316; Eleanor Maccoby and Carol N. Jacklin, *The Psychology of Sex Differences* (Stanford, CA: Stanford University Press, 1974); Eleanor Maccoby and Carol N. Jacklin, "Sex Differences in Aggression: A Rejoinder and Reprise," *Child Development* 51 (1980): 964 – 980; Bernice Lott, "Cataloging Gender Differences: Science or Politics?" in *Women, Men, & Gender: Ongoing Debates,* Mary R. Walsh, ed. (New Haven, CT: Yale University Press, 1997), 19 – 23.

47. See Brown, *Subversive Dialogues,* esp. 66, for a discussion of this "dynamic tension." See also Martha T. Mednick, "Currents and Features in American Feminist Psychology: State of the Art Revisited," *Psychology of Women Quarterly* 15 (1991): 611 – 621, esp. 616 – 617. For a view of constructivism, see Rachel T. Hare-Mustin and Jeanne Marecek, "Beyond Difference," in *Making a Difference: Psychology and the Construction of Gender,* Rachel T. Hare-Mustin and Jeanne Marecek, eds. (New Haven, CT: Yale University Press, 1990), 184 – 201.

48. See Janis Bohan's excellent discussion of psychology's relationship to gender essentialism in "Sex Differences and/in the Self: Classic Themes, Feminist Variations, Postmodern Challenges," *Psychology of Women Quarterly* 26 (2002): 74 – 88, esp. 80 – 81.

49. Sybil P. Hendrickson, "Women's Voices: A Guide for Listening to Chemically Dependent Women," *Women & Therapy* 12 (1992): 73 – 85.

50. Elizabeth D. Sperberg and Sally D. Stabb, "Depression in Women as Related to

Anger and Mutuality in Relationships," *Psychology of Women Quarterly* 22 (1998): 223 – 238, esp. 224.

51. Ibid., 235.

52. Ibid., 233 – 234.

53. Laurie N. Culp and Steven R. Beach, "Marriage and Depressive Symptoms: The Role and Bases of Self-Esteem Differ by Gender," *Psychology of Women Quarterly* 22 (1998): 647 – 663, esp. 649.

54. Ibid., 650, 658.

55. Ibid., 659.

56. Cheryl Rampage, in "Marriage in the 20th Century: A Feminist Perspective," *Family Process* 41 (2002): 261 – 268, esp. 263, argues, for example, that "current discourse in couple therapy has largely replaced feminism with a less politically charged interest in gender effects."

57. See Jennifer Radden, "Relational Individualism and Feminist Therapy," *Hypatia: A Journal of Feminist Philosophy* 11 (1996): 71 – 96. See also Carolyn Z. Enns, "Twenty Years of Feminist Counseling and Therapy: From Naming Biases to Implementing Multi-faceted Practice," *The Counseling Psychologist* 21 (1993): 3 – 87.

58. Laura S. Brown and Annette M. Brodsky, "The Future of Feminist Therapy," *Psychotherapy* 29 (1992): 51 – 57.

59. More recently, "self-in-relation" has also been called the "relational-self" or "being-in-relation." See Judith V. Jordan, "A Relational Perspective for Understanding Women's Development," in *Women's Growth in Diversity: More Writings from the Stone Center,* Judith V. Jordan, ed. (New York: Guilford, 1997), 9 – 24, esp. 14. Jordan also refers to self-in-relation theory as "the Stone Center relational perspective on human experience."

60. Brown, *Subversive Dialogues,* 66; Enns, "Twenty Years of Feminist Counseling," 48.

61. Gloria Steinem, *Revolution from Within: A Book of Self-Esteem* (Boston: Little, Brown, 1992). On personal as against "concrete" power, see Paula Johnson, "Women and Power: Toward a Theory of Effectiveness," *Journal of Social Issues* 32 (1976): 99 – 110, esp. 101.

62. Janet L. Surrey, "The Self-in-Relation: A Theory of Women's Development," in *Women's Growth in Connection,* Judith V. Jordan, Alexandra G. Kaplan, Jean B. Miller, Irene P. Stiver, and Janet L. Surrey, eds. (New York: Guilford, 1991), 51 – 66, esp. 56.

63. Miller, "The Development of Women's Sense of Self," 15, 16.

64. Marcia C. Westkott, "On the New Psychology of Women: A Cautionary View," in *Women, Men, and Gender: Ongoing Debates,* Mary R. Walsh, ed. (New Haven, CT: Yale University Press, 1997), 362 – 372, esp., 368. See also pp. 366 – 370 for further critiques of the mother-daughter relationship as conceptualized by the Stone Center psychologists on which my discussion, this paragraph, is based.

65. Miller, "The Development of Women's Sense of Self," 15.

66. Westkott, "On the New Psychology of Women," 365.

67. Hannah Lerman, "From Freud to Feminist Personality: Getting Here from There," in *The Psychology of Women: Ongoing Debates,* Mary R. Walsh, ed. (New Haven, CT: Yale University Press, 1987), 39 – 58, esp. 52, reprinted from *Psychology of Women Quarterly* 10 (1986): 1 – 18.

68. Westkott, "On the New Psychology of Women," 367, 370.

69. Arlie Hochschild, in *The Managed Heart: Commercialization of Human Feeling* (Berkeley: University of California Press, 1983), has coined this term and uses it differently

than I am using it here — to refer to labor in the marketplace that requires individuals (the majority of them women) "to induce or suppress feeling in order to sustain the outward countenance that produces the proper state of mind in others," (pp. 6 – 7). However, I think it is a term well suited to describe a variety of types of heavy emotional lifting performed by many women in relationships with others.

70. Thelma Jean Goodrich, "Women, Power, and Family Therapy: What's Wrong with This Picture?" in *Women and Power: Perspectives for Family Therapy,* Thelma Jean Goodrich, ed. (New York: Norton, 1991), 3 – 35, esp. 5.

71. See Judith Butler's discussion of Lacan in *Gender Trouble,* beginning on p. 44 (the Lacan quotation is on p. 45).

72. Westkott, "On the New Psychology of Women," 365, 367, 370.

73. Joan C. Tronto, "Women and Caring: What Can Feminists Learn about Morality from Caring?" in *Gender/Body/Knowledge: Feminist Reconstructions of Being and Knowing,* Alison M. Jaggar and Susan Bordo, eds. (New Brunswick, NJ: Rutgers University Press, 1989), 172 – 187, esp. 183.

74. See the previous discussion of Gillian Brown's *Domestic Individualism* in this book, chapter 5.

75. Tronto, "Women and Caring," 184.

76. Westkott, "On the New Psychology of Women," 370.

77. M. Brinton Lykes, "The Caring Self: Social Experiences of Power and Powerlessness," in *Who Cares? Theory, Research, and Educational Implications of the Ethic of Care,* Mary M. Brabeck, ed. (New York: Praeger, 1989), 164 – 179, esp. 169.

78. Rachel T. Hare-Mustin and Jeanne Marecek, in "Autonomy and Gender," detail the characteristics of male autonomy most frequently criticized by feminist psychoanalytic theorists (see esp. 208).

79. Patrice DiQuinzio, *The Impossibility of Motherhood: Feminism, Individualism, and the Problem of Mothering* (New York: Routledge, 1999), esp. 10.

80. Surrey, "The Self-in-Relation," 52.

81. In another, later, discussion of autonomy, Stone Center theorists Jean Baker Miller and Irene Stiver equate autonomy with "a sense of freedom and authenticity," and define authenticity as the ability "to represent [one's] experience . . . *and also* to respond authentically to the thoughts and feelings of others [italics in original]," in Jean Baker Miller and Irene P. Stiver, *The Healing Connection: How Women Form Relationships in Therapy and in Life* (Boston: Beacon Press, 1997), 44, 45.

82. Joan L. Griscom, "Women and Power: Definition, Dualism, and Difference," *Psychology of Women Quarterly* 16 (1992): 389 – 414, esp. 407.

83. C. B. MacPherson, *The Political Theory of Possessive Individualism: Hobbes to Locke* (Oxford: Oxford University Press, 1962). The Puritans, as well as John Locke, incorporated into their ideologies to some degree a "sense of the moral worth of the individual . . . with a sense of the moral value of community," pp. 2 – 3.

84. Adrie S. Kusserow, "Crossing the Great Divide: Anthropological Theories of the Western Self," *Journal of Anthropological Research* 55 (1999): 541 – 562.

85. See Adrie S. Kusserow, "De-Homogenizing American Individualism: Socializing Hard and Soft Individualism in Manhattan and Queens," *Ethos* 27 (1999): 210 – 234.

86. Surrey, "The Self-in-Relation," 52, 53.

87. Nancy Chodorow, in "Toward a Relational Individualism: The Mediation of Self through Psychoanalysis," in *Constructing Individualism: Autonomy, Individuality, and the Self in Western Thought,* Thomas C. Heller, Morton Sosna, and David E. Wellbery, eds. (Stanford, CA: Stanford University Press, 1986), 197 – 207, also uses the term "relational

individuality," but in a more limited fashion. She argues that object relations theory offers a way out of the intense preoccupation with the individual — what she terms "hyperindividualism" — in classical psychoanalysis. Her use of the term points up theoretical differences in the construction of self in object relations theory. The self is conceived of as both intrinsically social or related, both internally and externally, and "relational individualism" is meant to suggest the grounding of the self in a socio-historical matrix. She does not discuss "relationality" as a trait or tie it to gender in particular. In fact, Chodorow states categorically that "the grounding of the object-relational self" derives from "an . . . interpretation of experienced relationships and accordingly varies by individual, culture, period, gender, and so forth" (p. 204).

88. Jennifer Radden, "Relational Individualism," 88.

89. Ibid., 90.

90. On the subject of women's choices, see Kitzinger and Perkins, *Changing Our Minds,* 48 – 52.

91. Jordan, "A Relational Perspective," 15.

92. Philip Cushman, *Constructing the Self, Constructing America: A Cultural History of Psychotherapy* (Reading, MA: Addison-Wesley, 1995), esp. 259.

93. See chapter 1 of this book.

94. Hare-Mustin and Marecek, "Autonomy and Gender," 210.

95. Jane Flax, "Postmodernism and Gender Relations in Feminist Theory," in *Feminism/Postmodernism,* Linda J. Nicholson, ed. (New York: Routledge, 1990), pp. 39 – 62, esp. 55.

96. See Robert N. Bellah, Richard Madsen, William M. Sullivan, Ann Swidler, and Steven M. Tipton, *Habits of the Heart: Individualism and Commitment in American Life* (Berkeley: University of California Press, 1985/1996), esp. 131 – 132; see also Cushman, *Constructing the Self,* 141.

97. Laura Brown and Mary Ballou, eds., *Personality and Psychopathology: Feminist Reappraisals* (New York: Guilford, 1992), esp. xiii.

98. Brown, *Subversive Dialogues,* 25.

99. John W. Meyer, "The Self and the Life Course: Institutionalization and Its Effects," in *Human Development and the Life Course: Multidisciplinary Perspectives,* Aage B. Sørensen, Franz E. Weinert, and Lonnie R. Sherrod, eds. (Hillsdale, NJ: Lawrence Erlbaum, 1986), 199 – 216, esp. 205.

100. Miller, *Toward a New Psychology of Women,* quotations on pp. 116, 117, 118, 120.

101. For the concepts "power-to" and "power-over," see Steven Lukes, *Power: A Radical View* (London: Macmillan, 1974).

102. Westkott, "On the New Psychology of Women," 362 – 372, esp. 365; Jordan quoted by Westkott on p. 364. For an additional critique of the self-in-relation paradigm, see also Marcia C. Westkott, "Female Relationality and the Idealized Self," in *The Gender and Psychology Reader,* Blythe McVicker Clinchy and Julie K. Norem, eds. (New York: NYU Press, 1998), 239 – 250.

103. Miller, "The Development of Women's Sense of Self," 26.

104. Jean Baker Miller, "Women and Power," in *Women's Growth in Connection,* Judith V. Jordan, Alexandra G. Kaplan, Jean B. Miller, Irene P. Stiver, and Janet L. Surrey, eds. (New York: Guilford, 1991), 197 – 206, 200, 202 – 203.

105. Ibid., 204, 205.

106. Ibid., 202.

107. Ibid., 203.

108. In Jean Baker Miller and Irene P. Stiver, *The Healing Connection: How Women*

Form Relationships in Therapy and in Life (Boston: Beacon Press, 1997), Miller and Stiver maintain that mutual empowerment has a number of components, among them "zest," "vitality," "aliveness," "energy," and "action." Recently in Belle Liang, Allison Tracy, Catherine A. Taylor, Linda M. Williams, Judith V. Jordan, and Jean Baker Miller, "The Relational Health Indices: A Study of Women's Relationships," *Psychology of Women Quarterly* 26 (2002): 25 – 35, a measure of women's relationships based upon these ideas was developed and examined for reliability, but the question of the overall validity of these concepts was not challenged.

109. Miller and Stiver, *Healing Connection,* 31.

110. Ibid., 25.

111. Ibid., 36, 37.

112. Ibid., 38 – 39.

113. Ellyn Kaschak, "Growing Pains," *The Women's Review of Books* XV(6) (March 1998): 17 – 18. I thank Jeanne Marecek for bringing Kaschak's review to my attention.

114. Kitzinger and Perkins, *Changing Our Minds,* 40 – 41.

115. Miller and Stiver, *The Healing Connection,* 122.

116. Jane Flax, "The End of Innocence," in *Feminists Theorize the Political,* Judith Butler and Joan W. Scott, eds. (New York: Routledge, 1992), 445 – 463, esp. 459.

117. Mary Poovey, *Uneven Developments: The Ideological Work of Gender in Mid-Victorian England* (Chicago: University of Chicago Press, 1988).

118. Nancy Cott, *The Grounding of Modern Feminism* (New Haven, CT: Yale University Press, 1985), esp. 50.

119. See Hare-Mustin and Marecek, "Gender and the Meaning of Difference."

NOTES TO CHAPTER 7

1. In this paragraph, I owe a debt to Celia Kitzinger's discussion, "Therapy and How It Undermines the Practice of Radical Feminism," in *Radically Speaking: Feminism Reclaimed,* Diane Bell and Renate Klein, eds. (North Melbourne, Aus.: Spinifex Press, 1996), 92 – 101, esp. 98.

2. Gloria Steinem, *Revolution from Within: A Book of Self-Esteem* (Boston: Little, Brown, 1992).

3. Kitzinger, "Therapy and How It Undermines," 96.

4. bell hooks, "Feminist Politicization: A Comment," in *Toward a New Psychology of Gender,* Mary M. Gergen and Sara N. Davis, eds. (New York: Routledge, 1997), 533 – 539.

5. Barbara Cruikshank, *The Will to Empower* (Ithaca, NY: Cornell University Press, 1999), esp. 88.

6. The psychology of women, emerging from the women's movement of the 1960s and 1970s, gained recognition through the establishment of the Association of Women in Psychology in 1969, the formation of the women's division of the American Psychological Association in 1973, and the launching of the journal *Psychology of Women Quarterly* in 1977. For a discussion of the origins of women's psychology, see Martha T. Mednick and Laura L. Urbanski, "The Origins and Activities of APA's Division of the Psychology of Women," *Psychology of Women Quarterly* 15 (1991): 651 – 663.

7. See Phyllis Chesler's groundbreaking book *Women and Madness* (New York: Avon, 1972).

8. Celia Kitzinger and Rachel Perkins, *Changing Our Minds: Lesbian Feminism and Psychology* (New York: NYU Press, 1993), esp. 6, 7.

9. Martha T. Mednick, "Currents and Features in American Feminist Psychology: State

of the Art Revisited," *Psychology of Women Quarterly* 15 (1991): 611 – 621, esp. 612 – 613.

10. See, for example, David J. Castle, John McGrath, and Jayashri Kulkarni, eds., *Women and Schizophrenia* (Cambridge: Cambridge University Press, 2000); Jessica Wolfe and Rachel Kimerling, "Gender Issues in the Assessment of Posttraumatic Stress Disorder," in *Assessing Psychological Trauma and PTSD,* John P. Wilson and Terence M. Keane, eds. (New York: Guilford, 1997), 192 – 237.

11. Michelle Fine and Susan M. Gordon, "Feminist Transformations of/despite Psychology," in *Disruptive Voices: The Possibilities of Feminist Research,* Michelle Fine, ed. (Ann Arbor: University of Michigan Press, 1992), 1 – 25, esp. 23. Citation of Keller is on p. 23.

12. Ibid., 25. See also Arnold S. Kahn and Janice D. Yoder, "The Psychology of Women and Conservatism: Rediscovering Social Change," *Psychology of Women Quarterly* 13 (1989): 417 – 432, esp. 419.

13. Kahn and Yoder, "The Psychology of Women," 422.

14. Fine, *Disruptive Voices,*   14.

15. Celia Kitzinger, "Politicizing Psychology," *Feminism & Psychology* 1 (1991): 49 – 54, esp. 52.

16. Nathan Caplan and Stephen D. Nelson, "On Being Useful: The Nature and Consequences of Psychological Research on Social Problems," *American Psychologist* 28 (1973): 199 – 211.

17. Barbara S. Wallston and Kathleen E. Grady, "Integrating the Feminist Critique and the Crisis in Social Psychology: Another Look at Research Methods," in *Women, Gender, and Social Psychology,* Virginia E. O'Leary, Rhoda K. Unger, and Barbara S. Wallston, eds. (Hillsdale, NJ: Lawrence Erlbaum, 1985), 7 – 33, esp. 10.

18. Bruna Seu, "Change and Theoretical Frameworks," in *Feminism and Psychotherapy: Reflections on Contemporary Theories and Practices,* Bruna Seu and Colleen Heenan, eds. (London: Sage, 1998), 203 – 218, esp. 209, 211.

19. See Laura Brown, *Subversive Dialogues: Theory in Feminist Therapy* (New York: Basic, 1994), 32 – 33, 45.

20. Ibid., 32.

21. See Robert N. Bellah, Richard Madsen, William M. Sullivan, Ann Swidler, and Steven M. Tipton, *Habits of the Heart: Individualism and Commitment in American Life* (Berkeley: University of California Press, 1985/1996), esp. 131 – 132; see also Philip Cushman, *Constructing the Self, Constructing America: A Cultural History of Psychotherapy* (Reading, MA: Addison-Wesley, 1995), esp. 280.

22. Judith Myers Avis, "Power Politics in Therapy with Women," in *Women and Power: Perspectives for Family Therapy,* Thelma Jean Goodrich, ed. (New York: Norton, 1991), 183 – 200, esp. 183 – 184; see also Stephanie Riger's *Transforming Psychology: Gender in Theory and Practice* (Oxford: Oxford University Press, 2000).

23. Avis, "Power Politics," 188.

24. Thelma Jean Goodrich, "Women, Power, and Family Therapy: What's Wrong with This Picture?" in *Women and Power: Perspectives for Family Therapy,* Thelma Jean Goodrich, ed. (New York: Norton, 1991), 3 – 35, esp. 32.

25. Elizabeth Spelman, *Inessential Woman: Problems of Exclusion in Feminist Thought* (Boston: Beacon Press, 1988), esp. 178, 166, 167. See also Oliva M. Espín, "Feminist Therapy: Not for White Women Only," *The Counseling Psychologist* 21 (1993): 103 – 108.

26. See Kitzinger and Perkins, *Changing Our Minds,* 36 – 37; see also Jeanne Marecek and Diane Kravetz, "Power and Agency in Feminist Therapy," in *Feminism and Psy-*

chotherapy: Reflections on Contemporary Theories and Practices, Bruna Seu and Colleen Heenan, eds. (London: Sage, 1998), 13 – 29, esp. 21.

27. Lynne Segal, *Why Feminism? Gender, Psychology, Politics* (New York: Columbia University Press, 1999), 225, 226. See also Marcia Hill and Mary Ballou, "Making Therapy Feminist: A Practice Survey," *Women & Therapy* 21 (1998): 1 – 16, esp. 5.

28. Segal, *Why Feminism?* 227.

29. Ibid., 226.

30. Susan Brownmiller, *In Our Time: Memoir of a Revolution* (New York: Dial Press, 1999), 47 – 48.

31. Ibid., 79 – 80.

32. See Carolyn Enns, "Twenty Years of Feminist Counseling and Therapy: From Naming Biases to Implementing Multifaceted Practice," *The Counseling Psychologist* 21 (1993): 3 – 87, esp. 5, for a discussion of the reliance of many members on CR groups principally to achieve the personal goals of insight, support, and personal change. Brown, *Subversive Dialogues,* 32, on the other hand, looks back on consciousness-raising as having aroused anger rather than promoting action.

33. In Alice Echols, *Daring To Be Bad: Radical Feminism in America 1967 – 1975* (Minneapolis: University of Minnesota Press, 1989), esp. 83. In this paragraph I rely heavily on Echols' discussion of consciousness-raising, pp. 86 – 91.

34. Ibid., 6. The criticism came from Evelyn Goldfield in the August 1968 issue of *The Voice of the Women's Liberation Movement.*

35. Quote from Friedan in ibid., 87.

36. See Kathie Sarachild, quoted in Kitzinger and Perkins, *Changing Our Minds,* 77.

37. Annette Brodsky, "The Consciousness-Raising Group as Model for Therapy with Women," in *Female Psychology: The Emerging Self,* Sue Cox, ed. (Chicago: Science Research Associates, 1976), 372 – 378.

38. See Diane Kravetz, "Benefits of Consciousness-Raising Groups for Women," in *Women's Therapy Groups: Paradigms of Feminist Treatment,* Claire M. Brody, ed. (New York: Springer, 1987), 5 – 66, esp. 61, for a summary of the most frequently reported outcomes of CR. Kravetz makes the point that outcomes of the experience of members of a CR group were influenced by the groups' embeddedness in the women's movement. As a result, many women in the groups were engaged in feminist activities of various kinds and in reading feminist literature.

39. Diane Kravetz, "Consciousness-Raising and Self-Help," in *Women and Psychotherapy: An Assessment of Research and Practice,* Annette Brodsky and Rachel T. Hare-Mustin, eds. (New York: Guilford, 1980), 267 – 283, esp. 268. See also pp. 268 – 270 for a comparison of CR groups and psychotherapy.

40. Joy Rice and David G. Rice, "Implications of the Women's Liberation Movement for Psychotherapy," *American Journal of Psychiatry* 130 (1973): 191 – 196, esp. 192.

41. Ellen Herman, *The Romance of American Psychology: Political Culture in the Age of Experts* (Berkeley: University of California Press, 1995), esp. 303.

42. Brown, *Subversive Dialogues,* 95, 97.

43. See Enns, "Twenty Years of Feminist Counseling," 7 – 8. The quotation is from Tennov's 1973 article.

44. Miriam Greenspan, "On Being a Feminist and a Psychotherapist," *Women & Therapy* 17 (1995): 229 – 241, esp. 234 – 235.

45. See Enns, "Twenty Years of Feminist Counseling," 13.

46. See, for example, Sandra L. Bem, "The Measurement of Psychological Androgyny," *Journal of Consulting and Clinical Psychology* 42 (1974): 155 – 162.

47. Enns, "Twenty Years of Feminist Counseling," 16. For a critique of androgyny

research, see Martha T. Mednick, "On the Politics of Psychological Constructs: Stop the Bandwagon, I Want to Get Off," *American Psychologist* 44 (1989): 1118 – 1123. For a history and critique of the assertiveness training movement, see Mary Crawford, "The Reciprocity of Psychology and Popular Culture," in *Deconstructing Feminist Psychology,* Erica Burman, ed. (London: Sage, 1998), 61 – 89.

48. See Rice and Rice, "Implications of the Women's Liberation Movement"; see also Jeanne Marecek and Diane Kravetz, "Women and Mental Health: A Review of Feminist Change Efforts," *Psychiatry* 40 (1977): 323 – 329.

49. Rice and Rice, "Implications of the Women's Liberation Movement," 195.

50. Brown, *Subversive Dialogues,* 32.

51. Enns, "Twenty Years of Feminist Counseling," 39.

52. Diane Kravetz, Jeanne Marecek, and Stephen E. Finn, "Factors Influencing Women's Participation in Consciousness-Raising Groups," *Psychology of Women Quarterly* 7 (1983): 257 – 271.

53. Barbara Kirsh, "Evolution of Consciousness-Raising Groups," in *Women's Therapy Groups: Paradigms of Feminist Treatment,* Claire M. Brody, ed. (New York: Springer, 1987), 43 – 54, esp. 47. Also see Kitzinger and Perkins, *Changing Our Minds,* 80, 81.

54. See Enns, "Twenty Years of Feminist Counseling," 27 – 30, for a discussion of feminist psychoanalysis. A prominent critic of this trend was — and is — Hannah Lerman. See her book *A Mote in Freud's Eye: From Psychoanalysis to the Psychology of Women* (New York: Springer, 1986). See also Hannah Lerman, "From Freud to Feminist Personality Theory: Getting Here from There," in *The Psychology of Women: Ongoing Debates,* Mary R. Walsh, ed. (New Haven, CT: Yale University Press, 1987), 39 – 58.

55. John F. Longres and Eileen McLeod, "Consciousness Raising and Social Work Practice," *Social Casework* 61 (1980): 267 – 276, esp. 271, 272, 275.

56. See Enns, "Twenty Years of Feminist Counseling," 40.

57. Longres and McLeod, "Consciousness Raising and Social Work Practice," 271 – 272.

58. Greenspan, "On Being a Feminist," 239.

59. Ibid, 240.

60. Jeanne Marecek and Diane Kravetz, "Putting Politics into Practice: Feminist Therapy as Feminist Praxis," *Women & Therapy* 21(1998): 17 – 36, esp. 35.

61. Susan A. Thomas, "Theory and Practice in Feminist Therapy," *Social Work* 22 (1977): 447 – 454, esp. 452.

62. Ibid., 450, 451.

63. Ibid., 253.

64. Jeanne Marecek and Diane Kravetz , "Power and Agency in Feminist Therapy," in *Feminism and Psychotherapy: Reflections on Contemporary Theories and Practices,* Bruna Seu and Colleen Heenan, eds. (London: Sage, 1998), 13 – 29. Quotation on p. 17.

65. Ibid., 18.

66. Ibid., 24 – 25.

67. Brown, *Subversive Dialogues,* 30.

68. Ibid., 22.

69. Ibid, 19.

70. Others, too, have shown that feminist research and feminist practice are, in fact, increasingly estranged from each other, with practitioners increasingly adopting a more decontextualized, intrapsychic approach than academic feminists in psychology. See Martha T. Mednick, "Currents and Features in American Feminist Psychology." See also Mary Ricketts's study of academics and practitioners, "Epistemological Values of Feminists in Psychology," *Psychology of Women Quarterly* 13 (1989): 401 – 415.

71. Robert L. Woolfolk, *The Cure of Souls: Science, Values, and Psychotherapy* (San Francisco: Jossey-Bass, 1998), esp. 133.

72. Lynne Segal, *Is the Future Female? Troubled Thoughts on Contemporary Feminism* (New York: Peter Bedrick, 1987), esp. 139.

73. Charles B. Mark, "The Personal Relationship between Therapists and Their Theoretical Orientation," in *Women as Therapists: A Multitheoretical Casebook,* Dorothy W. Cantor, ed. (New York: Springer, 1990), 33 – 55, esp. 34.

74. I am indebted to Carolyn Enns's detailed discussion of feminist therapy, "Twenty Years of Counseling," esp. 44 – 45, for the discussion that follows.

75. Ibid., 44.

76. Brown, *Subversive Dialogues,* 47.

77. Ibid., 48.

78. See ibid., 45 – 46, for descriptions of these philosophies and pp. 46 – 48 for a discussion of how these philosophies have variously been integrated with feminist therapy.

79. Ibid., 48.

80. Cynthia E. Glidden and Terence T. Tracey, "Women's Perceptions of Personal versus Sociocultural Counseling Interventions," *Journal of Counseling Psychology* 36 (1989): 54 – 62.

81. Ibid., 60.

82. Ibid., 61.

83. RuthAnn Parvin and Mary Kay Biaggio, "Paradoxes in the Practice of Feminist Therapy," *Women & Therapy* 11 (1991): 3 – 12, esp. 7, 11.

84. See Cruikshank's discussions of the interpenetration of the private, the political, and the social in *The Will to Empower.*

85. Ibid., 39, 40, 41. "The professionalization of being human" is a phrase taken by Cruikshank from a chapter title in Theresa Funicello's *The Tyranny of Kindness: Dismantling the Welfare System to End Poverty in America* (New York: Atlantic Monthly Press, 1993).

86. Cruikshank, *The Will to Empower,* 72.

87. This phrase is taken from the title of Cruikshank's book.

88. Cruikshank, *The Will to Empower,* 51. Quotation of Octavia Hill is from "A Few Words to Volunteer Visitors among the Poor," in *Our Common Land* (London: Macmillan, 1877), 26 – 27.

89. Cruikshank refers to Frances Fox Piven's "Ideology and the State: Women, Power, and the Welfare State," in *Women, the State, and Welfare,* Linda Gordon, ed. (Madison: University of Wisconsin Press, 1990), 250 – 251.

90. Ibid., 67.

91. For examples, see Ann Bookman and Sandra Morgan, *Women and the Politics of Empowerment* (Philadelphia: Temple University Press, 1988); see also Barry J. Ackerson and W. David Harrison, "Practitioners' Perceptions of Empowerment," *Families in Society* 81 (2000): 238 – 244.

92. Cruikshank, *The Will to Empower,* 71.

93. Jean Baker Miller, "Women and Power: Reflections Ten Years Later," in *Women and Power: Perspectives for Family Therapy,* Thelma Jean Goodrich, ed. (New York: Norton, 1991), 36 – 47, esp. 46.

94. Arlie Russell Hochschild, *The Second Shift: Working Parents and the Revolution at Home* (New York: Viking, 1989).

95. Goodrich, "Women, Power, and Family Therapy," 23. See also Avis, "Power Politics," 183 – 184.

96. Goodrich, "Women, Power, and Family Therapy," 10.

97. This notion of power is associated with social psychologist Carolyn Sherif. It is discussed by Rhoda K. Unger, "Looking Toward the Future by Looking at the Past: Social Activism and Social History," *Journal of Social Issues* 42 (1986): 215 – 227, esp. 219 – 220.

98. Goodrich, "Women, Power, and Family Therapy," 23.

99. For the concepts "power-to" and "power-over," see Steven Lukes, *Power: A Radical View* (London: Macmillan, 1974); also see Marecek and Kravetz, "Power and Agency," 22, for discussion of study participants' views on power.

100. Marecek and Kravetz, "Power and Agency," 22.

101. See Rachel T. Hare-Mustin and Jeanne Marecek, "Autonomy and Gender: Some Questions for Therapists," *Psychotherapy: Theory, Practice, and Research* 23 (1986): 205 – 212, esp. 206. This idea was also discussed in chapter 6 of this book.

102. See Joan L. Griscom, "Women and Power: Definition, Dualism and Difference," *Psychology of Women Quarterly* 16 (1992): 389 – 414, esp. 406, for a discussion of the complex uses of power by women in parenting. See also Rachel T. Hare-Mustin, "Sex, Lies, and Headaches: The Problem is Power," in *Women and Power: Perspectives for Family Therapy*, Thelma Jean Goodrich, ed. (New York: Norton, 1991), 63 – 85.

103. Cindy B. Veldhuis, "The Trouble with Power," *Women & Therapy* 23 (2001): 37 – 56.

104. Kitzinger and Perkins, *Changing Our Minds*, 43.

105. Marecek and Kravetz, "Power and Agency," 21.

106. Ibid., 22.

107. Kitzinger, "Therapy and How It Undermines," 99.

108. Ibid., 99.

109. Cynthia L. Miller and A. Gaye Cummins, "An Examination of Women's Perspectives on Power," *Psychology of Women Quarterly* 16 (1992): 415 – 428.

110. Marecek and Kravetz, "Power and Agency," 23.

111. For instance, Cheryl Rampage, in "Marriage in the 20th Century: A Feminist Perspective," *Family Process* 41 (2002): 261 – 268, esp. 264, claims that these days, "gender issues in couple therapy, though more widely accepted as relevant, have often been removed from the political or power context in which feminists placed them."

112. This view was expressed by Veldhuis in "The Trouble with Power," 53.

113. Richard Powers, "American Dreaming: The Limitless Absurdity of Our Belief in an Infinitely Transformative Future," *New York Times Magazine* (May 7, 2000), 66 – 67.

114. Marecek and Kravetz, "Power and Agency," 19, 20.

115. Brown, *Subversive Dialogues,* 114.

116. See ibid., 116.

117. Hare-Mustin and Marecek, "Autonomy and Gender," 205 – 212.

118. Amy Rossiter, "Toward an Alternative Account of Feminist Practice Ethics in Mental Health," *Affilia* 13 (1998): 9 – 30, esp. 15.

119. Brown, *Subversive Dialogues,* 113 – 114.

120. See Elaine Showalter, *The Female Malady: Women, Madness, and English Culture* (New York: Pantheon, 1985), esp. 5. Showalter is vehemently opposed to a romantic view of women's madness.

121. Hare-Mustin and Marecek, "Autonomy and Gender," 206

122. Ibid., 206.

123. Kitzinger, "Politicizing Psychology," 52; Hare-Mustin, "Sex, Lies, and Headaches," 64.

124. Kitzinger and Perkins, *Changing Our Minds*, 48.

125. Michelle Fine, "Reflections on a Feminist Psychology of Women: Paradoxes and Prospects," *Psychology of Women Quarterly* 9 (1985): 167 – 183.

126. Kitzinger and Perkins, *Changing Our Minds,* 39 – 40.

127. Quoted by Ackerson and Harrison in "Practitioners' Perceptions," 238, from *The Social Work Dictionary,* 2nd ed. (Silver Spring, MD: NASW Press, 1991).

128. Ackerson and Harrison, "Practitioners' Perceptions," 239, 241.

129. Ibid., 240, 241. This sort of difficulty on the part of social workers was also discovered in a similar 1995 study to which the authors refer, conducted by Gutierrez, DeLois, and GlenMay.

130. Ibid., 241. The authors refer to Murdach's article, "Beneficence Re-Examined: Protective Intervention in Mental Health," *Social Work* 41 (1996): 26 – 32

131. Amnon Boehm and Lee H. Staples, "The Functions of the Social Worker in Empowering: The Voices of Consumers and Professionals," *Social Work* 47 (2002): 449 – 460.

132. Ackerson and Harrison, "Practitioners' Perceptions," 243.

133. Marcia B. Cohen, "Perceptions of Power in Client/Worker Relationships," *Families in Society* 79 (1998): 433 – 442, esp. 434.

134. Brown, *Subversive Dialogues,* 52.

135. Ibid., 106.

136. Ibid., 106.

137. Ibid., 107.

138. Greenspan, "On Being a Feminist," 240 – 241.

139. Kitzinger and Perkins, *Changing Our Minds,* 82 – 83, 86, 87.

140. Brown, *Subversive Dialogues,* 104 – 105.

141. Goodrich, "Women, Power, and Family Therapy," 32.

142. See Fine, "Reflections on a Feminist Psychology," 175 – 176.

143. Goodrich, "Women, Power, and Family Therapy," 32.

NOTES TO CHAPTER 8

1. Brent W. Bost, *The Hurried Woman Syndrome* (New York: Vantage, 2001). See also http://abcnews.go.com/sections/GMA/HealthyWoman/ GMA021210Hurried_woman _syndrome.html.

2. See Sander L. Gilman, *Disease and Representation: Images of Illness from Madness to AIDS* (Ithaca, NY: Cornell University Press, 1988); see also Peter Conrad and Joseph W. Schneider, *Deviance and Medicalization: From Badness to Sickness* (Philadelphia: Temple University Press, 1992).

3. Celia Kitzinger and Rachel Perkins, *Changing Our Minds: Lesbian Feminism and Psychology* (New York: NYU Press, 1993), especially Carol Travis's comments on the language of stress, cited on p. 10.

4. Ralph Swindle, Kenneth Heller, Bernice Pescosolido, and Saeko Kikuzawa, "Responses to Nervous Breakdowns in American over a 40 – Year Period: Mental Health Policy Implications," *American Psychologist* 55 (2000): 740 – 749.

5. Ibid., 747.

6. Derek L. Phillips and Bernard E. Segal, "Sexual Status and Psychiatric Symptoms," *American Sociological Review* 34 (1969): 58 – 72; see also Ronald C. Kessler, Roger L. Brown,, and Clifford L. Broman, "Sex Difference in Psychiatric Help-Seeking: Evidence from Four Large-Scale Surveys," *Journal of Health and Social Behavior* 20 (1981): 2 – 16.

7. Nikolas Rose, *Inventing Ourselves: Psychology, Power, and Personhood* (Cambridge: Cambridge University Press, 1998), esp. 65, 82.

8. Patricia Marx, "The New Anxiety Antidotes," *Self* (January 2002), 60.

9. On the relationship between stressors associated with these factors and women's

depression, see Deborah Belle and Joanne Doucet, "Poverty, Inequality, and Discrimination as Sources of Depression among U.S. Women," *Psychology of Women Quarterly* 27 (2003): 101–113.

10. American Psychiatric Association, *Diagnostic and Statistical Manual of Mental Disorders, 2nd ed.* (Washington, DC: Author, 1980).

11. See Dana Becker, "Posttraumatic Stress Disorder: Panacea or Problem?" in *Bias in Psychiatric Diagnosis,* Paula J. Caplan and Lisa Cosgrove, eds. (New York: Jason Aronson, 2004). See also Dana Becker, "When She Was Bad: Borderline Personality Disorder in a Posttraumatic Age," *American Journal of Orthopsychiatry* 70 (2000): 422–432.

12. American Psychiatric Association, *Diagnostic and Statistical Manual of Mental Disorders, 3rd ed.-Revised* (Washington, DC: Author, 1987), esp. 236.

13. Michael R. Trimble, "Post-Traumatic Stress Disorder: History of a Concept," in *Trauma and its Wake: The Study and Treatment of Post-Traumatic Stress Disorder,* Charles R. Figley, ed. (New York: Brunner/Mazel, 1985), 5–14.

14. American Psychiatric Association, *Diagnostic and Statistical Manual of Mental Disorders, 4th ed.-Revised* (Washington, DC: Author, 1994); American Psychiatric Association, *Diagnostic and Statistical Manual of Mental Disorders IV-TR* (Washington, DC: Author, 2000).

15. *DSM-IV-TR,* esp. 467.

16. Herb Kutchins and Stuart A. Kirk, *Making Us Crazy: DSM: The Psychiatric Bible and the Creation of Mental Disorders* (New York: Free Press, 1997).

17. Jeanne Marecek found that the feminist therapists she interviewed frequently believed that PTSD was the only acceptable diagnosis for their women clients. She noted that in some cases PTSD was represented to clients as a diagnosis that, as one therapist put it, "says right in the definition that this is a normal response to trauma that most people would have." See Jeanne Marecek, "Trauma Talk in Feminist Clinical Practice," in *New Versions for Victims: Feminists Struggle with the Concept,* Sharon Lamb, ed. (New York: NYU Press, 1999), 158–183, esp. 163.

18. See, for example, Michele M. Murburg, Alexandra E. Ashleigh, Daniel W. Hommer, and Richard C. Veith, "Biology of Catecholaminergic Systems and Their Relevance to PTSD," in *Catecholamine Function in Posttraumatic Stress Disorder: Emerging Concepts,* Michele M. Murburg, ed. (Washington, DC: American Psychiatric Press, 1994), 175–188. For further examples, see Ann M. Rasmusson and Matthew J. Friedman, "Gender Issues in the Neurobiology of PTSD," in *Gender and PTSD,* Rachel Kimerling, Paige Ouimette, and Jessica Wolfe, eds. (New York: Guilford, 2002), 43–75.

19. Nancy C. Andreason, "Posttraumatic Stress Disorder: Psychology, Biology, and the Manichean Warfare between False Dichotomies," *American Journal of Psychiatry* 152 (1995): 963–965.

20. See Jessica Wolfe and Rachel Kimerling, "Gender Issues in the Assessment of Posttraumatic Stress Disorder," in *Assessing Psychological Trauma and PTSD,* John P. Wilson and Terence M. Keane, eds. (New York: Guilford, 1997), 192–237, esp. 202.

21. Becker, "When She Was Bad." The option not to give traumatized women a diagnosis of mental disorder is problematic because American insurance companies require that a *DSM* label be supplied in order for clients to be reimbursed for the cost of psychotherapy. Equally troublesome is the fact that the enormous popularity of the PTSD diagnosis may lead therapists to make trauma and abuse *the* central issues in therapy, at the expense of examining other salient problems in women's lives. On this latter subject, see Janice Haaken and Astrid Schlaps, "Incest Resolution Therapy and the Objectification of Sexual Abuse," *Psychotherapy* 39 (1991): 39–46.

22. See Wolfe and Kimerling, "Gender Issues in the Assessment of Posttraumatic Stress

Disorder"; see also Rasmusson and Friedman, "Gender Issues in the Neurobiology of PTSD."

23. Shelley E. Taylor, Laura C. Klein, Brian P. Lewis, Tara L. Gruenwald, Regan A. Gurung, and John A. Updegraff, "Biobehavioral Responses to Stress in Females: Tend-and-Befriend, Not Fight or Flight," *Psychological Review* 109 (2000): 411 – 429.

24. Shelley E. Taylor, *The Tending Instinct: How Nurturing is Essential for Who We Are and How We Live* (New York: Henry Holt, 2002), esp. 3, 4.

25. See ibid., 23, for a description of Repetti's research at UCLA.

26. See Victoria L. Banyard and Sandra A. Graham-Berman, "Can Women Cope? A Gender Analysis of Theories of Coping," *Psychology of Women Quarterly* 17 (1993): 303 – 318, for a suggested reformulation of theories of coping that would include a focus both on women's diverse experiences as well as on the effects of sexism, racism, access to power, and other social forces upon women's coping.

27. See Taylor, *The Tending Instinct*, 26. As Janice Yoder and Arnold Kahn have pointed out, most researchers who have made gender comparisons have assumed that descriptions of difference are, ipso facto, causal explanations, and, having made this assumption, they imply that those differences are basic and psychologically hardwired. However, an alternate means of making gender comparisons in order to better understand them is to carefully examine the social context in which those gender differences exist. See Janice D. Yoder and Arnold S. Kahn, "Making Gender Comparisons More Meaningful: A Call for More Attention to Social Context," *Psychology of Women Quarterly* 27 (2002): 281 – 290.

28. Pauline M. Millard, "Girl Power Brings on Brand New Kinds of Pressures," *Pocono Record* (October 11, 2002), B-15. The author cited is Joann Deak.

29. Susan Faludi, *Backlash: The Undeclared War against American Women* (New York: Doubleday, 1991).

30. See note 43, chapter 3 in this book for citation.

31. Elaine H. Carmen, Nancy F. Russo, and Jean Baker Miller, "Inequality and Women's Mental Health: An Overview," *American Journal of Psychiatry* 138 (1981): 1319 – 1330.

32. Jean Baker Miller, "The Construction of Anger in Women and Men," in *Women's Growth in Connection*, Judith V. Jordan, Alexandra G. Kaplan, Jean B. Miller, Irene P. Stiver, and Janet L. Surrey, eds. (New York: Guilford, 1991), 181 – 196.

33. Rachel T. Hare-Mustin, "Sex, Lies, and Headaches: The Problem is Power," in *Women and Power: Perspectives for Family Therapy*, Thelma Jean Goodrich, ed. (New York: Norton, 1991), 63 – 85.

34. Stacey Colino, "Shifting Gears: How to Go from Stressed-Out Professional to Way-Calm Mom during Your Drive Home," *Working Mother* (December, 2000), 37 – 38. No less than nine "expert" sources are mentioned in this very brief article.

35. Arlie Russell Hochschild, "The Working Wife as Urbanizing Peasant," in *Families in the U.S.: Kinship and Domestic Politics*, Karen V. Hansen and Anita I. Garey, eds. (Philadelphia: Temple University Press, 1998), 779 – 790, esp. 786.

36. Arlie Russell Hochschild, *The Second Shift: Working Couples and the Revolution at Home* (New York: Viking, 1989).

37. Hochschild, "The Working Wife," 787.

38. See for example, Phyllis Chesler's *Woman's Inhumanity to Woman* (New York: Penguin, 2003). I am indebted to one of my social work graduate students, Amy Poppel, for drawing my attention to another example, Leora Tanenbaum's *Catfight: Women and Competition* (New York: Seven Stories Press, 2003).

39. See Lisa Belkin, "The Opt-Out Revolution," *New York Times Magazine* (October 26, 2003), 42 – 48, 58, 85 – 86, for one such discussion.

40. Allison Pearson, *I Don't Know How She Does It: The Life of Kate Reddy, Working Mother* (New York: Knopf, 2002). See also Kate Betts's review of the book in the *New York Times Book Review* (October 6, 2002), 7.

41. See such fare as Barbara Reinhold's *Toxic Work: How to Overcome Stress, Overload, Burnout and Revitalize Your Career* (New York: Dutton/Plume, 1997); M. J. Ryan's *365 Health and Happiness Boosters* (New York: Conari Press, 2000); Jennifer Bett Meyer, "The Best Stress-Busters," *Harper's Bazaar* (September 2003), 278; Sara Brzowsky, "How to Be Stress-Resilient," *Parade Magazine* (October 12, 2003), 10 – 12, esp. 12; Colino, "Shifting Gears," 38.

42. Deborah Hutton, "How to Reduce Your Stress," *Harper's Bazaar* (September 2003), 274 – 278, esp. 274.

43. Ibid., 274 – 278.

44. Wendy Simonds, *Women and Self-Help Culture: Reading between the Lines* (New Brunswick, NJ: Rutgers University Press), esp. 199.

45. Ibid., 193.

46. Elayne Rapping, *The Culture of Recovery: Making Sense of the Self-Help Movement in Women's Lives* (Boston: Beacon Press, 1996), esp. 7.

47. Ann Withorn, *Serving the People: Social Services and Social Change* (New York: Columbia University Press, 1984), esp. 89. I rely on Withorn's observations on "worker stress" in the discussion that follows.

48. Ibid., 90.

49. For a discussion of the contemporary medicalization of welfare, see Sanford S. Schram, "In the Clinic: The Medicalization of Welfare," chapter 3 in *After Welfare: The Culture of Postindustrial Social Policy* (New York: NYU Press, 2000), 59 – 88.

50. The article, written by Helen Epstein, was entitled "Enough to Make You Sick?" *New York Times Magazine* (October 12, 2003), 75 – 81, 98, 102 – 107.

51. As is commonly the case in such pieces, the exclusive representation of African Americans in discussions of poverty lead to a consistent confounding of class and race.

52. Epstein, "Enough to Make You Sick?" 79.

53. Ibid., 81.

54. Ibid., 81.

55. Ibid., 98.

NOTES TO THE AFTERWORD

1. AOL message from June 27, 2001.

2. Nikolas Rose, *Inventing Ourselves: Psychology, Power, and Personhood* (Cambridge: Cambridge University Press, 1998), esp. 79.

3. Irene J. Philipson, *On the Shoulders of Women: The Feminization of Psychotherapy* (New York: Guilford, 1993), esp. 151.

4. Larry Beutler, "Dreams and Nightmares about the Next Big Revolution in Psychotherapy," *Psychotherapy* 37 (2000): 354 – 358, esp. 360.

5. Kurt Salzinger, "Psychology Is Science: Spread the Word," *Psychological Science Agenda* (January/February 2002), 3.

6. Beutler, in "Dreams and Nightmares," puts his concern about prescription privileges this way:

A classical analyst might see in our [psychologists'] seemingly compulsive trek down a road that is marked by the footprints of the declining profession of psychiatry an example of identifying with the aggressor. But . . . all I can see . . . is a future in which psychotherapy becomes an increasingly nondescript, generic, and colorless activity practiced by technicians, not artists. . . . This profession of my nightmare is committed to the pursuit of linear logic, a search for magic potions, a devaluing of human relationships. (361)

7. Ann Withorn, *Serving the People: Social Services and Social Change* (New York: Columbia University Press, 1984), esp. 8.

8. John H. Ehrenreich, *The Altruistic Imagination: A History of Social Work and Social Policy in the United States* (Ithaca, NY: Cornell University Press, 1985), esp. 229 – 230.

9. Andrew J. Polsky, *The Rise of the Therapeutic State* (Princeton, NJ: Princeton University Press, 1991), esp. 55.

10. Steven Brint, *In an Age of Experts: The Changing Role of Professionals in Politics and Public Life* (Princeton, NJ: Princeton University Press, 1994), esp. 212.

Index

Ackerson, Barry, 163–164
Advertising: magazines and, 86; appeals to women, 87–89
Agrarian tradition, American, 82
Ahlstrom, Sydney, 197n. 14
Alcott, William, 86
Ally McBeal (TV program), 109
Americans View Their Mental Health surveys, 170
Anderson, Sherwood, 211n. 55
Androgyny, model of, 145
Anker, Roy, 39
Anti-ritualism, 78–79
Aristotle, 24
Assertiveness training, 145
Association of Women in Psychology, 221n. 6
Atlantic, 88
Augustine (Saint), 22
Autonomy: client, 160, 162; and relatedness, 128–129, 219n. 81; in religion, 38
Avis, Judith Myers, 139

Backlash. *See* Feminism
Baker, Ray Stannard, 47
Ballou, Mary, 129
Bartky, Sandra, 34
Beard, George M., 49, 63, 69–75, 170–171
Becker, Dana, 173, 228n. 21
Beecher, Henry Ward, 39
Belenky, Mary, 116, 119
Belkin, Lisa, 108
Bellah, Robert, 12, 23, 26–31
Beneficence, 162, 164
Bentham, Jeremy, 15, 30, 126

Berger, John, 93–94
Bergson, Henri, 51, 201n, 84
Beutler, Larry, 187–188, 230n. 6
Biaggio, Mary Kay, 153
Biological clock, 108, 112
Bio-power, 32
Blustein, Bonnie Ellen, 207n. 68
Boehm, Amnon, 164
Bordo, Susan, 217n. 38
Bowling Alone (Putnam), 12
Breuer, Joseph, 200n. 76
Brint, Steven, 189
Brown, Gillian, 20, 84, 209n. 17
Brown, Laura, 129, 146, 150–152, 160–161, 165–166
Brownmiller, Susan, 141–142
Burckhardt, Jacob, 19
Burnham, John C. 202n. 101, 202n. 109
Butler, Judith, 115

Cabot, Richard C., 46–47
California Task Force to Promote Self-Esteem and Personal and Social Responsibility, 32
Capitalism, 83–84, 210n. 27
Caplan, Eric, 48
Care, caretaking, 27, 123–124; "ethic" of, beliefs about, 116–117, 140; valorization of, 116; as women's preserve, 123, 131, 174, 187
Case study, 53
Casework. *See* Social work
Character, American, 52; assessments of, 11–12, 25, 28; and shift toward personality, 24, 28–29, 56
Charcot, Jean Martin, 200n. 76
Child Guidance Clinics, 101–102

233

About the Author

Dana Becker is Associate Professor at the Bryn Mawr College Graduate School of Social Work and Social Research, with degrees in both social work and psychology. She has been a therapist in private practice in Philadelphia, Pennsylvania, for over twenty years. She is the author of *Through the Looking Glass: Women and Borderline Personality Disorder.*